Climate
Risks

Founded in 1807, John Wiley & Sons is the oldest independent publishing company in the United States. With offices in North America, Europe, Australia, and Asia, Wiley is globally committed to developing and marketing print and electronic products and services for our customers' professional and personal knowledge and understanding

The Wiley Finance series contains books written specifically for finance and investment professionals as well as sophisticated individual investors and their financial advisors. Book topics range from portfolio management to e-commerce, risk management, financial engineering, valuation, and financial instrument analysis, as well as much more

For a list of available titles, visit our Web site at www.WileyFinance .com

Climate Risks

An Investor's Field Guide to Identification and Assessment

BOB BUHR

WILEY

Registered Office(s)
John Wiley & Sons, Inc., 111 River Street, Hoboken, NJ 07030, USA
John Wiley & Sons Ltd, The Atrium, Southern Gate, Chichester, West Sussex, PO19 8SQ, UK

Editorial Office
The Atrium, Southern Gate, Chichester, West Sussex, PO19 8SQ, UK

For details of our global editorial offices, customer services, and more information about Wiley products visit us at www.wiley.com.

Wiley also publishes its books in a variety of electronic formats and by print-on-demand. Some content that appears in standard print versions of this book may not be available in other formats.

Library of Congress Cataloging-in-Publication Data is Available:

ISBN 9781394187362 (Hardback)
ISBN 9781394187379 (ePDF)
ISBN 9781394187355 (ePUB)

Cover Design: Wiley
Cover Image: © Trismegist san/Shutterstock

Set in 10/12pt and Sabon LT Std by Straive, Chennai, India

SKY10043961_030623

*For my family, Jenni, Megan, and Susan,
and my grandkids, on whose behalf saving the
planet seems like a good idea.*

Contents

Preface

Occasionally, and usually against my better judgment, I look at the comments in *The Financial Times* on their wide range of climate coverage (which is generally excellent). I do this to check to see whether the denial and indifference to the notion of anthropomorphic climate change that seems to afflict so many *FT* readers, not to mention the financial community in general, is still with us. Sadly, it still is. However, this denial and indifference appears to be on the decline, although it's not gone yet. This is purely an anecdotal judgment, of course, but I would like to think it is also true.

This optimistic observation needs to be tempered by the fact that much of the political world, and that of public policymakers, has not yet caught up to climate reality. But investors and lenders, as well as a wide range of regulatory agencies, seem to be moving to an increased understanding that we may just be facing an existential crisis. We are not all Extinction Rebellion activists yet, although many of us are finding ourselves in the same ballpark at this point. Andreas Malm's stimulating *How to Blow Up a Pipeline* encapsulates some of the dilemma this presents—if you're facing an existential crisis, what sort of actions are appropriate?

In our case, we can at least try to get the numbers right. And that activity encompasses assessing the range of risks that are inevitably going to rise, and that will need to be dealt with. And at what cost will they be dealt with? In many cases, this is still contingent on public policymakers. They will certainly be in the trillions of dollars in the aggregate—but for most people, including those in the financial sector, as soon as one starts discussions of trillions of US dollars (or Euros, or pounds sterling), an air of unreality sets in. What do these numbers even mean? We can at least identify where the relevant financial risks are likely to materialize, and under what circumstances, and granulate these costs, to the extent possible, to real firms. This is our job, and what we are supposed to be good at.

This entire volume is premised on the notion that if we, as financial analysts and those who use such analysis, can deal with analyzing traditional business and financial risks successfully (which has generally been the case), we should be able to expand our horizons to encompass a new and significant class of risks—some of which, actually, are not so new. As is becoming increasingly clear, these risks are not trivial—they are increasingly systemic, and increasingly scary. Hopefully, this volume may make that process a bit more straightforward.

London,
November 2022.

CHAPTER 1

Introduction: Why We Need a Risk Taxonomy

The year 2022 has been another year of major economic upheaval due to the continued escalation of climate change (mainly global heating) impacts, most noticeably as natural catastrophes. The catalog of physical risks on display is considerable. Numerous droughts either continued or emerged: in the American Southwest there has been a record heatwave (over the past twenty years); a drought in China; a record drought in Chile; and a Northern European drought so severe that water levels in the Rhine dropped so much that river traffic, a critical element in Germany's export-dependent economy, was essentially blocked for several weeks. Water levels in rivers worldwide dropped to record or near-record levels, including in the western United States and China, and even the River Po in Italy and other areas in Europe.

Not to be outdone as a disaster category, record flooding in Pakistan, India, and Nigeria displaced tens of millions, produced significant amounts of topsoil loss and land destruction, and impaired crop production in many countries dependent on agricultural exports (not to mention serving domestic agricultural needs). In addition, significant flooding in Australia (again), parts of Brazil, and portions of the eastern United States (again) had significant negative economic impacts. Flooding associated with Hurricane Ian has proved to be Florida's largest economic disaster ever. The increase in flooding in Africa is particularly worrisome given the still-high dependence on local agricultural resources in many countries. The increased severity of extreme weather events is another concerning phenomenon. Japan, the Philippines, and Pakistan were each the victims of record or near-record-intensity storms over the course of the year.

At several points during the first nine months of the year there were so many simultaneous major extreme weather events around the world that one had to check to make sure whether one was reading about an existing disaster, or a new one. But extreme weather is simply the most obvious manifestation of the potential impacts of global heating.[1] Other less dramatic, but perhaps more significant, events and processes continued unabated. Glacial melt in both Greenland and Antarctica accelerated in both regions—these are the largest glacial areas in the world, and ice continues to disappear (turning into either water or water vapor) in both regions, with potentially major impacts on the earth's air and water circulation systems. Deforestation in critical forested areas—the Amazon, Africa, Southeast Asia, and northern areas such as Russia, Alaska, and Canada—continues through human activity, but also increased wildfires. Multiple places were subject to extremely hot temperatures, particularly India, Bangladesh and Pakistan, but also western China, which saw its worst heatwave in recorded history.

The human costs are, in terms of land displacement alone, significant, and will likely continue to rise. The current century is expected to be one of increased global migration on the back of environmental, usually climate-related, events and processes that will make portions of the planet increasingly unlivable for humans. Political and social conflicts relating to potential resource availability and scarcity issues are expected to increase. There is already evidence of intensifying competition for water resources in a number of places around the world, for example. The current rate of topsoil depletion suggests that topsoil could become another area of concern over scarcity. Climate impacts are expected to intensify competition for increasingly scarce natural resources.

Moreover, in October 2022 the United Nations Framework Convention on Climate Change (UNFCCC) issued a synthesis report indicating that signatories to the 2015 Paris Agreement are lagging considerably in meeting their climate commitments.[2] As noted in the report,

> The best estimate of peak temperature in the twenty-first century (projected mostly for 2100 when temperature continues to rise) is in the range of 2.1–2.9 °C depending on the underlying assumptions.

This is, of course, considerably higher than the 1.5 °C target agreed to in the 2015 Paris Climate Agreement, mainly because most signatories have not been meeting proposed Nationally Indicated Commitments. We are losing ground, in other words.

Thus far 2022 has also highlighted another disturbing trend, particularly for investors and lenders—the negative impacts of global heating are costing more than they did ten years ago. The impacts here are broad-based, ranging from individual homeowners to municipalities to state and national governments and, of course, businesses of all size, and their insurers. The US

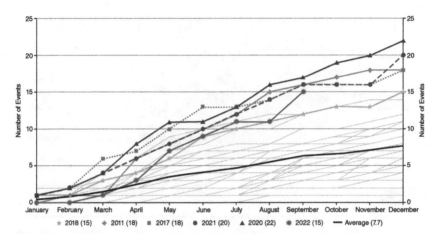

FIGURE 1.1 United States' billion-dollar disaster event count.
Source: National Centers for Environmental Information, National Oceanic and Atmospheric Administration, 2022.

National Oceanic and Atmospheric Administration (NOAA) has noted that for the United States alone the number of "billion-dollar natural disasters" through nine months of 2022 is running well above its historical average, and in fact appears to parallel years of all-time highs (although as NOAA points out, the financial impact has been below 2021, and the record year of 2017). The trend for this is shown in Figure 1.1.

As Figure 1.2 shows, the range of disasters is relatively broad, encompassing extreme weather, drought, and flooding in particular.[3]

On a global basis the narrative is fundamentally similar. As Swiss Re has noted,[4]

> The rise in insured losses maintained a long-term trend (based on 10-year moving averages) of 5–7% growth annually. Once again, secondary perils, including floods, were at the forefront, accounting for more than 70% of all insured losses. It was the first year ever that two separate secondary perils events—winter storm Uri in the US and the flood in western/central Europe in July—each caused losses in excess of USD 10 billion.

The impacts of these events, most of which are flood related, are socially and economically very broad-based, and in some parts of the world potentially catastrophic in terms of, for example, topsoil lost in excessive flooding.[5] For investors and lenders, the impacts will not be nearly as draconian.

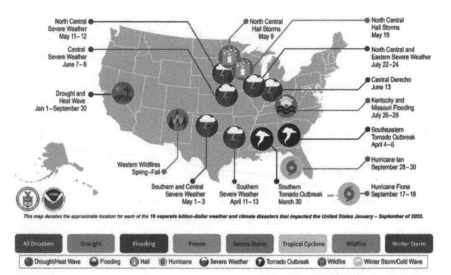

FIGURE 1.2   United States' 2022 billion-dollar weather and climate disasters.
Source: National Centers for Environmental Information, National Oceanic and
Atmospheric Administration, 2022.

Nonetheless, there is a broad spectrum of potential financial impacts that
may range from asset value destruction to revenue and profitability losses,
reduced tax revenues for governments, and higher insurance losses and costs.

For a number of observers, then, these developments have more than
a passing import. Investors, lenders, and financial regulators are paying
increasing attention to these potential costs, and to the risks underlying them.
Unsurprisingly, this is largely because it has become clear that these costs
will continue to rise as the impacts of global heating continue to grow. This
has resulted in multiple initiatives to try to capture and organize the factors
driving these costs, of which the Task Force on Climate-related Financial
Disclosures (TCFD) is probably the best-known example.[6] (We will discuss
these recommendations, and others, in more detail in Chapter 2.) This has
also led to considerable work on cataloging those areas where investors and
lenders can help facilitate a transition from our currently carbon-dependent
economy to an energy system considerably less reliant on carbon energy
sources, particularly with an overall target of reducing Greenhouse Gas
(GHG) generation by firms and sovereign entities. The EU's Sustainability
Taxonomy is perhaps the best-known example of this.[7] We note that much
of this work has taken the form of more detailed and robust tracking of
GHG emissions.

However, as we hope to make clear in this book, climate risk identification, assessment, and reporting may encompass a substantially broader landscape than simple reporting of GHG generation on an annual basis. For investors and lenders, climate change represents a medium- to long-term trend with the potential to have wide-ranging financial impacts on companies in a range of potentially affected industries, including on their credit profiles and/or share prices—or, indeed, their continued going-concern status. However, this knowledge is not necessarily helpful for lenders, investors, or regulators unless these potential risks can be granulated and quantified in terms of their scope and, more importantly, their timing and likelihood. A sufficient granulation of the potential risks being discussed here, along with some assessment of likelihood and timing of potential impacts, will facilitate an assessment of their specific financial manifestations, be it cash flows, asset valuations, margin impacts, or credit ratios, for example.

Moreover, increased concern among lenders, investors, and regulators over potential climate risks and some of the uncertainties associated with these risks has highlighted the need for a more rigorous assessment of just what those risks actually are.[8] This concern is being driven by two factors:

1. the increased frequency and severity of the impacts of global heating, particularly over the past decade, and
2. the increased likelihood of the need for the reporting of the potential impacts of these risks by firms.[9]

We have recently seen the emergence of various "Green" taxonomies, which largely reflect public policy objectives of facilitating financing for an energy transition to a zero-carbon economy. However, while "green taxonomies" classify the investment opportunities that may arise in a transition to a low-carbon economy, they often fail to capture and granulate the risks, and in particular the costs, associated with this shift.[10] These taxonomies are not designed to quantify specific risks and their impacts, of course—that's not what they were created for. Nonetheless, the need for a framework for such risk evaluation is obvious. One of the aims of climate risk analysis is identifying potential firm-specific climate risks *before* they cause reductions in asset utilization, stranded assets, reduced income and margins, impairments to cash flows, or other financial impacts.[11] These potential risks embody changes that translate into increased financial and credit risks, and these are likely to influence lenders' and investors' decisions about financial profiles.

Accordingly, this book presents a framework for classifying potential climate risks at the firm level, a climate risk taxonomy that captures a broad range of possible (and, in some cases, likely) physical and transition risks.

Note that this book is a not an inventory of these potential risks as they currently present themselves—rather, it is a potential framework for identifying where those risks are likely to materialize as climate change impacts become more significant. The main advantage of such a comprehensive climate risk taxonomy is that it would enable banks, investors, and regulators (including central banks) to assess the relative aggregate riskiness of portfolios that derive from climate and natural capital risks *at the firm level.* By financial risks, we specifically mean those financial events or trends that may affect, for example, a company's probability of default (PD), its credit rating, its share price, or its ability to internally fund necessary CAPEX (capital expenditure) because of a change in some critical financial measures (asset valuations, cash flows, leverage ratios, reserve levels, and margins being the most critical). Another advantage is that such a taxonomy can be built up using existing risk assessment frameworks and categories, as we will show.

Investors and policymakers have settled into a convention that subdivides potential climate risks into two traditional broad categories: physical risks and transition risks. Physical risks represent the range of impacts on landforms and infrastructure that will result from physical results of climate change—increased heat in certain regions, increased flooding from storm surge, and a range of other physical impacts. Transition risks are generally categorized into two further categories: adaptation and mitigation. Adaptation responses are designed to cope with the probable physical, societal, and economic consequences of global heating on populations and regions, particularly on infrastructure. Mitigation measures generally are designed to curtail the growth of GHG emissions, principally CO_2 and methane.

The granular taxonomy presented here encapsulates potential climate risks in terms of these three traditional climate risk categories, and also includes an additional category, natural capital risk. The overall framework, then, is as follows:

1. physical risks, both acute and chronic risks (and often both at the same time);
2. transition risks related to adaptation policies in response to physical risks;
3. transition risks related to mitigation, ranging from regulatory compliance risks to reputational and litigation risks; and
4. natural capital risks, which reflect mainly depletion of both renewable and nonrenewable resources that are themselves affecting, and being affected by, potential climate risk factors.

The objective of this comprehensive climate risk taxonomy is that it enables lenders, investors, and regulators to assess better the relative aggregate risk exposure of portfolios that derive from climate and natural capital risks *at the firm level*. Moreover, the categories and indicators presented here are, we believe, more granulated than those suggested in other models. They are certainly broader—most of the climate frameworks currently in effect take GHG emissions as the main risk to be solved. We hope to show that this is insufficient. Climate risk disclosure entails considerably more than simply cataloguing reductions in GHG emissions. The importance of developing this model for the analysis of firms is simply that the firm is what an investor invests in, either directly or indirectly (through index funds, for example). The firm is also what a lender lends to. Lenders do not lend to the chemical sector—they lend to individual firms in that sector.

We note that numerous entities undertaking climate risk analysis—financial analysts and rating agencies, for example—have been somewhat constrained in their analysis of potential climate risks by two factors:

1. the very limited historical base for many of these risks; and
2. the potentially uncertain horizons or impacts, many of which lie outside traditional analytical or rating horizons.

The first point is obvious. While some of these impacts have manifested themselves repeatedly through the planet's history, very few of them have posed material challenges for the survivability of humanity over the past 10,000 years, including the past several hundred years of industrial development on a planetary scale.

The second point is a bit more complicated. Potential climate risks pose a challenging issue for determining risk horizons, which is a central component of the financial analysis usually undertaken by investors and lenders. Specifically, potential climate risk may have a very high level of likelihood, but their timing and scale may both be uncertain, particularly regionally in terms of physical risks such as sea level rise. We know that sea level rise will have a range of significant regional impacts—but we may not know when these physical impacts will have financial implications, or at what scale. A fundamental issue with climate risk analysis, then, is dealing with these uncertainties. In many cases, particularly with reference to adaptation and mitigation risks (both being transition risks), the potential scope of these risks is contingent on public policy decisions.

The climate risk taxonomy presented here is essentially a toolkit for firms, and people who analyze them, to identify and assess the potential scope and impact of a wide range of potential risks *that would not necessarily appear in more traditional risk or credit analysis*. Importantly, the taxonomy presented here is intended to supplement, not replace, traditional financial analysis, which is useful—indeed, fundamental—for assessing situations with more determinate horizons. More specifically, a climate risk taxonomy should be organized according to increasing granulation of different types of risks and levels of potential materiality at the firm level. The EU's Green Taxonomy is a useful tool to define an investment opportunity set. However, it is limited in its potential utility as a risk monitor, partly because of its focus on industrial sectors, rather than firms, and partially because it generally does not assess the costs associated with the transition it seeks to encourage. The EU taxonomy is an excellent guide to investment, and is not unmindful of climate risks, but it is not necessarily a framework for risk assessment. There are, in fact, a number of potentially useful taxonomies for risk assessment that have emerged in recent years, but all have some limitations We note that the taxonomies proposed by Climate Bonds Initiative (Climate Bonds), the Sustainability Accounting Standards Board (SASB), and the Carbon Disclosure Standards Board (CDSB, now the ISSB)[12] have all proposed frameworks for assessing varying degrees of compliance with Paris Climate goals that are also useful for consideration of various levels of risk.[13] However, none have been developed as strictly a risk-based taxonomy.

There is, out of necessity, a wide range of risk categories being considered, and many are quite different from each other. Sea level rise is not the same sort of risk that carbon taxation is, although both have the potential for sizeable financial impacts on firms and their instruments. Since the proposed taxonomy is primarily designed to address potential risks attending to individual instruments—loans, bonds, and equities—we have sought to granulate risks to the level at which these risks have the potential to have a financial impact. This is, of course, partially a speculative exercise, but hopefully one informed by what experience we have with these potential risks to date.

In fact, since there is no pre-existing climate risk taxonomy for firms, we have had to create one. The specific categories chosen—physical and transition risks, the latter further granulated into adaptation and mitigation risks—are generally those found in any compendium of climate risks, although not all of these are organized along the same lines. Natural Capital Risks, on the other hand, represent, to our knowledge, an entirely novel taxonomy, although with the sharpened attention to biodiversity among investors and lenders we suspect it will take on increasing importance. Moreover, as we discuss in Chapter 2, the overall framework we have used for providing a context for this risk analysis is the traditional risk model employed by financial analysts over the past several decades.

The Physical Risk category in particular is the one that has been explored most thoroughly, for several reasons, particularly by the Intergovernmental Panel on Climate Change (IPCC). First, it is relatively straightforward—there is considerable overlap and duplication of categories across groups in their adoption of the specific categories. Second, these are the areas where potential financial risks are manifesting themselves most obviously at present. The categories presented here reflect a distillation of a broader range of risk and hazard categories. Our major risk categories are heat stress, water stress, extreme precipitation, sea level rise, and extreme weather. Other approaches may have a different number of general categories, but the overall scope of the analysis is essentially the same. There are actually only a limited number of possible physical risks categories that lend themselves to this approach, and only a limited number of ways to describe them. We have not necessarily included all physical risks—only those that are likely to manifest themselves as financial impacts at the firm level. We also retain the traditional distinction between acute and chronic physical risks: acute risks refer to episodic events that have the potential to inflict significant physical damage (e.g., wildfires, river and ocean flooding, and tropical storms), while chronic risks have a considerably longer duration (e.g., sea level rise and increases in global mean temperature) and may be understood as processes rather than events.

What investors and lenders are facing is the fact that what have traditionally been classified as idiosyncratic risks—natural disasters, for example—are becoming less idiosyncratic and more systemic. While the number of manmade disasters (aviation and maritime, for example) has declined from their high in 2005, natural catastrophes (particularly those associated with severe storms and flooding) continue to rise,[14] and this rise is attributed to global heating impacts. While most industries will have some exposure to physical risks, there are some industries that will have considerably more exposure than others. Since a considerable portion of humanity lives along the coast or on banks of rivers, and these are where the bulk of global economic activity takes place, it would be cavalier to assume that the impacts of the manifestations of these risks will not be felt broadly. Particular sectors at risk include: infrastructure, particularly utilities and ports; residential and commercial (including industrial) property; transport; financial institutions; and insurance.

This raises an issue that will likely arise during any risk analysis of physical risks—the potential for stranded assets. There is also the broader question of whether valuation of the firm is directly dependent on the valuation of its physical assets. Most industrial firms are not dependent on a single physical asset. However, there are sectors where there is a rationale for a particular physical location, or a concentration of them. For example, utilities are almost always located adjacent to bodies of water—be it the sea or rivers. Mines are located where the resources are to be found. It is also possible that physical assets in the aggregate may present risks that, individually, would be immaterial as a single property. This may be the case for property portfolios—single property risks may be small, but in the aggregate these risks may become potentially material for lenders and/or investors.

Discussions of modeling and scenario analysis lie outside the scope of this book, although these are now regarded as integral tools for assessing the potential impacts of climate factors (in particular, global heating) on firm evaluations. Though the classification of physical risk categories is relatively straightforward, there are nonetheless several issues that make modeling these risks a complex process, even as they are becoming increasingly important in climate risk analysis. Critically, it is important to recognize that potential climate risks are not necessarily independent of each other—there is no such thing as orthogonal climate risks. The potential extent to which feedback loops may need to be included in any sort of modeling is a complex issue, but to some extent these will be model- and scenario-specific, and potentially significant. What this book outlines are those potential risks that should be the subject of scenario analysis—if the appropriate risk categories are not being modeled, then it is not clear what purpose the analysis serves.

Adaptation risk categories are also relatively consistent, since the physical changes expected to emerge are well identified, so issues associated with adapting to these impacts should be also well understood, at least conceptually. However, we note that there have been only moderate attempts to codify these potential risks in the climate risk literature, unlike, for example, the urban planning literature. This category, then, represents a constructed set of risks that seem most directly relevant to the Adaptation process and its potential costs. This category also entails some discussion of resilience, which is often used as a target to which adaptation should aim to achieve. This will be discussed in more detail in Chapter 5.[15]

We note that most of the specific potential adaptation risks outlined here derive directly from specific risk indicators used in traditional financial analysis. All five of our categories—Asset Valuation Risks, Operational Impairments, Cost of Business adjustments, Regulatory Changes, and Subsidy loss risks—are categories assessed in the normal course of determining the credit risk of any potential investment, for example. We have chosen these as being the areas where specific potential risks relating to adaptation efforts are most likely to manifest themselves. Note also that two of the adaptation risk categories—Subsidy Loss Risk and Asset Valuation Risk—appear more than once in the overall taxonomy. This will be a recurring issue—*specific financial risks can result from more than one potential climate impact.*

Adaptation costs, and who will bear them, are an important element of this assessment. Adaptation risks encompass the impacts of adapting to climate change on the physical environment, and the potential financial impact such risks may carry for individuals, governments, and corporations. Note that these risks may take the form of the costs associated with various adaptation actions—but there will also be potentially significant costs associated with inaction. Rising ocean levels and increased flooding will pose actual risks to coastal areas, for example, including port facilities and railroads. If left unmanaged, these risks have the potential to produce potentially significant asset devaluations, if not outright stranded assets. Adapting to these impacts, either by accommodation or displacement, is likely to entail substantial costs. At present, these costs, when actually incurred, are generally being borne by governments and insurance companies.

Of the Adaptation Risks discussed, the potential from Stranded Assets remains one of the most uncertain, but one with a potentially large tail risk. In part this reflects the uncertainty over the potential timing of Adaptation costs being expended—there is often a long lead time, but the costs may be significant in any event. For example, consider what might be involved in adapting transport systems (including the potentially necessary land infrastructure replacement, particularly rail). It will be some time before there is a better picture of what assets will be involved, or not, in significant adaptation impacts. However, current assessments are not comforting—a recent study has suggested that the fossil fuel industry may be facing a stranded assets impact of US $1 trillion.[16]

Loss of financial subsidies remains a significant potential risk as well, although one not generally discussed, since the political realities of cutting subsidies are complicated. Subsidy risks actually span three risk categories being discussed in this report: Adaptation, Mitigation, and Natural Capital risks. Subsidies generally enable economic producers and consumers to avoid paying the genuine economic costs of the extraction and usage of various resources. To the extent that subsidies contribute to financial indicators of interest to investors and lenders—earnings and cash flows in particular—any loss of these subsidies could prove to be financially punitive. Most industries actually receive a range of producer and consumer subsidies, but some industries—agriculture, fossil fuels, metals and mining, and construction—appear to be more significant beneficiaries of government generosity than others. In particular, agriculture could be significantly affected by major subsidy changes, especially those related to water availability. We are already seeing potential water conflicts in the Southwestern United States between farmers and urban residents over water allocation issues.[17]

There are numerous industries that have some degree of exposure to adaptation risks and their associated costs—in fact, most industrial firms have some physical exposure to potential climate impacts. These include utilities, property and real estate, energy, ports, transportation (particularly rail transport), refineries, cement and building materials, including steel, and manufacturers in a wide range of industries that benefit from the proximity to transit hubs. Potential exposure will clearly vary by country and by sector. In addition, industries with significant and occasionally complicated supply chains may also be vulnerable to these risks. We note that in some cases, sovereign government financial profiles could be negatively affected by adaptation costs, assuming they can be adopted. For numerous emerging markets (EM) sovereigns, this may not be feasible.[18]

The mitigation category being presented here has the least amount of external validation if that means aligning with other taxonomies. This is simply because there are no external taxonomies where these potential risks are articulated broadly above and beyond emissions reductions, although the respective taxonomies of SASB and CDSB include elements of various transition mitigation risks, and the TCFD indicates some suggested risk categories (all discussed in Chapter 2). The major exception is the area of "Energy Transition," where many of these potential risks have received varying degrees of attention and where ongoing debates over appropriate future energy trajectories remain lively.[19] As in the case of adaptation risks, we have generally adopted indicators of potential risk from more traditional credit analysis—again, there turns out to be a number of potential climate impacts that can be expected to manifest themselves in these various categories. Technology risks and litigation risks relating to climate risk both present interesting and potentially expensive issues—but these risk categories are pretty standard in any sort of financial analysis of firms.

While the mitigation risk category represents the most diverse collection of specific risks of the whole taxonomy, there is a recurring theme to these specific risk indicators, which we mentioned with respect to adaptation risks: *their potential impact is directly derivative of human activity in response to potential climate impacts.* Such costs are usually the result of public policy decisions adopted by governments and/or regulators, and these can change as well. There is a broad range of potential mitigation efforts being considered at various government levels, and some are even being implemented. Much of this activity has the potential to increase financial risk to firms.

Our principal risk categories in this collection are regulatory risks, technology risks, going-concern risks, water risks, and subsidy risks (again). These categories encompass eighteen separate proposed risk indicators, but we have every expectation that this number will be revised at some point.

Currently, the main mitigation risk is from the regulatory front, as regulation of carbon and other greenhouse gases seems increasingly likely and will certainly remain a topic of debate. Regulatory risks also encompass other potential regulatory measures, particularly those related to water availability and noncarbon pollution. Of the other risk indicators of this group, many have considerable uncertainty attached to them. In some cases, such as litigation, the risks may be simply binary: risks will either be low or high. In other cases, such as removal of subsidies or failure to maintain social license to operate, risks may be more industry specific. Many of these risks are already materializing, in some cases in surprising scale (e.g., the emergence of consumer demand for nonmeat products, which is having an impact on the food industry, or the enthusiasm for electric vehicles).

The range of going-concern risks—risks related to simply running the business—is probably surprising, but these represent traditional risk categories that have been exacerbated by potential climate impacts. This group consists of commodity price changes, changes in consumer preferences, reputational and license to operate risks, litigation risks, and supply chain risks. We also note that this category can include a range of possible offsets. These may be industry specific—reforestation programs from the paper and forest products sector, for example. Many of these seem to involve carbon capture and storage (CCS) proposals, although we note considerable uncertainty remains as to whether this will be a successful approach to carbon offsets. We will discuss this point in our section on technology risks. Note that the recent surge in interest in "net-zero" targets relies heavily on the use of these potential offsets.

Not surprisingly, the main industries potentially affected by mitigation risks are industries we have already encountered: transportation; metals, mining, and construction; and energy and utilities, including oil and gas. In particular, these are industries that rely on heat to generate their product— cement and steel, for example. We also note that the automobile industry is facing some industry-specific transition challenges. We will discuss these in more detail in Chapter 6. Nonetheless, it is difficult to envision an industry that will not be engaged in mitigation and transition measures, even if it is only through supply chain disruptions, although sector costs may vary widely.

The fourth category in this taxonomy, natural capital risks, represents an entirely novel concept and, we believe, the first attempt to codify such risks into an organized taxonomy (although, we admit, a relatively simple one). While conceptually different from climate risks, many of these risks are currently being exacerbated by climate impacts, and in turn may be accelerating some potential climate risks—the impact of land use changes on the incidence of drought, for example, or of natural resource depletion in the case of declining water aquifers globally. In essence, these reflect potential risks to asset values, profitability, cash flows or margins from natural events that may be accelerated because of some form of natural capital depletion or disruption.

For example, the apparent increase in the number of droughts worldwide is having a short-term impact on some industries (e.g., agriculture in California, supply chain issues in Germany). But droughts can also have longer-term financial impacts, some of which are emerging in the Southwestern United States and portions of Mexico.[20] In addition, these potential risks may have a geopolitical impact, as evidenced by many events in North Africa and the Middle East over the past decade, where climate impacts have had a role in economic affairs and social unrest. Many of these risks appear to be more frequent, more numerous, and perhaps more predictable than they used to be. In fact, there is every reason to believe that many natural capital risks will increase in intensity in the next two to three decades.[21] Many of these risks also, obviously, encompass risks to human societies.

The four major natural capital risk indicators chosen—subsidy loss risks, depletion risks, boundary condition risks, and geopolitical event risks—are, in fact, all manifesting themselves at present, although these are less directly tied to specific firms than the other types of potential risks being discussed in this book. We believe these four general metrics accommodate the wide range of natural capital issues currently unfolding, many of which are receiving increased attention from investors—recent emerging concerns about biodiversity reflect this, as do concerns about metals required for electric vehicle batteries. As with both types of transition risks, several of these natural capital risks derive from multiple sources. Of particular concern is that numerous forms of natural capital—in fact, most—are being depleted more rapidly than they are being replenished, if they are renewable resources such as forests, fisheries, and farmland topsoil. Moreover, if we are referring to nonrenewable resources such as minerals and, perhaps, the capacity of the atmosphere and the oceans and atmosphere to absorb CO_2 without untoward effects, the narrative becomes even more complex, but currently seems to be trending in the wrong direction.

We thus distinguish between renewable and nonrenewable depletion risks, given that these reflect two different types of resources. We also discuss water risks as being perhaps the most significant depletion risk. Water never goes away, it simply changes its state. And at present the trend is for much of the world's water to move from ice to liquid water to water vapor, accelerating the process of evaporation globally: "Water always wins."[22] Industries likely to be affected by either the continuation of current Natural Capital Trends, or efforts to moderate these trends, include most major global industries. All industries are dependent on water—but some industries are thirstier than others. While the global food system is the most likely to be affected in the near term, other potential candidates for disruption include: energy (principally oil and gas production); metals and mining; electric utilities; paper and forest products; and chemicals. Much of this risk exposure derives from industrial dependence on high levels of water consumption in the manufacturing process.

In addition to the above, we also cite the potential impact of global heating on the state of natural resources. In the case of global heating, the concern here is with the impacts of those physical impacts on other natural capital trends—particularly the depletion of forest, agricultural land, particularly topsoil loss trends, and other renewable resources. The desertification of parts of the world will likely be accelerated under more draconian global heating scenarios. Negative biodiversity impacts are expected to accelerate as climate change impacts become more severe.[23] The cost of global deforestation to firms, mainly agricultural firms, may exceed $53 billion, according to CDP.[24]

While it is difficult to envision these trends manifesting themselves as firm-specific financial impacts in the near term, other than water availability issues in some regions, especially for large, well-capitalized corporations, the outlook for EM sovereign governments is considerably more uncertain. This is particularly the case for those dependent upon resource development and exports for economic growth. Agencies and organizations have addressed the issue of the possible impact of climate change on a range of EM sovereigns, particularly those with a high dependence on natural resource or agricultural exports, or those with substantial exposure to physical climate risks. These are sectors where the macroeconomic financial impacts are generally believed to be potentially negative.

In summary, the taxonomy being presented here is designed to improve the assessment of potential financial risks to firms posed by the physical and transition risks associated with climate change. Many of the specific categories chosen mirror those found in any compendium of climate risks, although not all of these are organized along the same lines. On the other hand, many had to be imputed based on traditional risk frameworks employed by financial analysts. All of these potential risks can be assessed within the general approach to risk undertaken by financial analysts, portfolio managers, and lenders.

It should be clear at this point that what we refer to as climate risks actually constitute a broad collection of risks of various types. Even more critically, climate risk can no longer be viewed as idiosyncratic risks that can be diversified away from. Rather, these are now increasingly regarded as systemic risks. Granulating these risks into a taxonomy can help us assess not only the specific impacts of those risks in isolation, but also the complex relations and overlap between them, more effectively. The potential for feedback loops here is high, and in many cases not well understood.

The assessment of the financial impacts of climate risks is as much an art as a science at present. In part, this reflects horizon issues; assessing risks that may not manifest themselves for several years, or even decades, is indeed a highly speculative process. However, there is the further complication that the emergence of most of these risks, at least the physical risks, is pretty much a certainty. We know that something is highly likely to occur, but we are not certain about the timing, or the scope. Droughts are likely to become more severe. Extreme weather is expected to become even more extreme in parts of the world. Sea level rise is likely to occur at an accelerating rate. We believe analysis of these risks should not be supplemental to fundamental risk analysis over the longer term. This sort of analysis should be integral to the financial analysis of firms.

Note that this book is not a set of recommendations or procedures on modeling or scenario analysis. It is more basic than that. This book is simply a review of the range of potential risks that may need to be considered when constructing these models and scenarios. Moreover, we make no claims as to the relative weighting of each of these potential risks should they arise from one sector to another. We believe industry analysts and lenders themselves are best positioned to distinguish between the climate risk profiles of, say, steel producers as opposed to those of supermarket chains. There will be overlaps; there will also be significant differences. Industry analysts are the best positioned group for those assessments. We hope that this book provides some useful tools for that process.

NOTES

1. See, for example, Intergovernmental Panel on Climate Change (IPCC). *Fifth Assessment Report: Climate Change 2014: Impacts, Adaptation and Vulnerability*, 2014; *Global Warming of 1.5°C, Summary for Policymakers*, 2018; Summary for Policymakers. In IPCC *Special Report on the Ocean and Cryosphere in a Changing Climate*, 2019; *The Concept of Risk in the IPCC Sixth Assessment Report: A Summary of Cross-working Group Discussions; Guidance for IPCC authors*, September 2020; *Climate Change 2022: Mitigation of Climate Change, Working Group III—Contribution to the Sixth Assessment Report of the Intergovernmental Panel on Climate Change. Summary for Policymakers*, 2022.
2. United Nations Framework Convention on Climate Change. *Nationally Determined Contributions under the Paris Agreement: Synthesis Report by the Secretariat*, October 26, 2022.

3. Note that NOAA's figures include Hurricane Ian, but not the financial impacts, which are still being developed. At the time that NOAA prepared this information (the first nine months of 2022) the cost of these disasters was relatively modest when compared to some years, particularly 2017. With Hurricane Ian shaping up to be the most expensive disaster in US history, these assessments will obviously change.
4. Bevere, Lucia and Federica Remondi. *Natural Catastrophes in 2021: The Floodgates Are Open—Losses from Flood Have Been on an Upward Trend Globally.* Zurich: Swiss Re Institute, 2022.
5. IPCC. *Climate Change 2022: Impacts, Adaptation and Vulnerability—Summary for Policymakers*, March 2022.
6. Task Force on Climate-related Financial Disclosures. *Final Report: Recommendations of the Task Force on Climate-related Financial Disclosures*, December 2016; *Task Force on Climate-related Financial Disclosures Status Report*, October 2021.
7. EU Technical Expert Group on Sustainable Finance. *Taxonomy: Final Report of the Technical Expert Group on Sustainable Finance*, March 2020; *Financing a Sustainable European Economy Taxonomy Report: Technical Annex*, March 2020.
8. Note that in the climate literature it is customary to distinguish between hazards, which are potential risks that have not yet occurred, and actual risks, where the manifestation of the issue in question is tangible enough to be quantifiable. We discuss this distinction in more detail in Chapter 2.
9. Many countries, including those in the EU and the United Kingdom, are requiring such disclosures, or are set to.
10. See, for example, Buhr, Bob. Green Is Easy, Brown is Hard. *Responsible Investor*, June 27, 2019.
11. TCFD. *Phase I Report of the Task Force on Climate-related Financial Disclosures*, March 31, 2016.
12. These will be discussed in more detail in Chapter 2. We note here that the Carbon Disclosure Standards Board in December 2021 merged with the IFRS Foundation to form the International Sustainability Standards Board (ISSB). CDSB no longer exists as a distinct organization, although its work is now collectively part of the ISSB effort, and the reports being referred to here are still available on the CDSB website.
13. Fox, Megan, Brendan Holmes, and Sally Yim. *ISSB's Proposed Climate Disclosures Add Momentum for Improving Climate Risk Data.* Moody's Investors Service, April 12, 2022.
14. Bevere, Lucia and Federica Remondi. *Natural Catastrophes in 2021: The Floodgates are Open—Losses from Flood Have Been on an Upward Trend Globally.* Zurich: Swiss Re Institute, 2022.
15. We note that there is much discussion of resilience and sustainability pretty much everywhere these days. Our approach regards resilience as embodying the state we want systems to be able to return to after expected or unexpected disturbance. Sustainability, on the other hand, is part of the toolkit that can be used to achieve resilience. These are not interchangeable concepts.

16. Semieniuk, Gregor et al. Stranded Fossil-fuel Assets Translate to Major Losses for Investors in Advanced Economies. *Nature Climate Change* 12: 532–538, 2022.

17. There are actually a number of areas globally where competition for water resources is already fierce—we will discuss these in more detail in Chapter 7.

18. Volz, Ulrich et al. *Climate Change and Sovereign Risk.* SOAS Centre for Sustainable Finance, ADBI Institute, WWF, 427, 2021.

19. We note that "energy transition" is not the same thing as an overall economic transition. There can be no transition, energy or otherwise, without significant mitigation activity.

20. According to a NOAA report, economic costs of this drought to the Southwest United States in *2020 alone* were in the range of US $11.4–$23 billion. See *NOAA Drought Task Force Report on the 2020–2021 Southwestern U.S. Drought*, September 2021.

21. H. M. Treasury. *Final Report—The Economics of Biodiversity: The Dasgupta Review*, April 2021.

22. Gies, Erica. *Water Always Wins: Thriving in an Age of Drought and Deluge.* Chicago: University of Chicago Press, 2022; Schwartz, Judith D. *Water in Plain Sight.* White River Junction, VT: Chelsea Green, 2017.

23. Meyer, A. L. S. et al. Risks to Biodiversity from Temperature Overshoot Pathways. *Philosophical Transactions of the Royal Society B, Biological Sciences*, April 2022.

24. DeSouza, Aggie. *Global Business Seen Facing $53 Billion Hit from Deforestation.* Bloomberg UK, March 22, 2021.

CHAPTER 2

What Should a Climate Risk Taxonomy Do?

A useful climate risk taxonomy should address potential climate risks that have specific financial implications, or that may affect diverse measures of financial performance, at the level of individual firms. Moreover, it should be organized taxonomically such that relations between risks, if any are observable, can be assessed within a hierarchical framework. By financial risks, we specifically mean those financial events or trends of such materiality[1] that may affect, for example, a company's PD, its credit rating, its share price or its ability to internally fund necessary CAPEX because of a change in some critical financial measures.[2] The PD metric is sensitive to a number of financial factors, including:

1. Change in a firm's credit rating deriving from weakened financial performance and ratios.
2. Change in a firm's asset valuations (e.g., through the emergence of significant stranded asset), such that the balance sheet profile or credit profile of a company is materially changed.
3. Change in a firm's required reserves for potentially material liabilities, for example deriving from increased regulatory compliance or litigation risk.
4. The potential for an increase in the cost of financing attributable to the potential realization of material climate risk factors.

There are a variety of financial indicators that financial analysts and others (particularly regulators) pay attention to, and substantial changes in the trajectories of these factors often determine buy or hold, or sell, decisions on specific financial instruments. Mapping climate impacts on to these financial indicators, especially given the increase in climate impacts globally on any number of industries, clearly would seem prudent.[3] In fact, this focus on climate risks is now regarded in many circles as being part of an investor's (or lender's) fiduciary responsibilities.[4] Moreover, as we will discuss later, it appears likely that reporting on financial risks will be increasingly mandated in numerous countries.

Quantifying climate risks and pricing them appropriately has thus become a central goal of climate finance. The taxonomy being proposed here addresses climate risks at the *firm level*. The main advantage of this approach is that since investment and lending decisions are likewise made at the firm level, it is at this level that risks are most likely to manifest themselves as risks to investors and lenders from impacts on financial measures. One does not, for instance, invest in or lend to the chemicals sector (except through funds of some sort); one invests in or lends to a specific firm.

There is, in fact, an increasing range of constituencies potentially interested in such a taxonomy. For example, the taxonomy could be of use to firms looking to present a standardized framework for identifying and assessing the potential financial impacts of relevant climate risks. These may follow such indicators as those suggested by the TCFD[5] (to be discussed in more detail later). Likewise, financial organizations preparing for the release and discussion of climate risks in financial reports may also benefit from a standardized risk taxonomy. From a regulatory perspective, banking supervisors, under the auspices of the Network for Greening the Financial System (NGFS, a consortium of central banks) have pressed for the development of a "brown" taxonomy (essentially a risk-based taxonomy) as a way of quantifying the potential economic losses associated with a transition away from fossil fuels.[6] Several other organizations (to be discussed) have proposed similar frameworks for risk assessment. But none of this occurs unless climate risks, and their likely financial impacts, are properly specified at the appropriate level—the firm—in the first place.

In addition, it appears likely that firms will be required by regulators to report on climate-related risks, as opposed to the current voluntary reporting model in nearly all countries. Both the United Kingdom and New Zealand now have legal requirements for reporting on such risks in financial statements in line with TCFD recommendations and requirements. The United Kingdom requires that these potential risks be a part of a company's Strategic Report. Additionally, the G7 has recommended that TCFD reporting requirements be adopted throughout the G7. In the United States, the Securities and Exchange Commission (SEC) has introduced a series of climate-related disclosure recommendations that, if adopted, would require a substantial increase in climate-related disclosure by firms and financial institutions. These would include a number of measures based on TCFD recommendations, including Scope 1 and 2 emissions, among other requirements. In Europe, the European Banking Authority (EBA) has recently revised several measures—particularly Capital Requirements Regulation—which will update reporting and disclosure requirements for European banks, effective June 2022.[7] Needless to say, there are a number of issues surrounding the question of mandatory climate risk reporting, particularly whether global governance systems are sufficiently aligned.[8] Note that there is a difference between simply "disclosing" a list of Scope 1 and 2 GHG emissions, for example, and an actual discussion of the firm-based financial implications for that production. Many companies regard such emissions disclosures as sufficient, although the TCFD recommendations, for example, are considerably broader.

Despite the increasing number of green taxonomies being published, there are considerably fewer climate risk–based taxonomies.[9] For convenience, we will distinguish between two categories of frameworks: "green" taxonomies, and "risk-based" taxonomies. The "green" category, which includes the EU sustainability taxonomy, the CBI taxonomy, and several others, typically involves a system of classification, often but not always binary, flagging whether or not a particular technology is "green," often with a set of graduated criteria for determining shades of green.[10] However, these taxonomies highlight the fundamental difference between green and risk-based taxonomies: the former is an investment opportunity set, and the latter is a set of risk assessments. *In other words, the two categories of taxonomies have different objectives.*

DEFINING RISK

We begin with the most recently revised definition of risk promulgated by the IPCC:

> The potential for adverse consequences for human or ecological systems, recognizing the diversity of values and objectives associated with such systems. In the context of climate change, risks can arise from potential impacts of climate change as well as human responses to climate change. Relevant adverse consequences include those on lives, livelihoods, health and wellbeing, economic, social and cultural assets and investments, infrastructure, services (including ecosystem services), ecosystems and species.[11]

We note that there is a distinction to be made between hazard and risk. A hazard is specifically defined by the IPCC as the

> potential occurrence of a natural or human-induced physical event or trend that may cause loss of life, injury, or other health impacts, as well as damage and loss to property, infrastructure, livelihoods, service provision, ecosystems and environmental resources.

Properly speaking, as the IPCC noted in 2020, ". . .The current definition of 'risk' related to climate change impacts has retained the notion of 'hazard' to describe the **climatic driver** of a risk" (our emphasis). In 2019, the IPCC commented that

> In the context of climate change impacts, risks result from dynamic interactions between climate-related *hazards* with the *exposure* and *vulnerability* of the affected human or ecological system to the hazards. Hazards, exposure and vulnerability may each be subject to *uncertainty* in terms of magnitude and *likelihood* of occurrence, and each may change over time and space due to socio-economic changes and human decision-making.[12]

The distinction between hazard and risk is a fruitful, and frequently necessary, distinction to be in made the context of the overall risk assessments being undertaken by the IPCC and related groups, particularly for physical climate impacts. Additionally, rating agencies may employ a similar distinction—Moody's, for example, distinguishes between exposure and impact in its environmental, social, and governance analysis, which includes the agency's climate risk assessments.[13]

However, this distinction in general is not very explicitly employed by investors or lenders, for whom the term "risk" covers a fairly broad range of uncertainties. For an investor, or a bank risk officer, risk categories tend to be largely predetermined—by rating agencies criteria for credit quality, by a set of financial performance criteria for asset or performance valuation for investors, or by specific financial targets by regulators, such as the Basel Pillar framework for banks. These almost always have proved sufficient for most risks before climate considerations began to manifest themselves in scale.

For this reason, while many of the specific categories might more properly be termed "hazards," that usage is likely an underused one in the target audience for this taxonomy. We will elide this distinction by using the concept "potential climate risk" as a convenience, keeping in mind that in some areas of discussion a more nuanced approach has proved necessary. As it happens, more recent IPCC reports have emphasized that risks apply to both "the *impacts of* and *responses to* climate change."[14] Our work is intended to deal with the implications of responses to climate change, since these are likely to be the most prevalent, and perhaps significant, financial impacts at the firm level.

In general, then, detailed potential climate risk assessment can be justified for two compelling reasons:

1. the potential impact of these risks on a firm's financial profile; and
2. the increasing likelihood that firms, banks, insurance companies and regulators will be obligated to identify and assess the range of climate risks attendant to firms, and, accordingly, to financial and industrial sectors.

Further, some recent research details how climate risks may negatively impact the global financial system, including by increasing the frequency of banking crises, which can be considerable. Hence the strong interest from Central Banks as embodied by the NGFS.[15]

We note that some of the proposed frameworks for capturing potential climate risks represent a combined effort from both investors, nongovernmental organizations (NGOs), and regulators. While some of what follows derives from a single NGO or regulatory source, investor involvement in this process, particularly NCFD and the EU taxonomy, has been significant.

GREEN TAXONOMIES

EU Sustainable Taxonomy

There are several approaches to organizing climate criteria relating to firms or sectors. In particular, the EU has been at the forefront of regulatory interventions that would classify economic activities and associated financial flows for investment purposes according to their climate impact. Specifically, EU energy and sustainability policies currently are directed at transitioning away from a carbon-intensive economy in line with Paris agreement goals, mostly through aggressive GHG emission reductions. The Sustainability taxonomy reflects these goals by classifying economic activities, and then assessing whether these activities (and the firms that perform them) are aligned with Paris goals.[16] This results in a framework that classifies activities by their positive attributes—do these economic activities *facilitate* a desired energy (and other) transition?—especially in relation to achieving Paris agreement goals. This is the motivation behind the EU's Sustainability taxonomy.[17] This taxonomy has been revised since it was first introduced in 2019, and we expect these revisions will continue. This will especially be the case now that the Corporate Sustainability Reporting Directive (CSRD; discussed later) has been ratified.

The EU's Green Taxonomy has been widely acknowledged to be a significant effort.[18] The development of this taxonomy required several years' consultative work, led by a Technical Expert Group, whose final report was published March 20, 2020,[19] with several reports being published previously. In fact, the whole exercise represents an effort to define and institutionalize criteria for "sustainability" and "sustainable finance," in line with the EU's Sustainability Directive. In that sense, the taxonomy represents as much a political agenda as an investment one. Note that the first list of such activities relating to climate ("mitigation and adaptation objectives"), released in June 2019, concerned only mitigation activities—since then, a number of adaptation factors have been added. Note also that, at present, this taxonomy is mainly (although not exclusively) a taxonomy of industrial sectors by ranking their potential for contributing to decarbonization. Firms within the EU will need to begin reporting on their activities in terms of the taxonomy in 2022, in line with the three operating metrics of revenues, CAPEX and operating expenses (OPEX), and whether these are taxonomy eligible. Financial institutions will begin reporting these in 2023.

The objectives that the EU taxonomy and legislation embody are:

1. climate change mitigation,
2. climate change adaptation,
3. sustainable use and protection of water and marine resources,
4. transition to a circular economy, waste prevention, and recycling,
5. pollution prevention and control, and
6. protection of healthy ecosystems.

And the EU's taxonomy does exactly that, or most of it. The result is a taxonomy that basically represents an investment opportunity set, primarily in the energy sector. This is an admirable goal, and investors have been receptive to the guidance this represents. This is understandable—the energy sector is where carbon reductions are most needed, and most achievable. The EU's proposed Green Taxonomy is binary in the sense that it flags whether a particular technology is "green" according to whether it contributes to CO_2 reduction in particular, and "sustainability" activities in general. In particular, it seeks to allow for the determination of potential alignment between an economic activity and its potential alignment with Paris objectives through the assessment of specific financial metrics: revenues, CAPEX, and OPEX. Potential alignment with Paris objectives is determined through an analysis of these financial metrics with the six objectives of the taxonomy listed above over time. Reduction in GHG is, after all, one of the central goals of the taxonomy. The taxonomy does have some other criteria, mostly relating to water availability and discharge—but CO_2 reduction over time in line with Paris objectives is the primary goal here.

The taxonomy is not unmindful of risk factors. In fact, the technical expert group (TEG) specifically identified four types of climate hazards that should enter consideration of sustainable economic activities, specifically those related to adaptation.[20] These are:

1. water,
2. temperature,
3. wind, and
4. mass movements.

These are all physical climate hazards, and can be granulated further as suggested in the Figure 2.1.[21]

Note also that the taxonomy only encompasses a selected range of targeted industries at present, although more will be assessed going forward. At present, these are:

1. Forestry;
2. Environmental protection and restoration activities;
3. Manufacturing;
4. Energy;
5. Water supply, sewerage, waste management, and remediation;
6. Transport;
7. Construction and real estate;
8. Information and communication;
9. Professional, scientific, and technical activities;
10. Financial and insurance activities;
11. Education;
12. Human health and social work activities; and
13. Arts, entertainment, and recreation.

The EU has published a lot on the "Electricity, gas, steam, and air condition supply" sector as an economic sector, which would fall under number four in the preceding list: Energy. This is what the NACE (nomenclature statistique des activités économiques dans la Communauté européenne) codes were initially developed for, actually—economic reporting at a specific level of activity. In fact, the EU Green Taxonomy is most granulated changes in climate patterns and in the frequency/severity of climate-related events that are:

	Temperature-related	Wind-related	Water-related	Solid mass–related
Chronic	Changing temperature (air, fresh water, marine water)	Changing wind patterns	Changing precipitation patterns and type (rain, hail, snow/ice)	Coastal erosion
	Heat stress		Precipitation and/or hydrological variability	Soil degradation
	Temperature variability		Ocean acidification	Soil erosion
	Permafrost thawing		Saline intrusion	Solifluction
			Seal level rise	
			Water stress	
Acute	Heat wave	Cyclone, hurricane, typhoon	Drought	Avalanche
	Cold wave/frost	Storm (including blizzards, dust and sand storms)	Heavy precipitation (rain, hail, snow/ice)	Landslide
	Wildfire	Tornado	Flood (coastal, fluvial, pluvial, ground water)	Subsidence
			Glacial lake outburst	

FIGURE 2.1 Granulation of EU sustainable taxonomy physical climate risks.
Source: EU Technical Expert Group on Sustainable Finance, *Using the Taxonomy*, Supplementary Report, June 2019.

in this area. Of the sixty-seven industry sectors initially surveyed by the Green Taxonomy TEG in its first report, the vast majority were in the Energy sector.

We expect that more sectors (consumer products or agriculture, for example) will be added over time—that is the stated intent of the taxonomy, in fact. Interestingly, there are several sectors that have a potential range of green to brown characteristics that future taxonomic work will need to encompass. Transportation, for example, has both green and brown characteristics as a category in the aggregate. A taxonomy that does not capture these differences won't be particularly helpful in terms of risk analysis or achieving the targeted aims of the Sustainability taxonomy either, which is why granulation is essential.[22] For a number of years there has been interest in a brown taxonomy. However, it is unclear at present what this term actually means—is it simply a list of companies that are less green in terms of the Sustainability taxonomy but where the climate risk exposure is relatively low, or is it a taxonomy based on the inherent climate riskiness of the firm's operations? In the taxonomy being proposed here we have taken the latter approach as a starting point—but we cheerfully admit that other permutations are certainly possible.

One very positive result of the discussions leading up to the adoption of the Sustainability taxonomy has been the considerable progress made over the past several years in identifying policies that will lead to decarbonization and, indeed, carbon neutrality by firms and governments, net-zero targets, in other words. This has become an important discussion point for several reasons. First, it is a potentially useful framework for organizing business and government policies and actions aimed at decarbonization. Second, it allows for some flexibility in the timing of adoption of gross reduction of GHG emission targets—this is a "net-zero" target, not a "gross-zero" one. However, this aspect of net-zero has also raised concerns, that mainly relate to the practice of using potential offsets to carbon production (usually in the form of "carbon credits") in net-zero calculations. As we will discuss in Chapter 6, there is some potential for greenwashing impacts here that investors and lenders need to be mindful of.

OTHER GREEN TAXONOMIES

There are also, presently, a number of other such efforts. Many of these, like the EU taxonomy, are directed at defining what is meant by terms such as "green" and "sustainable" for investment purposes. For this reason, we will discuss the most significant proposed frameworks in some detail, since they shed important light on the process for identifying potential climate opportunity and risk factors.

Like the EU taxonomy, the CBI taxonomy is intended to capture whether some technology does or does not contribute to meeting Paris agreement goals.[23] CBI's main metric is whether their taxonomic categories are 2-degree compliant, that is, a 2-degree decarbonization trajectory is in place at a firm. CBI's categories are internally developed (with considerable external guidance) and reflect some of the industrial categorizations embodied in various

IPCC and International Energy Agency (IEA) reports. The taxonomy is pretty broad, and covers most relevant industry groups—although the level of granularity and categorization may differ from other approaches (EU, SASB, etc.). The primary focus, unsurprisingly, is GHG emissions.

The most recent version dates from September 2021. It's a proper taxonomy, moving from general to specific levels of analysis. Like the EU taxonomy, it is a taxonomy organized by industrial sector, which makes it a useful tool for a range of purposes (but not necessarily risk assessment at the firm level). In fact, like nearly all of the green taxonomies discussed here, it is simply not designed for risk assessment in the first place, and it never pretends to be anything other than an assessment tool for achieving movement toward meeting Paris agreement goals. Figure 2.2 provides a summary of the major sector categories that the Climate Bonds taxonomy has analytic tools and criteria for.

Note that they have identified some areas where the sector or use of proceeds is inconsistent with green objectives. This is pretty binary—there is no attempt at weighting, other than to subdivide green criteria into "automatically compatible" and "compatible if compliant with screening indicator." The screening indicators are pretty well defined, although one might quibble at some in terms of the threshold of acceptability in terms of criteria.

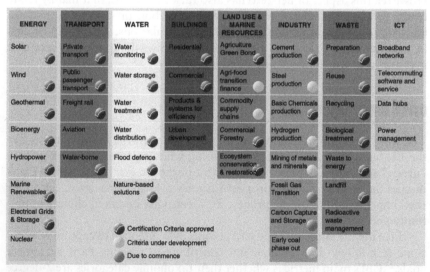

FIGURE 2.2 CBI's taxonomy categories and status.
Source: Climate Bonds Initiative, September 2021.

There are two other major frameworks, from the SASB and the CDSB, that merit attention. SASB's approach to this issue is comparably granulated, and reflects a greater degree of detail, perhaps to be expected from an organization consisting mostly of accountants. SASB currently provides assessment criteria for seventy-seven industries, a pretty broad spectrum. SASB's materiality map and its more recent Materiality Finder[24] both have good taxonomic classifications, in large part because of alignment with Financial Accounting Standards Board (FASB) and TCFD criteria. Again, the overall organization is by industrial sector and subsector, against which a series of environmental (and other) risks are assessed.

SASB does rank different environmental criteria—GHG emissions, Air Quality, and Energy Management (and several additional environmental criteria, principally related to water). SASB determines a three-dimensional weighting system, dividing companies by whether:

1. the issue is likely to be material for more than 50% of industries in sector;
2. the issue is likely to be material for fewer than 50% of industries in sector; or
3. the issue is not likely to be material for any of the industries in sector.

The implication of "material" here is negative, and is the usual accounting and reporting one.

Two comments are in order here. First, this is an accounting framework, developed by accountants, so it really is addressed at materiality and disclosure. While it may prove to be a useful framework for the type of weightings investors may wish to pursue in various scenario analyses, that's not its intention. Second, it's a US outfit, and therefore works in conjunction with FASB in the United States, although it is formally an International Financial Reporting Standards (IFRS) affiliate.[25] While there is considerable overlap between FASB and International Accounting Standards Board (IASB[IFRS]), this can't necessarily be assumed, especially for the financial sector.

Finally, the CDSB developed a set of criteria for environmental reporting by companies, often in conjunction with SASB and the TCFD goals.[26] Environmental information was defined as information about the reporting organization's:

- Natural capital dependencies;
- Environmental results;
- Environmental risks and opportunities;
- Environmental policies, strategies, and targets;
- Performance against environmental targets.

The principal criteria were the following:

- GHG emissions;
- Renewable/nonrenewable energy generation, use, and consumption;
- Land use, land use change, and forestry (LULUCF);
- Non-GHG emissions to air, land, and water, for example, noise, odor, particulates, pollutants;
- Renewable and nonrenewable material resource use, for example, forest products, fish stocks, minerals, metals;
- Water use and consumption; and
- Waste and spillages, for example, mining and hazardous waste, radiation, and industrial by-products.

This is both a broader, and slightly different, set of criteria, and is quite similar to many of the risk indicators to be discussed. Note that this is a complicated and quite mixed listing of concerns. Only one issue (land use change) has any bearing on physical risks, one (material resource risk) is a straightforward Natural Capital risk, and the remaining concerns are all basically transition risks that have differential impacts on various financial measures. It's a good list, but not necessarily an organized taxonomic one. The general thrust is to provide a framework for financial reporting to include a wide range of environmental risks, of which climate risks are just one (albeit major) risk category.

CDSB also offered the following as a set of potential risk and opportunity categories to be assessed and incorporated in financial reporting. It is a very good summary of a range of potential risks of interest to the reporting firms themselves, as well as investors and lenders:

Climate change related risks and opportunities are potentially wide-ranging, direct or indirect (e.g., affecting markets and supply chain), and can include:

- Regulatory risks and opportunities from current and/or expected regulatory requirements, including known or expected effects of:
  - GHG emissions limits,
  - energy efficiency standards,
  - carbon taxation,
  - process or product standards, and
  - participation in GHG trading schemes.
- Risks and opportunities from the physical effects of climate change, including known or expected effects of:
  - changing weather patterns,
  - sea level rise,

– shifts in species distribution,
– changes in water availability,
– changes in temperature, and
– variation in agricultural yield and growing seasons.

This list, among other things, identifies some of the issues to be dealt with when assessing candidate definitions of climate risk. In particular, these listings provide a pretty solid overview of issues that should be flagged as potential risk categories. However, there is no overall organization to these issues that would make risk assessment more straightforward. It's a very good list, but it's not a taxonomy.

Other taxonomies continue to appear, particularly among investors, and various firms are incorporating taxonomic approaches based on the Green Taxonomy internally.[27] However, we note that like the EU's Green taxonomy, these generally represent candidates for investment and are organized by industrial sectors and are largely silent on risk classifications.

This is, at present, a voluntary process in most countries (other than the United Kingdom and New Zealand), as are all these taxonomies, although if climate risk reporting becomes mandatory, as appears to be the case, that is likely to change. Whether any of the current systems are suitable for a generic non-Green—or Green, for that matter—global taxonomy (beyond the EU, for example) remains to be seen. What is needed at present is a purported organization of these risks for identification and assessment by investors and lenders. What follows is an attempt to do just that.

PROPOSED RISK FRAMEWORKS

There have been a number of proposals for a framework for this sort of potential risk assessment. By far the most important of these are the general models presented by the TCFD and the NGFS.

Task Force on Climate-related Disclosures

The reports presented by TCFD since 2016 have been by far the most important driver of climate risk reporting—or at least forcing firms, exchanges, and regulators to think about it.[28] They were originally presented at the Paris COP meeting by the UK's Financial Stability Board (which continues to oversee TCFD operations) with the specific objective of providing a framework for financial reporting of climate risks. Since then, the TCFD recommendations have been widely accepted, and this process continues to grow. In addition, in some markets (particularly the United Kingdom) the TCFD is now intended to be a driver and framing provider of scenario

Industry	Percent
Energy	43%
Materials and Buildings	42%
Banking	41%
Insurance	41%
Ag., Food, and Forest Products	37%
Consumer Goods	33%
Transportaion	32%
Technology and Media	15%

FIGURE 2.3   Average percentage of climate risk disclosure by industry.
Source: TCFD. *Annual Status Report,* 2022. https://assets.bbhub.io/company/
sites/60/2022/10/2022-TCFD-Status-Report.pdf

analysis. In the United Kingdom, entities now required to report climate related items include a range of financial entities, particularly premium listed companies, asset managers, and insurance companies. In its Annual Status Report for 2022, TCFD notes that TCFD disclosure in a range of firms has been increasing annually, with several potentially affecting sectors reporting relatively high levels of climate risk disclosure, as shown in Figure 2.3.[29]

So what is being disclosed? TCFD's original eleven recommendations concentrated on disclosure in four key areas:

1. governance;
2. strategy;
3. risk management; and
4. metrics and targets.[30]

This is the essential framework by which TCFD encourages the disclosure of climate-related risks. TCFD's own reports, including the most recent Status Report, adopt this framework for the bulk of their discussion.

As is the case with other framework developers, TCFD adopted the overall framework of two distinct classes of climate risks: physical risk and transition risks. The six risk categories are:

1. Acute physical risks
2. Chronic physical risks
3. Transition risks – policy and legal risks
4. Transition risks – technology risks
5. Transition risks – market risks
6. Transition risks – reputational risks

In addition, TCFD also catalogued five categories of what it termed climate opportunities:

1. resource efficiency,
2. energy source,
3. products and services,
4. markets, and
5. resilience (mainly in the context of resilience of firm strategy).

The overall goal is for firms to note developments in all eleven areas on an annual basis, with an eye toward assessing potential financial impacts on the back of an itemization of climate-related risks and opportunities. TCFD proffers the theoretical framework for adopters shown in Figure 2.4.

Clearly the TCFD is meant to recognize that potential climate risks can also have corresponding offsets (this is, in fact, the basis of many net-zero frameworks at both firms and governments). In its 2022 Status Report, TCFD notes that not all these potential offsets receive comparable attention by reporters. Resilience, in fact, despite receiving increased attention over the past three years, still scores the lowest in terms of disclosure. In general, it is difficult to assess the potential impact of these potentially positive opportunities and how they are integrated into overall assessments—the 2022 Status

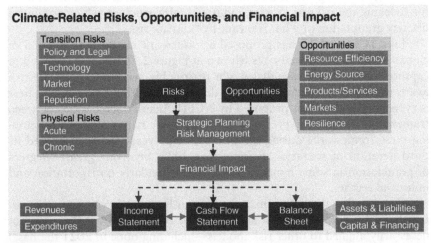

FIGURE 2.4 TCFD flow of climate risks and opportunities to financial risks.
Source: TCFD, *Recommendations of the Task Force on Climate-related Financial Disclosures: Final Report*, June 2017.

Report has little information on the extent to which these are broadly disclosed. However, the information presented in the report is almost entirely in terms of the four major goals, with only sporadic attention paid to disclosure of the eleven actual risks and opportunities outside case studies.

There is no question that TCFD has been wildly successful in spurring interest in the identification and assessment of climate-related risks. Whether these proposals offer enough granularity to achieve a thorough cataloguing of such risks is a bit uncertain, especially given some of the qualitative uncertainties associated, in particular, with those factors mentioned in the Opportunities column. Given the number of current publications offering advice on how to implement TCFD recommendations, we suspect that this issue will eventually be accommodated.

Network for Greening the Financial System

As mentioned, the NGFS has been pressing for the development of a more granulated risk taxonomy as a way of quantifying the potential economic losses associated with a transition away from fossil fuels. Such a taxonomy could be of use for employing the recommendations by the TCFD.[31] However, it seems likely that the range of risks to be assessed is considerably broader than those accompanying the so-called "energy transition." Moreover, any attempt to define the scope of a broad economic transition or a more targeted energy transition should, at a minimum, include a mechanism for reducing the risks of existing industrial infrastructure, which requires a discrete granulation of what is meant by "climate risks."[32]

Like TCFD, NGFS has proposed a framework for the transmission of climate risks into financial risks (shown in Figure 2.5), which is intended to capture some of the issues that might reasonably arise in any climate risk assessment. The first thing to note is that the Transition risk category here is even smaller than that proposed by NCFD. Again, discrepancies between frameworks are to be expected at this point—we have only been developing these frameworks during the past six or so years. NGFS proposed its third iteration of scenarios in September 2022, involving greater degrees of granulation in some nonenergy sectors, particularly transportation and industrial sectors.

We note that the list of financial risks in Figure 2.5 represents the current Basel framework for risk assessment by banks, and that these are not necessarily aligned to other risk models—including ours. In 2021 the Basel Committee on Banking Supervision (BCBS) issued a statement indicating it saw no need to provide any special accommodation for climate risks at present.[33] This decision has not gone unchallenged, and we expect it will remain

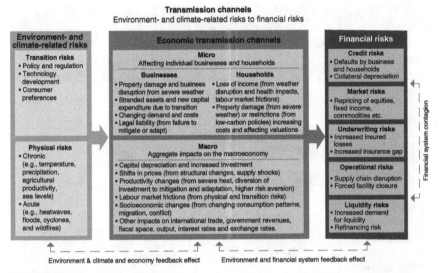

FIGURE 2.5 The NGFS framework for the transition from environmental to financial risks.
Source: NGFS Climate Scenarios for Central Banks and Supervisors, 2020.

a topic of discussion going forward.[34] There remains the issue of reconciling any proposed set of climate risks, including the one being presented here, with the Basel categories. This lies outside the scope of this book but will eventually need to be undertaken. Our approach is somewhat different from the Basel Commission's, although we suspect that the range of potential environmental risks to be accommodated (the Transition and Physical Risks left-hand boxes in the framework shown in Figure 2.5) will be very similar to the categories embodied in our proposed taxonomy.

There is considerable overlap between the two, which should not come as a complete surprise—both are geared to scenario analysis and financial reporting. Note that it is difficult to see how the financial risks assessment of the NGFS framework can be accomplished without attending to the financial metrics identified in the TCFD framework.

This represents a general pattern that we are still in the middle of—frameworks and models get more granulated, as they need to be, to accommodate a broader spectrum of risks. Our view, to be expanded in Chapter 3, is that climate risk identification and assessment needs to be granulated to the level of the financial measure the potential risk is manifesting itself in.

Likewise, another approach to such an analytical framework has been offered by the World Resources Institute (WRI) and the United Nations Environment Programme (UNEP) Finance Initiative.[35] This framework,

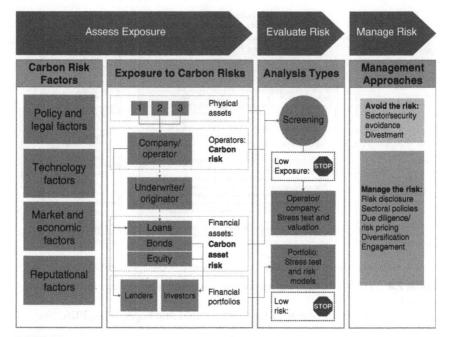

FIGURE 2.6 WRI/UNEP framework for addressing carbon risk.
Source: World Resources Institute and UNEP Finance Initiative, *Carbon Asset Risk: Discussion Framework*, 2020.

shown in Figure 2.6, is a more granular version of the framework proposed in Figure 2.5, and has a narrower focus of carbon risk exposure.[36] The model also builds on traditional economic and financial measures, but with a specific carbon risk objective.

The WRI/UNEP approach in general resembles the EU taxonomy approach to classifying economic activities in terms of their environmental sustainability.[37] In each case, the goal is to determine how aligned the instrument (e.g., bond, loan of share) is with a specific targeted objective. In the case of the EU taxonomy, the objective is alignment with Paris Agreement objectives for investment purposes. In the case being modeled by the framework (Figure 2.6), the objective is risk assessment with a focus on managing the risk of the asset (e.g., in absolute terms or in terms of portfolio alignment). Much of the analytical work, however, will be the same. Note that in the WRI/UNEP framework, the categorizations of the actual risks to be assessed are left open, and ultimately seem to rely on stress testing for risk quantification. We believe this is a common characteristic of these (and similar) frameworks: they are designed, in part, to allow for the type of scenario analysis that is increasingly required to calculate potential financial impacts of climate risks. We also note that these frameworks differ from each other, but not in particularly meaningful ways. All have specifications of climate risks to varying degrees, and all have identified the financial measures that are likely see a potentially measurable impact.

Over the past several years SASB, CDSB, and TCFD (primarily the latter two organizations) have published, individually or cooperatively, several guides on assessing approaches to climate risk, particularly in terms of the financial reporting of these risks.[38] Among other things, these reports are intended to provide practical guidance in implementing TCFD and related measures. Should TCFD reporting become mandatory, as seems increasingly likely, we expect these processes to receive even closer scrutiny.

Some Observations

There are several points worth considering at this juncture. First, as seen earlier, there seems to be a wealth of possible candidates for risk categories and risk instances, including many that have not yet been suggested, in some areas (transition risks) and less flexibility in others (physical risks). Since much climate risk assessment in the past has been geared to macroeconomic impacts and scenario analysis, this granulation of risk categories is a welcome development. It is also a relatively recent development, primarily within the past decade. It is not surprising, therefore, that there may be some nonagreement across different risk categorization systems on particular risk categories, just as standard industrial classification systems can also vary widely in their degree of granulation. We suspect that over time we will see a gradual consolidation of proposals to a relatively standardized set of climate risk criteria.

On this point, we note in passing that there is an increasing number of guides to climate risk assessment available for firms and analysts for constructing risk and disclosure models, and we expect the number of such guides to continue to increase.[39] This potential expansion raises an issue, however, one which we have already encountered in our brief discussion of risk categorization—how to ensure interoperability across various reporting landscapes. As has been pointed out, there is no uniformity for corporate governance models, which limits the potential uniformity of climate disclosure frameworks.[40] If TCFD is more aligned with one shareholder model (say, that of the United States) than it is with another (say, those of Asia and Europe), does this have corporate disclosure and reporting implications? This issue requires further investigation.

Second, note also that the above categories contain risks that are not the same—in CDSB's taxonomy, for example, sea level rise is not the same sort of risk that carbon taxation is, although both have potentially sizeable financial impacts on firms and their instruments. It is therefore important to ensure that the granulation of risk categories achieves a certain level of consistency. This consistency may be partially achieved in the classification of the risks themselves—by not, for example, conflating certain risk categories that should be kept separate (extreme weather and extreme precipitation, for example). However, it may also be achieved through the delineation of where and when these risks manifest themselves—by an analytical focus of, for example, cash flow impacts across a range of physical and transition potential risks. As previously indicated, the taxonomy proposed is primarily designed to address potential risks attending to individual instruments—loans, bonds, and equities, through specific financial measures such as cash flows and operating margins.

Third, the risks we envision being captured here are often longer-term risks. They do not lend themselves to comparable quantification and analysis as shorter-term risks, in part because the track record is simply not there in most cases, and because of the horizon issues discussed previously. These climate risks are the type, for example, that TCFD envisions being captured by scenario analysis.[41] The taxonomy proposed here is designed to at least identify where long-term mischief might arise. A recent report from the Bank for International Settlements suggested that climate risks are a "Green Swan" event, one in which past risk models will prove insufficient for appropriate risk assessment, and where tail risks may be considerable.[42] As we noted earlier, we haven't been here before.

Fourth, there is little discussion of the implication of losing government subsidies in potentially affected industries in any of these frameworks. This includes industries that benefit enormously from generous government subsidies (e.g., fossil fuels and agriculture) that may see those subsidies reduced or even eliminated, which in many cases would generate financial implications that could only be described, in some cases, as "startling," to say the least. These industries are particularly vulnerable to potentially aggressive regulatory action on carbon pricing, although these industries are politically contentious as well. This makes predictions about potential changes to subsidy levels a difficult call. In short, the range of potential risks is broad, but action on these remains uncertain, leaving financial institutions, in particular, broadly exposed. These potential risks need to be included in any climate-related taxonomy. Subsidy issues occupy a fair amount of the risk discussion in this book.

There is, then, a need for an ambitious risk taxonomy, one that would span diverse industrial sectors and provide some guidance as to where financial risks—and not just opportunities—reside at the firm level.[43] It should also allow the aggregation of the relative riskiness of various industrial sectors that may be exposed to significant changes in asset values, for example. However, many historic attempts to measure climate financial risks at the sector level typically have derived from broad integrated assessment models, which are geared to macro-level analysis of climate impacts.[44] Most such models, are, frankly, of limited use to investors and lenders when it comes to individual firm investments or loans. The approach taken here is very much a bottom-up approach.

There are many industrial sectors where the current regulatory structure is likely to become more stringent in terms of developments such as carbon pricing or mandated GHG reductions. Such restrictions will in turn increase regulatory, and perhaps litigation, risks for those industries that currently generate high levels of GHGs. Naturally, this group includes the energy and power sector, and it is this sector that has received considerable scrutiny to date. However, other industries that may be affected include transportation (mainly autos and trucks), the maritime shipping and airline industries (which share a number of attributes), the cement and building products industry, and metals and mining, including the steel industry. Many share a common thread—because their industrial processes require generation of significant amounts of heat (process heating), they are extremely energy consumptive, and are therefore more exposed to the costs associated with an energy transition. Transition will clearly involve different costs for different sectors.

We suspect this issue will rise in importance in the near term in the United Kingdom as the Bank of England (BoE) begins to require banks to undertake climate stress tests for the first time.[45]

The BoE has provided an elegant summary of what it regards as climate risks that encapsulates where we believe most regulators are likely to end up.[46] It's not nearly as granulated as the frameworks discussed above, but it doesn't need to be—the onus for assessment will still reside with listed companies, banks, and insurers. One assumes, however, that regulatory bodies such as the BoE and others over time will gain sufficient expertise to be able to assess the quality of such reporting and disclosure.

Finally, it would be desirable if a risk model was capable of predicting tipping points—in this case, either physical tipping points (which are becoming more important as climate impacts expand), or social ones, or, for present purposes, financial ones.[47] This is such an embedded concept in financial analysis that its importance is frequently overlooked—but recognizing tipping points is what financial analysis is *for*. Tipping points are those indicators that warrant a change in recommendation, and analysts do this regularly. The proposed taxonomy simply adds a new collection of risk indicators that may manifest themselves in sufficient strength so as to lead to changes in share price or credit rating assessments. To oversimplify, this is what analysts do. And they are finding that increasingly they need to include climate factors in this assessment. Predicting the financial impact of climate tipping points will increasingly be part of the process, just as any number of considerations affect that process now. In many cases, some of these risks and tipping point considerations apply only to certain sectors—litigation risk in the pharmaceutical and tobacco industries, for example. For climate-related issues, this is a difficult process, in part because of uncertainty over timing, and, in the case of a number of potential transition risks, their likelihood. It seems clear, however, that the number of potential climate tipping points continues to rise, as will the concomitant financial risks associated with them.[48]

As we mention elsewhere, some climate risks are relatively certain—a whole raft of physical risks, for example. Other risks, however, are contingent on human responses to climate risks. Many transition risks are contingent on public policy decisions, which in many cases have not yet been made—a global price for carbon, for example, or resilience requirements for shoreline infrastructure. This fact will, of course, complicate any sort of analysis of the financial impacts of climate risks—since we are not in a position yet to determine those financial impacts. However, we may still be able to speculate on what financial indicators those impacts are likely to manifest themselves as, even if we can't determine yet the likely scope of theses impacts.[49] Additionally, many transition risks can be anticipated and planned for, which may make those costs more manageable, depending on the potentially available time frame. Much of our discussion throughout the book will reflect these varying levels of uncertainty.

NOTES

1. By "material," we reflect the International Accounting Standards Board's (IASB's) revised definition of materiality released October 18, 2018: "Information is material if omitting, misstating or obscuring it could reasonably be expected to influence the decisions that the primary users of general-purpose financial statements make on the basis of those financial statements, which provide financial information about a specific reporting entity."
2. "Probability of Default" is simply a measure of the potential for a firm to default on obligations. It underlies lending assessments in particular, but also has a broader utility in financial analysis in general.
3. Monnin, Pierre. *Integrating Climate Risks into Credit Risk Assessment—Current Methodologies and the Case of Central Banks Corporate Bond Purchases*, December 20, 2018. Council on Economic Policies, Discussion Note 2018/4.

4. *Principles for Responsible Investment and UNEP FI*. Fiduciary Duty in the 21st Century, 2019.

5. TCFD. *Final Report: Recommendations of the Task Force on Climate-Related Disclosures*, June 2017.

6. On the grounds that "brown" industries, unlike "green" industries, are those most associated with GHG production, as well as other forms of environmental pollution.

7. Hafner, Katherine and Frederick Winter. EBA Finalises Rules on Climate Risk Disclosures for Banks. *Linklaters Sustainable Futures*, February 2022.

8. Griffin, Paul and Amy Myers Jaffe. Challenges for a Climate Risk Disclosure Mandate. *Nature Energy* 7, 2–4, 2022.

9. OECD. *Developing Sustainable Finance Definitions and Taxonomies: A Guide for Policymakers*, October 2020.

10. Climate Bonds Initiative. *Climate Bond Taxonomy*, January 2020.

11. Reisinger, Andy et al. *The Concept of Risk in the IPCC Sixth Assessment Report: A Summary of Cross-Working Group Discussions*. Intergovernmental Panel on Climate Change, Geneva, Switzerland. September 2020.

12. IPCC. Summary for Policymakers. In *IPCC Special Report on the Ocean and Cryosphere in a Changing Climate*. Edited by H.-O. Pörtner et al., 2019.

13. Moody's Investors Service. *General Principles for Assessing Environmental, Social and Governance Risks Methodology*, December 14, 2020.

14. IPCC. *The Concept of Risk in the IPCC Sixth Assessment Report: A Summary of Cross-working Group Discussions*, Guidance for IPCC authors, September 2020.

15. Francesco Lamberti et al. The Public Costs of Climate-induced Financial Instability. *Nature Climate Change* 9: 829–833, November 2019.

16. There are a number of existing frameworks for organizing and classifying economic activity. The TEG's approach reflects the framework used throughout most of the EU, the NACE (Nomenclature of Economic Activities) system for economic organization and statistics. Use of NACE is mandated within the European statistical system. There is considerable overlap between NACE and the International Standard Industrial Classification of All Economic Activities (ISIC), which is intended by the United Nations to be the international reference classification of productive activities.

17. EU Technical Expert Group on Sustainable Finance. *Taxonomy: Final Report of the Technical Expert Group on Sustainable Finance*, March 2020.

18. Quinson, Tim and Tom Freke. *Europe's 'Taxonomy' May Set Global Standards for Green: Q&A*, Bloomberg, November 13, 2019.

19. European Commission. *TEG Final Report on the EU Taxonomy*, March 2020. The taxonomy was formally adopted by the European Parliament on June 19, 2020, and went into effect shortly after that.

20. EU Technical Expert Group on Sustainable Finance. *Using the Taxonomy, Supplementary Report*, June 2019.

21. . . . or, from our perspective, potential climate risks. As mentioned previously, we are being casual about this distinction.

22. This is usually done according to NACE code in Europe, or the North American Industry Classification System (NAICS) in North America.

23. Climate Bonds Initiative. *Climate Bond Taxonomy*, September 2021. Note that this is a different endeavor than the process underling the Climate Bonds Certification process, which is more limited.

24. SASB Standards. *SASB Implementation Supplement—Greenhouse Gas Emissions and SASB Standards*, October 2020; SASB Standards. *ESG Integration Insights*, 2021 edn, December 2021.

25. Effective August 1, 2022, the Value Reporting Foundation—parent of the SASB—consolidated into the IFRS Foundation, which previously had established the International Sustainability Standards Board (ISSB), in November 2021 when it incorporated CDSB.

26. Carbon Disclosure Standards Board. *CDSB Framework for Reporting Environmental and Climate Change Information*, December 2019; *EU Environmental Reporting Handbook,* February 2020.

27. Martindale, Will. *Taxonomies a Revolutionary Shift in ESG*, Top1000funds.com, September, 2020.

28. We note that proposed reporting requirements for areas such as natural capital and biodiversity are currently being prepared by the Task Force for Nature-related Financial Disclosures (TNFB). We will discuss these in more detail in Chapter 7.

29. TCFD. *Annual Status Report*, 2022. This report is replete with case studies of how firms in a broad range of sectors have implemented TCFD disclosure recommendations.

30. TCFD. *Recommendations of the Task Force on Climate-related Financial Disclosures: Final Report*, June 2017.

31. TCFD. *Recommendations of the Task Force on Climate-related Financial Disclosures,* December 2016; *Final Report: Recommendations of the Task Force on Climate-related Financial Disclosures,* June 2017; *2022 TCFD Status Report: Task Force on Climate-related Financial Disclosures*, October 2022.

32. Donovan, Charles, Milica Fomicov, and Anastasiya Ostrovnaya, *Transition Finance: Managing Funding to Carbon-intensive Firms,* Centre for Climate Finance and Investment, September 2020.

33. Thompson, Douglas. Existing Risk Categories Can Capture Climate Risk Drivers, Basel Says. *Global Banking Regulation Review*, April 16, 2021. From a broader perspective, current regulations and legislation governing risk weightings, which are mostly based on the Basel II and Basel III reforms in Europe, generally do not factor in climate factors. In part, this is because they were not designed to do so; in most cases, the horizons involved would be longer than can be assessed from a Basel framework.

34. Thiruchelvam, Sharon. Basel Playing Catch-up on Climate Risk, Say Experts. *Risk.net*, April 26, 2021.

35. World Resources Institute and UNEP Finance Initiative. *Carbon Asset Risk: Discussion Framework*, 2020.

36. There is a considerably broader risk landscape that investors, lenders, and regulators need to be mindful of.

37. We suggest that the proposed taxonomy in this book fits most easily into the third column of Figure 2.6.

38. SASB and CDSB. *Converging on Climate Risk: CDSB, the SASB, and the TCFD*, September 2017. CDSP. *Uncharted Waters*, March 2018; TCFD. *Status Reports* 2018–2022; CDSB, *Materiality and Climate-related Financial Disclosures*, 2018; CDSB and SASB. *TCFD Implementation Guide*, 2019; CDSB and SASB. *CDSB Framework for Reporting Environmental and Climate Change Information*, December 2019; CDSB and CDP. *EU Environmental Reporting Handbook*, February 2020;

39. See, for example, Principles for Responsible Investment. *Climate Risk: An Investor Resource Guide*, 2022; Umwelt Bundesamt. *How to Perform a Robust Climate Risk and Vulnerability Assessment for EU Taxonomy Reporting? Recommendations for Companies—Draft*, August 2022.

40. Griffin, Paul and Amy Myers Jaffe. Challenges for a Climate Risk Disclosure Mandate. *Nature Energy* 7(1): 1–3, 2022.

41. TCFD. *Technical Supplement: The Use of Scenario Analysis in Disclosure of Climate-related Risks and Opportunities*, June 2017.

42. Bolton, Patrick et al. *The Green Swan: Central Banking and Financial Stability in the Age of Climate Change*. Bank of International Settlements, Basel, January 2020.

43. European Central Bank. Climate Change and Financial Stability. *Financial Stability Review*, May 2019.

44. NGFS. *Guide to Climate Scenario Analysis for Central Banks and Supervisors*, June 2020.

45. Noonan, Laura. Banking Regulators Start Climate Stress Tests. *The Financial Times*, April 15, 2021.

46. Bank of England. *Enhancing Banks' and Insurers' Approaches to Managing the Financial Risks from Climate Change*. October 2018. See the appendix in particular.

47. Herr, Alexandria, Shannon Osaka, and Maddie Stone. Points of No Return. *Grist Magazine*, April 2021.

48. Lenton, Timothy L. et al., Climate Tipping Points: Too Risky to Bet Against. *Nature* 575: 592–595, 2019.

49. Although in some cases we are beginning to be able to provide such pricing information. Loans for renewable energy projects have become cheaper over the past several years, while loans for coal projects have become more expensive (although the Ukraine invasion may temporarily have distorted this picture somewhat). See Zhou, X. Y., C. Wilson, and B. L. Caldecott. *The Energy Transition and Changing Financing Costs*. Oxford: Smith School of Enterprise and the Environment, 2021.

CHAPTER 3

The Climate Risk Taxonomy and Its Constituents

How was this taxonomy constructed? Specifically, what criteria were employed for determining its constituents, and its overall form? Since this process overall has not been peer-reviewed (although certain constituents have been), providing external validation for this approach becomes an important part of the process. Unless this taxonomy is well motivated, it will serve little purpose.

RISK CLASSIFICATIONS

Investors and policymakers, as mentioned, have settled into a convention that subdivides potential climate risks into two traditional broad categories: **physical risks** and **transition risks**. Physical risks represent the range of impacts on landforms and infrastructure that will result from the physical effects of climate change. Transition risks arise from preparing for, responding to, and attempting to limit the impacts of physical risks—in other words, getting from Point A (where we are now) to Point B (where we want to be). These transition risks have generally been categorized into two further categories: **adaptation** and **mitigation**. Adaptation responses are designed to cope with the probable physical, societal, and economic consequences of global heating. Mitigation measures are designed to curtail the growth of factors producing global heating, particularly (but not exclusively) GHG emissions.

In the absence of any pre-existing climate risk taxonomy for firms, we have elected to create one. The specific categories chosen here largely reflect those found in most compendia of climate risks, although not all of these are organized along the same lines. There also are a number of indicators and categories that are not normally found in such compendia, even while we maintain a general recognition of the differences between physical risks and transition risks. Our classification of natural capital risks, however, represents a novel contribution, and will certainly evolve over time, given increasing interest in issues such as biodiversity loss.

We provide a short summary of the taxonomical categories, reserving our more detailed discussion of actual indicators of these categories and their possible sectoral impacts for the remaining chapters of this book.

THE TAXONOMY RATIONALE

"Climate risk" is a broad rubric, covering a range of more specific risks which must be decomposed to become more financially meaningful. The taxonomy proposed here is based on Buhr (2014, 2017) and retains the major categories proposed at that time, as shown in Figure 3.1.[1]

We have taken as our point of departure the framework employed by rating agencies for basic risk assessment. All are variations of a basic theme—organize potential risks into business risks and financial risks. Obviously, these are not independent of each other. But as a basic framework, traditional credit analysis covers a lot of ground and has remained a durable model as a framework for risk assessment. Standard & Poor's (S&P) provides a formulation (circa 2013) of the basic approach to analyzing risks by overall category (see Figure 3.1). More recently, S&P has granularized the overall risk categories, but the fundamental approach remains similar.[2] However, this approach does not lend itself easily to identifying and assessing potential risks with indeterminate horizons. Note that rating agencies have recently been incorporating ESG factors into this basic framework where relevant—but the basic model remains the same.[3]

For our purposes we have simply expanded this approach, as indicated in Figure 3.2.

Taken together, the two Buhr papers articulate a vision for analyzing a new suite of credit risks composed of three categories:

1. *Traditional risks*, meaning the risks usually captured by traditional business risk and financial risk analysis. This is the risk assessment process that financial analysts are trained to undertake.
2. *Climate risks*, subdivided into physical and transition risks, with the latter relating mainly to climate mitigation and adaptation.
3. *Natural capital risks*, intended to capture renewable and nonrenewable resource depletion and certain geopolitical risks (particularly risks associated with water resources).

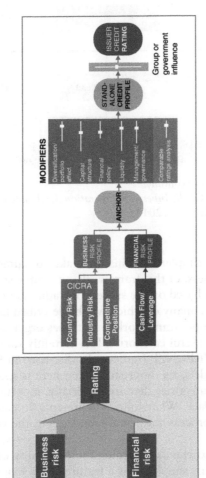

FIGURE 3.1 S&P credit frameworks (2013 and 2015).
Source: Standard & Poor's Rating Services.

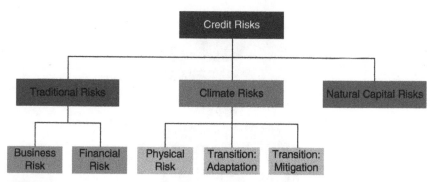

FIGURE 3.2 The basic risk taxonomy.
Source: Buhr, B. *ESG for Credit Investors: Operational, Climate and Natural Capital Risks.* Paris: Société Générale, 2014.

It doesn't get much simpler than this. We make no claims as to the potential import, or uniqueness, of this framework—it simply strikes us as being a motivated one that is based on the success of traditional business risk and financial risk categories, many of which will be described later in this book. It is actually a very simple framework, but it does organize potential indicators into potentially useful categories. It is certainly simple as compared with the TCFD and WRI/UNEP frameworks discussed in Chapter 2. With reference to those models, the approach taken here is geared to identifying the potential risk categories that are materially important enough to be modeled in the first place. What follows represents an elaboration of this basic approach. The process framework underlying the current model is shown in Figure 3.3.

Again, we make no claims regarding the originality of this approach, and we frankly regard its simplicity as a feature, not a bug. We expect that, over time, the various climate risk adjustments to be made will be more fully integrated into what we term "traditional" financial analysis, and that these will reflect the sorts of accommodations embodied in Figure 3.2. As we mention elsewhere, we would eventually expect that the climate risks column (and that of its financial manifestations at the far right) will be integrated into the left-hand side of this model. At present, however, most work in this area is concerned with identifying the actual range of potential risks embodied in this column.

As illustrated in Figure 3.3, each of the four main subcategories of risk has at least one representative financial indicator. In fact, there will usually be multiple potential financial indicators in actual practice. It is difficult,

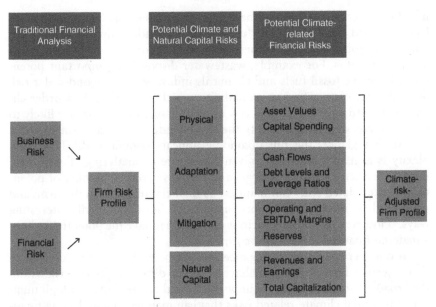

FIGURE 3.3 Deriving a climate-risk-adjusted firm model.
Source: Buhr, B. *What Is Climate Risk? A Field Guide for Investors, Lenders and Regulators.* London: Centre for Climate Finance and Investment, Imperial College Business School, February 2022.

for example, to envision each of the major risk categories as *not* having an impact on asset valuations, for example. Note also that while we have observed the acute/chronic distinction customarily used in these frameworks, this distinction is easily blurred. Many of the potential risks presented in the taxonomy may manifest as *both* acute and chronic. Note that in all the proposed risk categories, the right-hand column is always a representative physical or financial indicator. As mentioned previously, several of these potential risk candidates span multiple risk categories, reflecting the intertwined nature of both climate impacts and the financial responses to them. For instance, water stress can be found as both a physical risk and a natural capital risk and manifest themselves in a wide range of potential risk categories. Similarly, carbon-based assets are particularly at risk since the numerous risks that these assets face stem from diverse mitigation causes. In each case, we have tried to assess the relevant risk level that would trigger a financial impact, although in some cases this attempt may be somewhat speculative.

It should be noted that some of the potential risks categorized as Climate Risks are not strictly so. Some are broader environmental risks that may be exacerbated by global heating concerns, such as air pollution. We have included these under the "climate risks" heading simply because the impact of global heating on these risks may become disproportionate to its current status. For example, wastewater disposal, an important potential risk for the fossil fuels and chemicals industries, is a second-order risk derived from issues of water availability, which is clearly a first-order climate risk (and a natural capital risk as well). Issues of this sort are likely to become increasingly important to the mining industry in water-scarce areas.

At first glance, the full taxonomy appears complicated.[4] This complexity is arguably inevitable, given the nature of analyzing climate risk: inputs are often uncertain; a large (and perhaps variable) number of potential climate-related risks can manifest as financial impacts on the firm; and many of them intertwine in poorly understood but undoubtedly interesting ways.[5] However, its unifying focus is on risks that have the potential to have a material financial impact *at the firm level*.

If one were aspiring to elegance, this framework would hardly satisfy that objective. For one thing, we have mixed up different types of risk within the broader categories. This is simply because there are indeed a high number of potential climate-related risks that can manifest themselves as financial impacts on the firm—it's not just CO_2 emissions reductions that are meant to be captured by risk reporting. Our taxonomy looks complicated because the analysis of potential climate risks was always going to be complicated. This is a complex analysis with often uncertain inputs.

In addition, there are certain kinds of risks that are not captured here in a straightforward manner. This aspect of the proposed taxonomy reflects a necessary distinction between proximate and distal causation. For example, glacial melt is clearly a physical risk, in terms of its potential contribution to rising sea levels on a global basis (as we discuss in Chapter 4). In this case, sea level rise is the proximate risk, and glacial melt one of several likely distal causes. In turn, glacial melt is a physical risk that is itself the result of another, larger, more distal risk that adds to increasing global temperatures. In fact, most of the risks we discuss derive, either directly or indirectly, from a small handful of what we might call "primary" risks—primarily those associated with increased regional and/or global temperatures, with a wide range of regional variations, that derive directly from the accumulation of GHGs in the atmosphere. While this is certainly true, it is the granulation of these mostly derivative risks to the level of their financial impacts that is relevant to the target audience here. As we mention elsewhere in this book, simply referring to "Climate Risk" is not actually that useful an exercise in and of itself for investors, lenders, or regulators.[6]

PHYSICAL RISKS

The physical risk category has been the most thoroughly explored to date, for several reasons. First, it is relatively straightforward. For all their given uncertainties in terms of timing and scale, physical risks are the easiest to understand and measure. Second, these are the areas where potential risks are manifesting themselves most obviously at present. Much of the general work in this area derives from various IPCC reports (noted previously), for example, where risk categories emerged early on and have remained more or less the same over successive reports. The categories presented here reflect a distillation of a broader range of risk and hazard categories, mainly drawn from the aforementioned reports, but also from other sources. The approach that the taxonomy being presented here most closely resembles is that proposed by Four Twenty Seven, Inc., which has six major climate risk indicators: heat stress, water stress, extreme precipitation, wildfires, sea level rise, and hurricanes and typhoons.[7] Even at this foundational level, however, we have made some adjustments in our taxonomy (e.g., we have categorized wildfires as an instance of acute heat stress). We also retain the broad distinction between acute and chronic risks. As we discuss in more detail in Chapter 4, there are only a finite number of possible ways to organize these risks, and there are only a limited number of terms that can be employed to describe them. "Drought" pretty much means the same across a wide range of climate risk assessments.

TRANSITION RISKS

Adaptation Risks

Since the physical changes that are expected to emerge are well identified, it follows that measures for adapting to these impacts should also be at least somewhat understood. Thus, adaptation risk categories across taxonomies are also relatively coherent. The IPCC definition of Adaptation is elegantly straightforward:

> In *human systems*, the process of adjustment to actual or expected *climate* and its effects, in order to moderate harm or exploit beneficial opportunities. In natural systems, the process of adjustment to actual climate and its effects; human intervention may facilitate adjustment to expected climate and its effects.[8]

However, there has been little effort to codify these potential risks in a risk taxonomy, including in various IPCC reports and the planning literature.[9] This means this adaptation risk category represents a constructed set of risks that seem most directly relevant to it, that is, physical risks. Critically, such an approach tends to overlook the fact that, like mitigation risks, adaptation risks are transition risks—getting from where we are now to where we want to be is always a transition. And like mitigation risks, there may be substantial costs associated with the effort.

As we go on to discuss, most of the specific potential risks outlined here derive directly from risk indicators used in traditional financial analysis. All five of our adaptation risk indicators are categories used in the normal course of assessing credit or lending risk of an investment or loan, for example:

1. asset valuation risks,
2. operational impairments,
3. cost of business adjustments,
4. regulatory changes, and
5. subsidy loss risks.

We identify these as the areas where specific potential risks relating to adaptation efforts are most likely to manifest themselves. Significantly, adaptation efforts, in which risk assessment is a critical component, represent an iterative process, as we discuss in the adaptation risks chapter.

Mitigation Risks

The mitigation category has the least external, specifically climate-related validation; this is simply because:

1. it is by far the most diverse risk category, and
2. there are no external taxonomies where these potential risks are articulated (except for the area of the energy transition, where many of these potential risks have received varying degrees of attention).[10]

As with adaptation risks, we have generally adopted indicators of potential risk from more traditional financial analysis. Technology risks, regulatory risks, and going-concern risks, for example, are integral components of traditional analysis. We have highlighted them here because they currently have some climate-specific impacts with potentially material financial implications. This focuses mitigation efforts on those measures designed to *reduce* GHG gas generation (as opposed to adapting to them). We believe this is important, but insufficient in and of itself as an indicator of the broad spectrum of mitigation concerns. There are clearly potential climate risks associated with land use[11] policies and water access that require substantial mitigation efforts in and of themselves. Again, we can expect several potential climate impacts to manifest themselves across various indicators.

NATURAL CAPITAL RISKS

This category of risks is the most speculative of those proposed here, largely because, as noted, we know of no previous attempt to codify such risks into an organized taxonomy. We would expect this category to evolve as our understanding of natural capital risks increases. Likewise, we would expect this proposed taxonomy to be modified over time as the extent to which these risks are accelerating becomes more widely known. The major indicators chosen are, in fact, all manifesting themselves at present:

1. subsidy loss risks,
2. depletion risks,
3. boundary condition risks, and
4. geopolitical event risks.

We believe these four general metrics accommodate the wide range of natural capital issues currently unfolding, many of which (e.g., biodiversity loss and ocean acidification) are receiving increased attention from investors. Further, as is the case for adaptation and mitigation risks, several of these may derive from multiple sources.

Although natural capital risks have not figured prominently in past analyses, this may be changing. In credit analysis, for example, Moody's has begun to incorporate natural capital issues into ESG assessments.[12] Moody's basic environmental issuer profile score now consists of five "exposures": carbon transition, physical climate risks, water management, waste and pollution, and natural capital. We expect this trend to continue. Moreover, natural capital is becoming a growing focus among investment managers. In January 2021, HSBC, Mirova, and Lombard Odier established what will eventually be a US $10 billion investment fund to provide natural capital investments across a broad range of asset classes.[13]

ASSESSING RISK

Recent reports from the IPCC have emphasized that risks apply to both "the *impacts of* and *responses to* climate change."[14] Our work is intended to deal with the implications of responses to climate change, since these are likely to generate the most prevalent, and perhaps significant, financial impacts at the firm level. For an investor or a bank risk officer, risk categories tend to be largely predetermined (e.g., by rating agencies' criteria for credit quality, or by specific financial categories by regulators, such as the Basel three-pillar framework for banks). In most cases, these categories have proved sufficient for most risks before climate considerations began to manifest themselves in scale.

Any taxonomy construction project is an exercise in judgment. In this proposed framework, we note the distinction between potential risks from climate impacts on a physical or social level, as opposed to the specific potential risks being addressed in the proposed taxonomy. The socially desirable outcome of reducing GHG emissions and implementing various adaptation measures can emerge as a potentially significant risk for an investor or lender, since addressing these issues may require very high levels of spending by firms and governments. The taxonomy is intended for investors, lenders, and perhaps regulators with that in mind.

Note also that we do not distinguish between varying levels of uncertainty, which is a standard feature of scenario analysis. Some of these potential risks are virtually locked in, such as temperature increases, or sea level rise. On the other hand, some risks are highly contingent on issues such as regulatory aggressiveness—the impacts of a potential carbon price mechanism can vary widely, depending on the level of desired pricing, and the extent to which its impacts are moderated by subsidies and potential offsets. These are public and economic policy decisions—often contentious ones. This means that some of these assessments of potential financial impacts may be highly contingent on developments that have not yet occurred.

We expect, then, that over time this taxonomy will undergo some modifications. Should glacial melt be a specific risk category? If it proves to be potentially useful as a category relating to financial risk, the answer is yes. May some of these risk categories drop out if they prove to be less useful than expected? Again, yes. We have attempted to create a taxonomy that is both complete and consistent. Whether this proves to be the case in its current form remains to be seen.

Finally, we previously noted that this approach is meant to be supplemental to what we referred to as "Traditional" risk analysis. However, it is clear that it should not be supplemental—it should be integral as the potential scale of the financial impacts of climate risks becomes more evident. It is currently supplemental only because investors and lenders have not done the necessary work of integrating climate risks into traditional risk analysis—largely because of some of the impediments mentioned earlier. We suspect this will occur, and soon—the rapid uptake of the EU Sustainability taxonomy, and of TCFD recommendations for financial reporting, indicate that this is happening right now. Over the past decade the perception of potential climate risks among the financial community has changed, moving from idiosyncratic to non-idiosyncratic, or systemic, risks, increasingly difficult to diversify away from. Green taxonomies are not sufficient—more systematic risk taxonomies are equally important. And as the scale of potential risks becomes clearer, we expect that risk taxonomies such as this one will become more widely used as part of the process of integrating potential climate risks into general risk analysis.

NOTES

1. Buhr, Bob. *ESG for Credit Investors: Operational, Climate and Natural Capital Risks.* Paris: Société Générale, 2014; Buhr, Bob. Assessing the Sources of Stranded Asset Risk: A Proposed Framework. *Journal of Sustainable Finance & Investment* 7(1): 37–53, 2017.
2. Gillmor, David. *Standard & Poor's Rating Process*, December 2, 2015.
3. Moody's Investors Service. *General Principles for Assessing Environmental, Social and Governance Risks*, January 2019; S&P Global Ratings. *The Role of Environmental, Social, and Governance Credit Factors in our Ratings Analysis*, September 12, 2019; Fitch Ratings. *What Investors Want to Know: ESG Relevance Scores for Corporates*, February 20, 2020.
4. It is often overlooked how complex fundamental financial analysis of the firm actually can be—there are LOTS of moving parts. The traditional SWOT (Strengths/Weaknesses/Opportunities/Threats) model broadly employed by financial analysts can often have many dozen independent indicators to be assessed. A figure of the full taxonomy in a slightly altered version can be found here: https://www.imperial.ac.uk/business-school/faculty-research/research-centres/centre-climate-finance-investment/research/what-climate-risk-field-guide-investors-lenders-and-regulators/
5. Fiedler, T. et al. Business Risk and the Emergence of Climate Analytics. *Nature Climate Change* 11: 87–94, 2021.
6. More specifically, telling an investor that "climate risk" is going to have a specific impact on global economic stability at the end of the century sounds great, but is actually not that useful, especially if the investor is trying to decide whether or not to buy or sell a bond issued by, say, a cement company. A fundamental issue in this sort of analysis, of which this book is just one current attempt, is the mismatch between climate horizons and firm risk horizons.

7. For example, as presented in *Measuring Physical Climate Risk in Equity Portfolios*, Deutsche Asset Management, November 2017. In this case, the number of categories was six. But this number is clearly a moving target—other classifications have more, and some have fewer.
8. IPCC. Summary for Policymakers. In *IPCC Special Report on the Ocean and Cryosphere in a Changing Climate*. Edited by H.-O. Pörtner et al., 2019.
9. There is, however, a considerable literature on adaptation mechanisms, as well as on resilience, which is a necessary component of any adaptation effort. That is a somewhat different endeavor than our attempt to map out actual adaptation risks in the taxonomy, although the degree of overlap is substantial.
10. The fact that the energy transition has received considerable attention over the past few years is not surprising given its importance to efforts to reduce GHG growth; however, this should be regarded as just one component of a broader transition of economic activity. Any "transition" that does not encompass the broaching of the boundary conditions that support planetary life, or even a simple metric such as topsoil loss, really should not be called a transition.
11. Pongratz, Julia et al. Land Use Effects on Climate: Current State, Recent Progress, and Emerging Topics. *Current Climate Change Reports* 7: 99–120, 2021.
12. Moody's Investors Service. *General Principles for Assessing Environmental, Social and Governance Risks Methodology*, December 14, 2020; Moody's Investor Services. *Sovereigns—Global. Explanatory Comment: New Scores Depict Varied and Largely Credit-negative Impact of ESG Factors*, January 18, 2021.
13. Taylor, Madeleine. *Natural Capital at Centre of New USD 10 Billion Investment Alliance*. Institutional Asset Manager, January 12, 2021.
14. IPCC. *The Concept of Risk in the IPCC Sixth Assessment Report: A Summary of Cross-working Group Discussions*. Guidance for IPCC authors, September 2020.

CHAPTER 4

Physical Risks

The physical effects of climate change continue to affect landforms and infrastructure in increasingly obvious ways. As a result, the physical risk category has been more deeply explored than other categories, particularly by the IPCC. Much of the financial interest in physical climate risks traditionally has been associated with the insurance sector,[1] but investors and banks increasingly are developing tools to examine physical risk in both corporate and retail exposures. These tools overlap with those of the insurance sector in many ways, but also differ somewhat, in that the risks that lenders face may be broader and stem from enterprise activities, rather than from contingent possibilities relating to specific locales. Moreover, as with transition scenarios, data uncertainty and knowledge gaps affect the development of such tools.

It is fair to say that most impressions of climate change impacts tend to focus on physical risks. In part, this is because many of these risks are already occurring, and, moreover, appear to be accelerating. Unsurprisingly, these risks are not evenly distributed, including in the industrial sector: Moody's has estimated that the three largest sectors with exposure to physical risks are oil and gas, mining, and chemicals (although these are not necessarily the top three in terms of carbon transition risk).[2] Most of the manifestations of increased climate risks tend to be water related,[3] at least in terms of their financial impacts—and since water itself is not evenly distributed globally,[4] neither will the risks or impacts be evenly distributed. One-third of insured losses in 2022 derived from floods, for example.[5] This encompasses the impacts of increased extreme weather, which we saw much of in 2022. However, all of the risk categories indicated below have been manifesting themselves robustly over the past several years. Most have significant implications for human society, particularly agricultural production.[6]

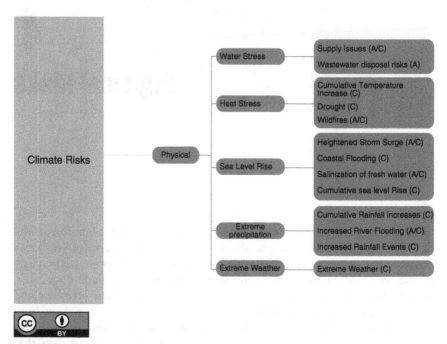

FIGURE 4.1   Physical risk taxonomy.
Source: Green Planet Consulting Ltd. *What Is Climate Risk? A Field Guide for Investors, Lenders and Regulators.* London: Centre for Climate Finance and Investment, Imperial College Business School, February 2022.

The taxonomy we are proposing for physical risks is shown in Figure 4.1. Note that some indicators are categorized acute (A), others chronic (C), and still others fall within both categories (A/C). This categorization reflects those included in the current risk literature, but some of these may evolve over time—especially in a world where some of these risks become more frequent. Any attempt to construct a taxonomy where none has previously existed should be expected to display a certain degree of fluidity.

The categories presented here reflect a distillation of a broader range of risk and hazard categories, granulated to those risks that can have a potential financial impact at the firm level.

Climate change is now well understood to pose both physical and economic risks. Moody's has neatly summarized the types of climate issues likely to be felt by countries (but these apply to firms and economic sectors as well):

The physical effects of climate change can be broadly grouped into two categories: climate shocks and climate trends. Climate shocks, in the form of storms, floods, droughts, and other climate-related disasters, are acute, costly and more conspicuous than trends. While climate trends including higher global temperatures and rising sea levels are multi-decade phenomena and less visible from one year to the next, one of the manifestations of climate trends is a higher frequency of shocks.[7]

Current approaches[8] to linking weather and climate risks to economic impacts focus on several specific factors:

1. Direct loss from damage to equipment and infrastructure.
2. Loss from business disruption.
3. Wider political and socioeconomic considerations.

These factors, of course, can (and probably should) be granulated into more specific risks associated with spheres of activity, or with specific locations. A number of factors affect the ability to model physical events and calibrate these to damage functions. These include:

a. Limited data on historical events and climate uncertainty that can affect the reliability of results.
b. Location databases are needed to identify vulnerable assets.

There has been considerable development in these areas in recent years, particularly the second area. However, data are still limited, especially in emerging markets. Obtaining property damage information is relatively straightforward in Florida, or Southern California. Data from, say, Vietnam or Bangladesh might not be as complete. In addition, much of the modeling work in this area has been hampered by the fact that a wider range of scenarios still needs to identify weaknesses based on analysis of established or anticipated resilience, and to map the channels of transmission from an extreme weather event to a wider range of physical and financial impacts. As mentioned earlier, risks rarely exist in isolation. Of interest here is Moody's recent introduction of an analytical tool that allows for the assessment of bank loan portfolios in terms of their physical risk exposure.[9]

ACUTE RISKS

Acute physical risks refer to events or specific episodes that have the potential to inflict significant physical damage (e.g., wildfires, river and ocean flooding, and tropical storms, to pick some recent events). Such events are occurring with greater frequency on both a regional and a global basis, as shown in Figures 4.2 and 4.3.[10] Risks that have traditionally been classified

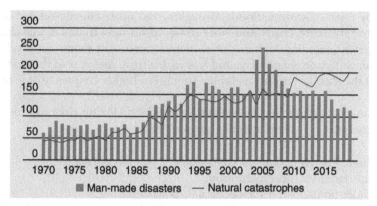

FIGURE 4.2   Number of catastrophic events, 1970–2019.
Source: Swiss Re Institute; Swiss Re sigma 2/2020. *Natural Catastrophes in Times of Economic Accumulation and Climate Change*, April 8, 2020.

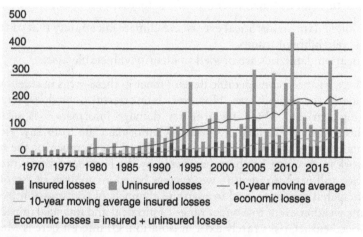

FIGURE 4.3   Insured vs. uninsured losses, 1970–2019.
Source: Swiss Re Institute; Swiss Re sigma 2/2020. *Natural Catastrophes in Times of Economic Accumulation and Climate Change*, April 8, 2020.

as idiosyncratic, such as natural disasters, are becoming less idiosyncratic and more systemic. While the number of manmade disasters (e.g., aviation and maritime disasters) has declined from its high in 2005, natural catastrophes—particularly those associated with severe storms—continue to rise. Figure 4.2, which shows a table from Swiss Re, summarizes the trend for natural catastrophe events from 1970 to 2019.

Unsurprisingly, as shown in Figure 4.3, the number of associated damages, both insured and uninsured, also continues to rise steadily.

CHRONIC RISKS

As their name suggests, chronic physical risks are those that carry a range of physical impacts of considerably longer duration than those posed by acute risks. They are best understood as processes, not events. To date, it has proven difficult to assess whether any of these risks has actually generated significant financial impacts for firms. In most cases, these impacts are localized (e.g., droughts) but there is some likelihood that chronic risks will become more meaningful over the longer term in highly vulnerable areas, such as the US Gulf Coast with its deep range of petrochemical processing facilities. We note that a number of emerging market sovereigns are exposed to many of these types of risks. On a country level, Syria has been used as an example of the longer-term impacts of physical climate impacts: a multi-year drought from 2006 to 2011 led to significant outmigration, creating a refugee crisis, and leading to significant political upheaval in the region. On the other hand, a multi-year drought in Honduras did not impede a rating upgrade in 2017. It is difficult to treat these climate processes in isolation, even though they can be identified and their potential implications assessed.

Note that there are a limited number of possible physical risk categories that lend themselves to this approach, and a limited number of ways to describe them. Where possible, we indicate in each category the sectors most likely to be at risk. However, in most cases of physical risk, the parties carrying the greatest potential risk exposures are likely to be lenders, particularly those with significant local and regional exposures; governments at all levels; property owners (both residential and commercial); transportation companies; and insurance companies.

WATER STRESS

Water availability and water damage embody pervasive risks across several categories—and not just physical risks, as we discuss throughout this book. Thus, in addition to the physical risks discussed here, we also discuss water issues as they relate to adaptation and mitigation efforts and, most importantly, to natural capital depletion issues. In this section, we will focus on water as a risk in terms of (a) its potential availability, or lack of it, and (b) potential damage scenarios.

Water is, of course, fundamental to pretty much everything. Our culture and social systems, to say nothing of our economies, are all premised on the hydrological cycle—the regular flow of water through land, sea, and the atmosphere. Nearly all water is in the oceans, and therefore salty—only about 3% of water on earth is fresh water—and most of this is locked up in ice. This has led to a degree of predictability to the cycle. Water evaporates, and then returns to earth as rainfall—that's about it. Winds are important here—they can speed up the evaporation process. They can also move water around in ways that turn out to be relatively predictable—hence our understanding of weather, which we do not attribute to the gods, but to natural processes. Water that does not evaporate also sinks into the ground, forming aquifers and underground rivers.

Global heating is altering this cycle, primarily through increased temperatures in the lower atmosphere, which accelerates rates of evaporation.[11] Which means more water vapor in the atmosphere, which generally translates into more precipitation, often in more unpredictable ways. More rapid evaporation also can have the reverse effect—of making dry areas drier, again through accelerated evaporation—which means areas already subject to drought concerns have even more reasons for concern. All of this is the result of changes to the flow of water in the hydrological cycle—the cycle itself has accelerated, with increasingly predictable effects—more precipitation—but greater unpredictability in terms of the potential frequency of events, and their intensity.

All of which makes the expected ongoing increase of CO_2 concentrations in the atmosphere more worrisome. The greater the concentration, the more rapid the effects of increased evaporation. The physical effects will be manifold. To take just one example, glacial melt will accelerate, with two effects. First, the expected runoff will increase sea levels. Both Antarctic and Greenland glaciers are melting at increasing rates. Second, a sizable portion of humanity relies on glacial melt for water availability—for both agriculture and direct consumption. In addition, the availability of fresh water can determine the extent to which public health can be improved, or at least stabilized—loss of fresh water is usually associated with public health problems.

Supply Issues (Acute and Chronic)

Water availability and supply issues will become more severe over time, for several reasons. First, global consumption continues to increase, often more rapidly than population growth. In addition, continued development of, and paving over, land is limiting the ability of soils to absorb and store water, increasing runoff and preventing its potential for human consumption and agricultural use.

Second, as mentioned earlier, global heating is already having an impact on glaciers, including those in the Himalayas. In this region, glaciers supply fresh water for about 1 billion people. However, winter snowpack is evaporating more rapidly, and the glaciers themselves are evaporating and melting more rapidly, resulting in less running water due to insufficient replacement by annual snowfall.[12] This trend is likely to continue, leading to materially less water for a substantial and growing population. Moreover, the implications for irrigated agriculture are significant.[13]

Third, droughts appear to be increasing in frequency and severity as well, affecting local water supplies.[14] We discuss drought in more detail later.

Fourth, major aquifers are declining on a global basis,[15] with frequent uncertainty over the actual rate of depletion. In many parts of the world, it is unclear how much groundwater is actually left, and there are expectations that a number of wells will run dry worldwide.[16] Groundwater basins, or aquifers, are generally fed by underground water sources that ultimately derive from rainfall elsewhere. Two issues thus present themselves. First, as surface evaporation rates increase and the atmosphere gradually increases its moisture content, the amount of groundwater flowing into aquifers will likely decline. Second, human use of aquifers is draining them faster than they are being replenished. As noted, this is perhaps the most significant natural capital depletion risk and will be discussed in greater detail in Chapter 7. We note that currently there are some serious cultural and technological efforts to access and store water more efficiently, which are discussed in more detail in Chapter 7.[17] Whether these will have significant offsetting impacts other than at the local level remains unclear.

There are a number of organizations that track water use and availability on a global basis. For example, the AQUEDUCT model of country water stress,[18] developed by the WRI and other organizations, is one of the best-known models tracking water-related risks on a global scale. Figure 4.4 presents the most recent version of this model, with darker countries on the map carrying higher levels of water stress. Firms operating in those regions are likely to be vulnerable to water-related risks.

The WRI has been updating this model regularly over the years. We do not expect significant improvements in the stressed areas—in all likelihood, stress levels will increase for the reasons discussed earlier.

A number of human economic activities, not to mention basic human functions, rely on the availability of fresh water. In addition, a number of

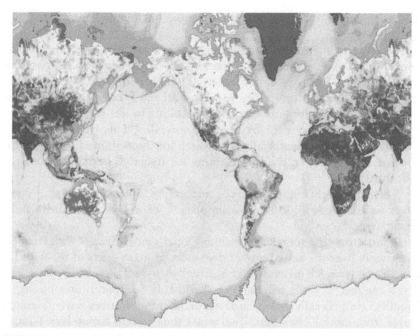

FIGURE 4.4 AQUEDUCT model of global water stress.
Source: World Resources Institute. *The New AQUEDUCT Water Risk Atlas: What's New and Why Does It Matter to You?* August 2019.

industries are relatively thirsty industries—they rely on the availability of fresh (or, at times, less than fresh) water for a range of industrial processes—usually those that generate heat in the processing of material. As noted later, there are a number of industries that are subject to this condition—utilities most obviously, but also industries such as steel, cement, chemicals, and, in many countries, transportation. All have the potential to be disrupted from a range of water-related risks.

Wastewater Disposal Issues

Firms need water, some more than others. Firms also need to dispose of water, often after significant chemical changes, and these changes are not always positive for human or animal lives. There are two ways in which global heating may affect this dynamic. First, impacts on water availability will clearly have an impact on the ability of firms to undertake activities that are water dependent—and this includes activities in such industries as mining where disposal is a critical part of the industrial process. There are simply parts of the world where industrial activities rely on water availability, and in many of these areas water is essentially disappearing for a variety of reasons—primarily increased evaporation and diminished aquifers.

Second, water availability issues may result in restrictions on water use by firms in a range of sectors. We have seen this dynamic play out in many areas in the United States where water issues have become important public policy discussions, especially with reference to certain industries. For some industries, such as energy, chemicals, and mining, wastewater disposal is a critical need. In many cases, these industries have been lightly regulated in the past, or have benefited from a benign regulatory structure, often because of nonenforcement of existing regulations (e.g., methane generation from fracking in the United States).[19] We note that methane regulations appear to be becoming more stringent in the US under the Biden administration.[20] However, as water scarcity issues increase in severity, they may face some significant logistical challenges. In particular, the chemical and the mining industries could face issues in areas where water availability may be constrained. Further, simple changes in some US regulations—such as those relating to fracking wastewater disposal—would generate significant additional costs for portions of the US fossil fuels industry.

The fracking industry in the United States provides an elegant case in point to how distortive subsidies of various sorts can be. Fracking is a very thirsty enterprise. Fracking, representing the combination of hydraulic fracturing (blowing up gas deposits in shale formations) and horizontal drilling, has been transformative for global energy markets. This result derives from the fact that fracking in the United States has changed the way pricing occurs in global energy markets. The US government, for which the notion of "energy independence" has great political (if not economic) appeal, has supported the development of the fracking industry wholeheartedly.[21] In particular, it has exempted the fracking industry from most wastewater disposal regulations, particularly through the passage of the Energy Policy Act in 2005. This allowed the industry to avoid the additional costs of disposing of fracking wastewater as a hazardous chemical waste—which is what it is, essentially.

Fracking uses significant amounts of water. Most oil and/or gas drilling involves pumping water into wells when the natural underground pressure becomes insufficient to move oil or gas up the well so that it can be recovered. However, shale oil and shale gas require significant amounts of water above and beyond the normal requirements of the industry. A "typical" well, for example, may involve 3–210 million gallons of water, and 1.5 million pounds of sand. Even by the standards of the water-hungry natural gas industry, these are prodigious amounts. In a number of US states, companies developing the Marcellus shale (the largest shale gas region in the United States) resorted to bringing in water by the truckload, in areas not noted for water scarcity.

Given the still uncertain composition of the chemical mixes used in fracking, this in itself raises some concerns for public interest groups. Coupled with the significant amount of water used, concerns have been raised about what regulations will be required to ensure the safe disposal of wastewater. Typically, anywhere from 10% to 40% of water injected in wells using fracking technology gets returned to the surface, and must be disposed of in some manner.

We note that there are a number of industries other than the oil and gas industry that are exposed to wastewater issues, particularly the manufacturing, electricity generating, and chemical industries, and especially mining. The legacy impact of mining is potentially significant:

> According to the United States Environmental Protection Agency's toxic release inventory . . . metals mining is the number one source of water pollution in the United States, with more than 1.4 billion releases, whereas coal mining is #14, with more than 8 million toxic releases. These problems are also emerging in Central and South America, and in Africa, around iron, copper, gold, and lithium mines. . .. Acid mine drainage is a pervasive problem around coal mines and metal mines. . .. Legacy mining activities in North America, Europe, Australia, and Asia have left a significant, unattended legacy of such sources.[22]

However, agriculture is also a major concern, given decades of runoff of agricultural chemicals. However, the impact of wastewater risks to agriculture are likely to be diffuse, whereas those for miners and manufacturers of other industrial commodities may be much more firm specific, depending on installed plant and its vulnerability to potential wastewater disposal risks.

Were water in abundant supply everywhere, these issues would not necessarily be a problem. However, it is not. In fact, in many parts of the world water is in short supply, and there is already intense competition for water resources between agriculture, energy resources, and urban development, particularly the latter. We would expect this competition to become more severe over time. Since the amount of water on the planet is finite, it's not as if more can be discovered.

HEAT STRESS

Cumulative Increase in Temperature

This refers to continued temperature increases that may have an impact on specific physical locations, which may have further impact on the economic

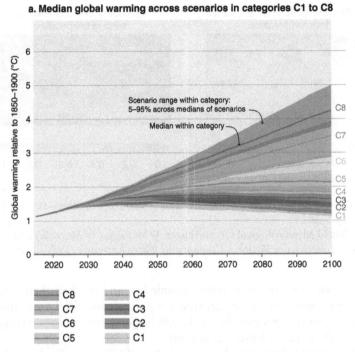

a. Median global warming across scenarios in categories C1 to C8

FIGURE 4.5 Range of assessed scenarios and 21st-century global warming.
Source: IPCC, *Climate Change 2002: Mitigation of Climate Change Working Group III—Contribution to the Sixth Assessment Report of the Intergovernmental Panel on Climate Change. Summary for Policymakers,* 2022.

elements associated with that location. Note that these impacts can be both specific—a particular coastal location, for example, or a port—or diffuse, where the physical impacts of increases in heating affect grain prices. The fundamental fact is that temperatures continue to rise, albeit unevenly on a global basis,[23] and the number of record heat days globally also appears to be increasing.

Predicting where and when temperature increases will occur depends critically on the sort of model one is assuming. Conventionally, presentations of future temperature projections embody several different scenarios; they are usually for overall global mean temperatures, and usually look something like the projections shown in Figure 4.5.

Note that Figure 4.5 embodies eight specific forecasts, representing a range of values—mostly the speed with which we reduce GHG emissions.[24]

More alarmingly, assessing these potential increases by region provides us with figures shown in Figure 4.6.

These two maps shown in Figures 4.5 and 4.6 indicate that the WMO expects a fairly significant increase in temperatures in a number of regions,

Ensemble mean forecast for 2021-2025
surface temperature

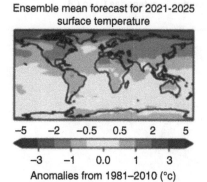

Probability of above average
surface temperature

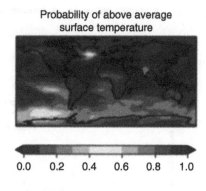

FIGURE 4.6   Mean temperature forecasts and assessments of above-average temper-
atures, 2021–2025.
Source: World Meteorological Organization. *WMO Atlas of Mortality and
Economic Losses from Weather, Climate and Water Extremes (1970–2019),* 2021.

and many of these are areas where people live and conduct their activities,
including economic ones. The greatest temperature increases are in the polar
regions, but in fact most of the world will be generating above-average temperatures (in terms of historical norms).

These temperature trends will have broad sector applicability, but the
most affected sectors are likely to be agriculture, property companies, and
property lenders. In addition, governments are likely to have to deal with
the implications of the need for increased services on reduced property
tax foundations, in the United States, for example. On a broader scale,
it is likely that over the next several decades an increasing area of the
planet will become physically uninhabitable.[25] It is not uncommon for
Iraq, for example, to see temperatures in the forties (Celsius) on a regular
basis, and this trend will certainly accelerate over time, with implications for agriculture and water availability, among others. In 2022 alone
we saw record high temperatures in much of the globe, including the
United Kingdom.

Wildfire (Acute and Chronic)

Wildfires appear to be an increasingly frequent natural disaster category,
although in many cases bad human planning has exacerbated the actual risk
levels. Current wildfires in both the Northern and Southern hemispheres,

and the steady increase in the number of such fires in locations where these had rarely occurred before (Siberia, Alaska) suggest a growing problem. In California, and Australia, the impacts have been dramatic, and have had substantial economic implications.[26] The economic implications in areas such as sub-Saharan Africa were less significant for major corporations, but these were certainly significant to inhabitants. These impacts will only increase over time.

Moreover, litigation issues associated with these may occur—witness the filing for Chapter 11 Bankruptcy protection by utility PG&E in 2019 over concerns about litigation costs associated with potential culpability over fire damage.[27] This may not be the last such case. Additionally, the insurance industry is encountering problems similar to those normally associated with increasingly strong hurricanes—getting insurance buyers to pay for the appropriate level of risk.[28] Unsurprisingly insurance purchasers have resisted, and so far the state of California has encouraged insurers to continue offering homeowner policies. Recently, however, several smaller insurers have declared bankruptcy, and several large insurers, including AIG and Chubb, have ceased underwriting of homes in California completely. Very much like insurance in Florida, where hurricane damage is a frequent (and increasingly expensive) event, we expect this situation to become even more complicated.

Since wildfires generally (but not always) occur in forests and woodlands, the economic activities of these areas will tend to be limited. However, economic costs can still be significant. Residential lending, home construction, and property insurance can expect significant economic impacts, although the construction industry may also see some pockets of increased demand. S&P Global has noted that the three major 2018 wildfires in California had an economic impact of about US $12.2 billion.[29] Other estimates are considerably higher—an earlier study suggested the total costs were in the range of US $148.5 billion, including out of state losses.[30]

We note that wildfires are acute events, but the trend to more frequent and geographically diverse suggests that the overall category should be regarded as chronic. Wildfires, particularly in the far north, are becoming decidedly chronic.[31] Going forward, it is expected that wildfire seasons will get longer, with the potential acreage vulnerable to wildfires expanding as well. Drought also plays an important role. The Western United States, for example, has been experiencing a multi-year drought that has exacerbated potential wildfire risks. Globally, fire seasons have increased, particularly in the northern boreal forests of Russia, Canada, and Alaska, and will likely continue to do so.

Drought (Chronic)

Significant droughts in 2022 included serious situations in:

1. Southwest United States and northwest Mexico, one that now has a 20-year history, with more to come—predictions are for a return to near-permanent drought in this region;[32]
2. Europe's worst drought in 500 years;
3. China's worst heatwave ever, with significant drought and the Yangtse River drying up; and
4. the Horn of Africa seeing its worst drought in forty years.

Expectations are for continued increases in drought as a direct result of climate change impacts[33]—particularly, increased global heating and reduced water availability. This trend will have a range of consequences for many regions of the globe.[34] Vulnerability remains high in a number of regions, including exposure to warm periods and natural capital depletion. A number of countries already regularly suffer from multi-year droughts, and these are expected to worsen. Droughts in the dry corridor of central America, for example (Guatemala, Nicaragua, Honduras, and El Salvador), have a direct impact on agricultural production, which employed much of these countries' population.[35] Droughts can destroy from 50% to 90% of the harvest in some areas in the dry corridor and may contribute to growing inequalities between the most vulnerable groups who are hardest hit.[36]

For many countries, agriculture still represents a significant percentage of exports, thus constituting an important source of foreign earnings and access to foreign capital. Key indicators of the potential economic impacts of climate-related drought risks will come from this economic sector. An impact of recurring droughts has been increased rates of deforestation. Guatemala, for example, has lost more than a quarter of its forests since 1990, with forest cover representing only 33% of total land area in 2015, down from over 44% in 1990.[37] Over the longer term, forest loss is a significant contributor to topsoil loss, so total land productivity tends to trend downwards. Second, while a number of food production categories are not necessarily critical to agricultural exports, these may well be critical to subsistence farming for much of the population. Third, the total amount of land devoted to agriculture, both for domestic consumption and subsistence and for export, is likely to be negatively affected by increasing drought severity and frequency. Finally, it now appears that anthropogenic climate change is responsible for a decline in agriculture productivity, particularly in warmer regions such as the Caribbean, Latin America, and Africa.[38]

In addition, water consumption trends appear to be running well ahead of the capacity of the water cycle to replenish adequate supplies, particularly in regions where global heating is expected to exacerbate water availability problems. This will also exacerbate drought impacts. This is even discounting the impact of what appear to be increasingly frequent droughts on a global basis. Droughts have significant economic impacts, of course; estimated annual costs may be as high as US $80 billion.[39] While this figure is relatively small in terms of the global economy, it is one that can reflect significant regional impacts. Moreover, it is a figure that is likely to rise, with potentially damaging impacts on global agriculture, and water availability in some regions. Drought is also expected to be one of the major contributors to environmental migration over the next several decades.[40]

Drought impacts can be significant. At the regional level, droughts can reduce food availability, threaten agricultural production, and affect local and regional economic performance. For firms, the effects are somewhat more diffuse. While packaged food companies are somewhat insulated from raw material costs, given that these are often a low percentage of the cost of product, they are not immune to these impacts. The United Kingdom's current "cost-of-living crisis" has been generated in part by increased food costs associated with the Ukraine invasion and the resulting concerns about global wheat availability—but this is also essentially similar to the impact of an extended drought in Ukraine. Some food categories, generally staples such as bread, can see significant increases. While companies generally pass these on to consumers, there are limits to their ability to do so. Likewise, trading companies can see reduced trading volumes having impacts on profitability, as Cargill experienced in 2012–2013.

More broadly, drought can have other negative economic impacts that put pressure on governments, both local and, in some cases, the sovereign governments as well. First, droughts have a clear social destabilization potential as evidenced by the increasing percentage of the global population being driven to migration as a result of drought. Additionally, the reduced tax base associated with declining agricultural production and declining land values can limit government effectiveness in dealing with drought impacts, particularly relating to water availability.

From the standpoint of firms, there appear to be several major categories of impacts. First, asset values of regional land and infrastructure can be devalued. This has the potential to have a negative impact on regional lenders—similar to the effects such lenders may experience as a result of flooding problems. This trend is already at work in some areas of the Southwestern United States, although at present it is being offset on a broader basis by continued migration to these areas.

Second, for many industries (particularly packaged food companies) that rely on agricultural feedstocks, the cost of these feedstocks may become inordinately more expensive, and may have a negative margin impact on firms that already have tight margins. In fact, potentially one-third of agricultural production could be significantly jeopardized by climate impacts (mainly drought) that food production moves outside a "safe climatic space."[41] (Note that this may apply to forest products as well.) And while agricultural production will likely move north (and south, in parts of the Southern Hemisphere), primary costs are still likely to increase.

Third, it is likely that transport systems will be disrupted, including both land-based systems and maritime shipping (both discussed elsewhere in this book). Not only might the costs of transport rise significantly, but its availability might also be curtailed. If large parts of a country are vacant because global heating has moved populations elsewhere, the costs of maintaining those transport links might be a constraint on the distribution of a range of products, but particularly agricultural produce that needs timely shipment. Food grown in California has to get to the US Midwest or the east coast somehow. The difficulty of that process, and the cost of doing it, could be likely to rise in regions where significant drought not only has taken farmland out of production, but has actually rendered the region with a subsistence population.

SEA LEVEL RISE

Sea level rise appears to be increasingly locked in over the next several decades, and likely more. The IPCC has repeatedly noted, in several major reports over the past decade or so, the following (published in 2013, but updates since then have confirmed the following):[42]

1. "Ocean warming dominates the increase in energy stored in the climate system, accounting for more than 90 percent of the energy accumulated between 1971 and 2010. . . .. It is virtually certain that the upper ocean (0–700 m) warmed from 1971 to 2010. . .and it likely warmed between the 1870s and 1971."
2. "Over the last two decades, the Greenland and Antarctic ice sheets have been losing mass, glaciers have continued to shrink almost worldwide, and Arctic Sea ice and Northern Hemisphere spring snow cover have continued to decrease in extent (high confidence) (see Figure SPM.3 [in original])."
3. "The rate of sea level rise since the mid-19th century has been larger than the mean rate during the previous two millennia. . . .."

4. "Changes in the global water cycle in response to the warming over the 21st century will not be uniform. The contrast in precipitation between wet and dry regions and between wet and dry seasons will increase, although there may be regional exceptions."

5. "The global ocean will continue to warm during the 21st century. Heat will penetrate from the surface to the deep ocean and affect ocean circulation."

6. "It is *very* likely that the Arctic sea ice cover will continue to shrink and thin and that Northern Hemisphere spring snow cover will decrease during the 21st century as global mean surface temperature rises. Global glacier volume will further decrease."

7. "Global mean sea level will continue to rise during the 21st century . . . the rate of sea level rise will very likely exceed that observed during 1971–2010 due to increased ocean warming and increased loss of mass from glaciers and ice sheets."

We have quoted at length because the extent of this problem still appears to be poorly understood by investors, lenders, and governments. This goes in one direction only.

What is actually generating a rise in sea levels? As Figure 4.7 indicates, it's from a combination of added water (primarily glacial runoff) and thermal expansion. Both of these causes are concerning. The larger contributor—added water—is of particular concern because of the acceleration of glacial melt in Antarctica and, particularly, Greenland. However, also of concern is the thermal expansion of ocean waters from solar radiation—it is unclear

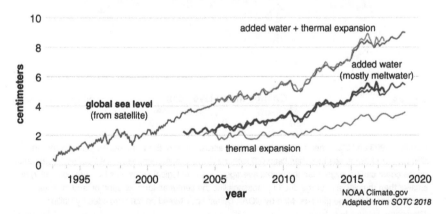

FIGURE 4.7 Contributors to global sea level rise 1993–2018.
Source: NOAA, 2022.

what the limits of the ability of the oceans to absorb solar heat actually are, and whether we may be approaching them.

What is also unarguable, however, is that the degree of sea level rise will vary considerably by region. There appears to be a pretty good understanding at present of where this risk is more pronounced than in other areas. The polar regions, for example, are melting faster than elsewhere on the planet—perhaps four times the global average warming. This alone will drive a certain level of sea level rise as glacial ice turns into water, which expands as it warms. Notably, sea ice melt does not necessarily increase sea level on its own, although exposing the ocean to direct solar radiation means the albedo effect is lost, and the sea itself it will heat up and expand faster.

As Figure 4.8 indicates, the rate of sea level rise is not distributed equally on a global basis.

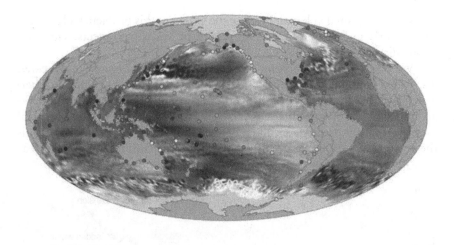

1993–2021   **Change in sea level** (cm)   NOAA Climate.gov Data: UHSLC

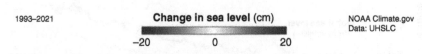

−20   0   20

Between 1993 and 2021 mean sea level has risen across most of the world ocean (blue colors). In Some ocean basins, sea level has risen 6-8 inches (15–20 centimeters). Rates of *local* sea level (dots) on the coast can be larger than the global average due to geological processes like ground settling or smaller than the global average due to processes like the centuries-long rebound of land masses from the loss of ice-age glaciers. Map by NOAA Climate.gov based on data provided by Philip Thompson, University of Hawaii.

FIGURE 4.8   Sea level change 1993–2021 is not evenly distributed. *Source:* NOAA, April 19, 2022.

The impacts of sea level rise are, unsurprisingly, generally negative. Since much of humanity lives on or near a coast, and much economic activity occurs there as well, there are clear vulnerabilities. Simply adapting infrastructure to higher sea levels will be an expensive process, as we discuss in Chapter 5. More worryingly is the knock-on effect on other physical impacts. Storm surge, for example, can be greater if sea levels are higher, and can travel further inland. Nuisance flooding (from high tides) can cause localized mobility and economic problems. Sea level rise can also put additional stresses on coastal ecosystems, many of which are already under pressure from human development. And, as we will discuss in more detail, salinization of fresh water increases.

Given these factors, it should not be surprising that pretty much all human activity along coasts has some degree of vulnerability to physical risk disruption. In some cases, there will clearly be a lot—for example, where coastal infrastructure, and even land, will be lost. In other cases, less so. In part this depends on the physical attributes of the affected area. However, vulnerability may be affected by the extent to which effective adaptation policies are implemented to reduce vulnerability and facilitate resilience.

Of interest is whether there are nature-based solutions that could counteract some of the rise in local areas. A long-term study on wetlands—and the race between seal level rise and plant growth in the wetlands—appears to be resolving in favor of the sea.[43] This turns out to be the case in other domains as well, particularly the migration of the tree line in northern Canada, Alaska, Scandinavia, and Russia where the impacts of global heating in higher latitudes is outpacing the ability of vegetation to adapt—in this case, the ability of the moving tree line to keep up.[44]

Heightened Storm Surge (Acute and Chronic)

Evidence suggests that storm surge impacts are becoming more frequent and more severe in areas where they are relatively common. While this is a global phenomenon, it poses the greatest economic risk in those areas that have the greatest concentration of economic investment—areas such as the US Gulf Coast, with its significant oil industry assets,[45] or Florida, with its significant property exposure on both coasts. Storm surge is often the most significant causer of damage, and of human mortality, associated with extreme weather. As extreme weather events have increased and strengthened in recent years, so too have storm surges, and also their economic and human impact. Perhaps most concerning, storm surge events are reaching further inland as the storms delivering them have increased in intensity.

As the World Meteorological Organization has pointed out, storm surge is simply "an abnormal rise in water generated by a storm." This fairly dry summary fails to do justice to perhaps the most dangerous aspect of storm surge—the speed with which it occurs. It is also a global phenomenon, and can arise in any extreme weather situation where seas rise in combination with significant wind. Of particular concern is storm surge in areas with significant river deltas and floodplains, which tend to be at sea level, such as in Vietnam, Bangladesh, and India. In these regions there is now an increasing risk that storm surges are pushing sea water further inland than in previous years. As we discuss later, this increases the salination of previously fresh water, affecting production of such staples as rice in these countries.

Industries affected are those also affected by increases in extreme weather and coastal flooding. The major sector affected here is likely the property sector, where both property lenders and insurers have some degree of potential vulnerability. While other sectors might see some impacts, we suspect it is likely to be region specific. This will be true of sectors such as ports and transportation, which will be vulnerable on a regional level, as well as industrial and manufacturing plants, again with some coastal exposure. Storm surges are, after all, regional in their impacts, and do not distinguish between different types of infrastructure. And as population densities and economic activities continue to increase on coastal regions over the near term, storm surge impacts are likely to continue to be economically significant.

Coastal Flooding (Acute and Chronic)

Coastal flooding[46] incidents are also increasing in frequency and severity on a global basis, particularly in areas where river flooding is already a concern, such as Vietnam, India, and Bangladesh. Since much of the world lives along coastlines, the potential for damages here is obviously high, and a number of areas along the US coast are at risk.[47] This is not just a US phenomenon, of course. As storm intensities continue to increase in all parts of the world, their effects on coastal flooding will be significant. As Erica Gies has noted,[48]

> Global economic losses from flooding rose from $500 million, on average in the 1980s to $76 billion in 2020. The World Meteorological Organization expects the number of people at risk from flooding to increase by nearly half a billion by 2050.

These numbers appear large, but they are not. Given that about 45% of humanity lives on coasts or river deltas, the surprising thing is that the number isn't higher.

The risk profile of potentially affected firms is pretty much identical to that of those vulnerable to storm surge. This is unsurprising, since the two impacts nearly always go together. We would note that most of the economic damage from Hurricane Ian in August 2022 in Florida was the result of coastal flooding. This is not unusual for US coastlines. Additionally, however, most of these losses were uninsured—hurricane insurance in Florida covers storm damage, but not flooding damage. This is not a widely employed model, though, some insurance company exposures could be higher in other regions. Property lenders, on the other hand, may not enjoy this distinction.

Salinization of Fresh Water (Acute and Chronic)

Increased intensity of storms and the potential for greater saltwater intrusion in rivers and wetlands are likely to disrupt the normal annual salinization cycle in some countries. In addition, inland monsoon flooding is likely to become an even greater risk. This is largely the result of storm surge and extreme weather moving seawater into freshwater sources, particularly river deltas such as the Mekong delta in Vietnam, or deltas in India, Pakistan, and Bangladesh.[49] But it will also be simply from the effect of sea level rise in many areas of the world. The main impact here is rendering water required for growing crops such as rice becoming too salty, diminishing agricultural yields. For much of the world, it is this agriculture that provides substantial subsistence for domestic populations. For example, according to the World Bank, salinization issues in Bangladesh will most likely lead to significant shortages of drinking water and irrigation problems by 2050, that may result in a 15.6% decline in rice yield.[50] Bangladesh is currently a net rice importer—this will only drive the demand for greater import levels even higher.

River deltas are not the only water source facing risks of salinization. There are, in fact, a range of causes of salination of freshwater supplies. Our concern here is mainly with two of these—storm surge impacts on river deltas, and groundwater salinization from groundwater depletion. If groundwater is consumed more rapidly than it is being replenished (which is often the case at this point), the saline content of groundwater simply increases as a result of the salts that have been deposited over geologic time in the pumped water settling back into the aquifer.

Groundwater is also at risk in many parts of the world, often as the result of irrigation for agriculture. An increase in this process would render groundwater largely unusable for agricultural use in many areas, to say nothing of availability to both domestic animals and wildlife. We note that desalinization processes, which are often offered as a process to reverse salinization trends, have improved over the past several decades, and costs have been declining. Nonetheless, these remain expensive, and probably out of reach for many countries potentially affected by salinization.[51]

The major industry at risk here is clearly agriculture. While we do not expect broad-based impacts on packaged and processed food companies outside some specific crops (specifically rice), implications for the sovereign governments of major rice-producing and rice-consuming countries are likely to be serious. Regional lenders and insurers may also bear some potential vulnerability to the extent that communities become unlivable as a result of increasing lack of fresh water. And as is the case for a range of physical risks to property, composition of REIT (real estate investment trusts) portfolios will be worthy of examination.

Cumulative Sea Level Rise (Chronic)

That sea levels will continue to rise as a uniform process globally is widely assumed and recognized as one the most significant (and even iconic) results of global heating. In fact, this rise is not uniform. There are substantial geographic differences in the amount of sea level rise at present, reflecting a range of geologic[52] and geographic constraints.[53] In fact, there are some regions (Sweden and Norway, for example) where land is currently rising faster than sea levels, as a result of ongoing land rise from the retreat of glaciers (termed glacial isostatic adjustment). Hotter oceans will tend to expand, but, as we have seen any number of times, this expansion is not equally distributed.

This uneven distribution of sea level rise raises an issue of specificity. Popular discussions of global heating and "sea level rise" often contain statements such as "sea levels may rise by two meters by the end of the century." It should be noted that there will be parts of the world that are severely impacted, such as the Arctic, and others that are less affected. On balance, however, the effect will occur, and it will have significant impacts in much of the world, particularly in major cities since most of these are located in coastal areas. Interested readers may refer to Moody's recently published report assessing the potential impact of sea level rise on US states and municipalities.[54]

Gradual cumulative sea level rise will have a range of impacts on landforms, fairly obviously, including more significant storm surge impacts, and more extensive coastal flooding. Coastal areas will be drastically affected, and many coastal communities globally are already preparing for these impacts (we discuss these preparations in Chapter 4). This includes major cities where much of the world's populations live. Higher sea levels also will result in greater storm damage to coastal areas, as well as coastal erosion. The ongoing receding of the Louisiana coastline is a case in point—the coast is basically washing away through the loss of wetlands, and the speed with which this is occurring is accelerating. Note that in this case, coastal erosion and recession has the potential to affect some of the world's major petrochemical processing areas. It should be noted that sea level rise is just one of several factors contributing to Louisiana's wetlands loss and coastal transformation; but as sea levels increase further, this rise will complicate future efforts to stabilize wetlands loss.

While Louisiana's current issues may appear extreme, they reflect much of the future development of coastal areas as a result of sea level rise. This will become a global problem, especially in major river deltas. Many major river deltas are at or below sea level. Major cities are vulnerable, including cities in China, Indonesia (where the government recently announced it was moving the capital for climate reasons), Japan, the Philippines, in addition to the United States and large portions of Europe. Sovereign governments will be facing some significant issues relating to displaced populations, not to mention economic activities.

There are numerous discussions of sea level rise available (some of which are included in our bibliography), and we do not intend to repeat them here. For our specific purposes, the task for analysts and lenders will be whether this process of economic migration can be managed efficiently as populations move. Perhaps the area that will receive the most attention, at least initially, will be transportation networks, many of which will need to be replaced. Much of this will depend on adaptation spending, and what form that will take. It is difficult to think of a coastal activity that will not be disrupted, in many cases dramatically and permanently. As is the case for many of the potential risks being discussed here, property lending and insurance companies may carry particular vulnerabilities.

EXTREME PRECIPITATION

Cumulative Rainfall Increases (Chronic)

Longer-term precipitation trends generally suggest stronger rainfall events over time in certain areas of the world—for example, in the Indian Ocean/ Southeast Asia region, where rainfall totals have increased over the past several decades. However, there is considerable variation in the occurrence of this trend. In some areas, it is increasing, but in others (e.g., Australia), rainfall totals have been gradually declining. Therefore, caution is advised in extrapolating such rainfall increases in order to ensure that regional specificity is observed.

Nonetheless, the increase in rainfall in some areas has been dramatic. As Erica Gies has noted,

> In the United States, the amount of precipitation falling during heavy storms has increased dramatically since 1958: by 55% in the Northeast, 27% in the Southeast, 42% in the Midwest, 10% in the Southwest, and 9% in the Northwest. For example, Hurricane Harvey dumped fifty inches of rain on Houston over four days in 2017, causing the area's third 500-year flood in three years.[55]

This pattern is being repeated elsewhere, with often dramatic and onerous costs—monsoon rains in India and Pakistan have become more intense over the past several decades, for example, with significant economic impacts. "Wet gets wetter" and "hot gets wetter" seem to be the applicable rules here. Moreover, evidence suggests that light-to-moderate rainfalls are diminishing, and heavy rainfalls are increasing.[56]

Of particular concern here is the apparent increase in the intensity of atmospheric rivers, as seen in California in early 2023.[57] These are bands of heavy moisture that seem to seek established wind patterns to direct increased moisture in the atmosphere into areas that normally see established rainfall levels. These have positive impacts in increasing potential water availability for snowmelt, for example. However, precipitation level impacts in a number of places—the west coast of the United States, for example, and the west coast of the Indian subcontinent—have the potential to intensify flooding impacts and surface erosion, for example, in coastal areas. As moisture continues to increase in the atmosphere, this phenomenon is expected to become increasingly problematic.

Again, there is considerable coverage of this area, and we do not intend to reproduce it. For our purposes, we note the impacts on human coastal infrastructure and on coastal landforms, with the predictable attendant risks to property lenders and insurers, not to mention municipalities and their ability to finance services. In addition, however, we would also note the impact of more extreme precipitation scenarios to regional agriculture, often through the impact of more rapid topsoil depletion, but also from increased potential for extreme flooding of farmland, making soils too saturated for crop production. These will, of course, vary country by country.

In an increasing number of countries, significant swings between periods of drought and periods of significant flooding from increased precipitation patterns—or their simultaneous occurrence—is becoming a more significant issue for domestic agricultural production.[58] Kenya, for example, is in exactly this place at present—it experiences both drought and flooding. In many respects, the impacts of extreme precipitation are similar to those of increased flooding—in fact, there is often a causal relationship there.

Increased River Flooding (Acute and Chronic)

Flooding is becoming an increasingly frequent problem in most parts of the world.[59] River flooding, specifically, is already a significant issue in countries such as India, Vietnam, and Bangladesh, and in the Midwestern United States. For example, as the World Bank has noted, climate-related risks are likely to depress agricultural activity by about 3% annually through 2050, with river flooding being a significant contributor to this trend. Again, Bangladesh serves as an important example as it contains the second largest river basin in the world and 80% of the country lies on floodplains. Equally problematic is the fact that about one-third of the land is exposed to tidal incursions (i.e., the mixing of saline and fresh water), and this is expected to increase as tidal zones spread inland from sea level rise. These factors equate to significant climate risk for Bangladesh and will almost certainly have an impact on its domestic rice production, which is already insufficient for domestic consumption needs.

Bangladesh is not alone. As Pakistan floods demonstrated in 2022, and significant US flooding in Yellowstone Park in the summer of 2022, this is increasingly a global problem, with increasingly punitive costs in terms of not just economic activity, but also population displacement. India, like Pakistan, is highly vulnerable. In fact, on a global basis, significant economic activity occurs on rivers—it is often a critical means of transport for a number of countries—Germany being a case in point, as it discovered again in 2022 when river levels dropped. But flooding can have a comparable impact, although perhaps not as long lived. Global economic losses to river flooding are significant, and expected to worsen over the next twenty years, especially in China.[60]

Rivers and their deltas have critical functions. For one thing, about 4% of humanity lives on major river deltas, often at heights that bring a range of flooding exposures.[61] In addition to providing fresh water and water disposal frameworks, rivers provide valuable ecosystem services. Additionally, and from our viewpoint most importantly, rivers provide countries with important transport networks. Disruption of these networks can cause significant economic damage,[62] just as droughts can. In the United States,

Hurricane Katrina, which stopped or slowed transport on the Mississippi river for several weeks, caused significant economic damage. While temporary, recovery took several months, and the disruption affected some critical US industries such as automobiles and steel, to say nothing of grain traffic.

Increased Rainfall Events (Chronic)

Evidence suggests that rainfall events, especially those associated with major storms, are increasing in both intensity and frequency. This trend has been particularly observable in areas where monsoons are a regular part of the agricultural year, but it is not geographically uniform; many parts of the world (e.g., California at present) are suffering an outright rainfall deficit. Again, this geographic diversity represents a key difficulty in assessing climate risks.

One expected result of increased precipitation is the increase in such events. Specifically, this refers to an actual increase in the number of weather events, not just their severity. This appears unclear. At present it is widely accepted that global heating is driving an increase in extreme weather events, tending to make them more extreme.[63] But what about ordinary weather trends? This is less certain, although what can be said at present is that global heating will exacerbate existing trends. As we mentioned earlier, "wet gets wetter," and "hot gets wetter." But the converse is also true—dry weather will more likely turn into droughts. In the United Kingdom, at least, this appears to be the case.[64]

EXTREME WEATHER (ACUTE AND CHRONIC)

The increasing frequency and intensity of cyclones, hurricanes, and typhoons represent both acute and chronic risks. In general, these extreme weather events are increasing, as shown in Figure 4.9 for the United States, but the global trend is similar. This trend is expected to continue, with resulting economic impacts also increasing. Some of this analysis is complicated by the apparent behavior of storms of moving more slowly than in previous years, allowing water vapor and windspeeds to increase more easily.[65]

The issue of whether tropical storms, specifically, are increasing in frequency and severity on a global basis is a complicated one, but one that has attracted considerable interest, particularly among vulnerable island nations such as Fiji. At present, it appears as if the trends are for increases in both frequency and severity, although there may be some regional differential between Atlantic and Pacific basins.[66] In the Pacific region, it seems that the frequency of storms (monsoons) is not necessarily increasing. However,

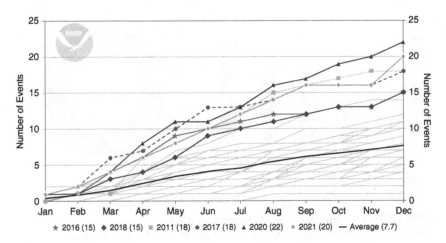

FIGURE 4.9 Rise in extreme weather disasters in the United States.
Source: US NOAA NCEI.

storms appear to be occurring with greater severity and frequency. In addition, storms seem to carry more rainfall.[67] In the Atlantic basin, all three of these factors appear to be increasing—frequency, severity, and earlier in the year.[68] Note that there can be considerable annual variation of these impacts—2022 was actually below the 1991–2020 average.[69]

Extreme weather has significant economic impacts at local and regional levels, and, increasingly, at sovereign levels in emerging markets. These economic impacts are likely to become more significant as weather patterns deteriorate. This analysis can be facilitated by the fact that we often know what the extreme weather pattern is—North Atlantic hurricanes follow a number of regular indicators, as do monsoons in the Indian ocean. In the latter case, recognizing these patterns is often a major ingredient of successful agriculture.

Cost estimates of the impacts of extreme weather continue to escalate. The Pakistan floods of 2022, during which one-third of the country was under water, initially carried cost estimates of US $10 billion, but these were immediately acknowledged to be too low. And in fact, the more current estimates are in the range of US $40 billion.[70] Floods in German and other European countries caused about US $43 billion in damages. The list could easily go on. Ongoing extreme weather events globally have generated estimates of increasingly high numbers. Figure 4.10 sourced from the World Meteorological Organization (WMO)[71] is representative.

Note that the losses shown in Figure 4.10 are actual damages, not estimates of future costs. Note also that total economic costs for the period

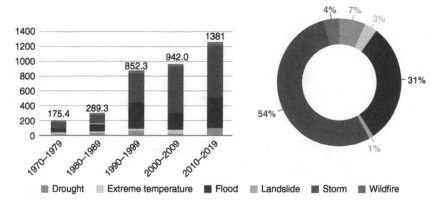

FIGURE 4.10   Economic losses from extreme weather.
Source: World Meteorological Organization 2021/ World Meteorological Organization.

were about US $3.6 trillion. However, it would be somewhat nonsensical to expect this trend to do anything other than continue its upward trajectory. Expected future damages are, to a considerable extent, contingent on adaptation spending and resilience targets, the subject of Chapter 5. But they will still be high. As we have seen in some other areas, the speed with which extreme weather is occurring has been more rapid than anticipated even a few years ago.[72]

SOCIOECONOMIC VULNERABILITY

While not actually physical risks in and of themselves, socioeconomic vulnerabilities (i.e., social unrest, migration, and economic disruption derived from, or exacerbated by, climate change) deserve mention here as they are certainly the result of such risks. "Climate migration" is becoming an increasingly accepted term for the impact that global heating is having on certain populations, particularly in geographically warm regions such as the Middle East or Saharan Africa.[73] The migration "crisis" facing Europe and North America is frequently associated with drought occurrences in places such as Syria and Guatemala. Such climate impacts as drought are, it should be remembered, invariably local in their impacts. There is every reason to believe that these trends will continue, even within wealthy countries. For instance, the potential for longer-term drought in the Southwestern United States could drive residents to other parts of the country for a range of reasons, starting with water availability issues.[74]

Currently, we would expect the most obvious impact to be on the sovereign governments that are affected—either on those of the emigrants (if there is an impact on a nation's financial and economic profile) or on the destination nations. These shifts will be a major problem, but it is extremely difficult to isolate any particular sector, other than sovereigns and local governments, that may be specifically affected. As we note in our discussion of natural capital risks, resource competition is likely to intensify both within and across sovereign boundaries.

McKinsey has recently published a report providing a suggested overview of the socioeconomic implications of physical climate risks.[75] The report notes that climate change is already having substantial physical impacts in a number of regions. McKinsey's climate risk typology is similar to those of other investigators assessing the potential of these risks, and, in line with those other investigations, the conclusions are not encouraging. Moreover, the report notes that "the socioeconomic impacts of climate change will likely be nonlinear as system thresholds are breached and have knock-on effects"—in other words, crossing certain climate tipping points will likely produce significant and frequently dramatic reactions. The report's authors highlight five particular areas of potential impacts:

1. livability and workability,
2. food systems,
3. physical assets,
4. infrastructure services, and
5. natural capital.

The economic systems supporting these categories of human activity will all be under varying degrees of pressure, not to say outright risk, on current climate trends. The case studies discussed in the McKinsey report suggest the potential complexities of addressing these issues.

OTHER POTENTIAL RISKS

We note that there are a number of potential physical risks that we have not included in our taxonomy. Essentially, at this point, it is difficult to see these risks having specific financial impacts *at the firm level,* which is the focus of this work. This does not mean that these risks will not manifest themselves more specifically in the future—simply that we do not view them as being potentially material in any particular horizon at present. The two such risks that receive the most attention are ocean acidification and glacial melt.

Ocean Warming Limits and Acidification

As global heating has expanded over the past two centuries, much of the excess heat in the atmosphere has been absorbed by the world's oceans.[76] This warming has had a number of consequences for the oceans themselves and for possible future impacts of global heating (e.g., will the oceans continue to absorb heat at the same rate that they have historically?).

In addition, there are other impacts of raised global ocean temperatures, particularly increased acidification, which have the effect of altering local sea life populations (often with negative consequences, such as for coral reefs). More broadly, there has been a significant impact on global and regional fish stocks, many of which are in substantial decline (although much of this decline stems from overfishing). This decline has impacts not only in terms of the availability of fish stocks to supply sustenance to much of the world's population (particularly Indigenous groups) but also in terms of threatening the livelihoods of coastal communities.

Glacial Melt

There are increasing concerns among climate scientists about the potential impacts of feedback loops. For example, as glacial melt accelerates in Greenland, resulting cold water is likely affecting the position of the Gulf Stream, which keeps much of Northern Europe warmer than it would otherwise be. This displacement could trigger, as one of its many consequences, an acceleration of glacial melt in Greenland as feedback loops kick in.

As indicated above, the implications of glacial melt for ocean circulation are of considerable concern; however, that is not the only,[77] or even the major, concern relating to glacial melt, which is sea level rise. Glacial melt is happening at an alarming rate, more rapidly than was expected even a few years ago.[78] In fact, it is now occurring at levels previously considered to be the worst-case scenario.[79] This suggests that ocean current systems may be disrupted sooner than expected and sea level rise impacts may increase. Addressing this issue will require more intensive assessment by coastal governments, as well as affected industries such as utilities. In addition, glaciers provide a source of fresh water for a wide range of human populations, particularly in Asia and Latin America. As melting accelerates, glaciers retreat, and much of this melt turns into water vapor,[80] meaning it is not available as a water source for affected populations. This scenario is just one of many possible implications.[81]

Although ocean acidification and glacial melt are both significant and concerning, their impacts are diffuse, which is why they are not included in this taxonomy. Moreover, causation is always a bit tricky in some of these risk categories. For instance, sea level rise, which we have identified as one of the primary risks emanating from global heating, has multiple causes, with glacial melt being just one. Hence, we have chosen to stick to risks that could be considered proximate causes. We note, however, that the rates of ocean acidification and glacial melt have been accelerating in recent years.

IMPLICATIONS FOR SELECT SECTORS

It is probably premature to assess the potential impacts of physical risks of climate change on a specific set of industrial and economic sectors (even though this has not inhibited a wide range of prognosticators from doing exactly that). However, it appears likely that a number of candidate sectors can be identified, including:

1. infrastructure, particularly asset valuation adjustments and the potential need for replacement;
2. property, including residential, municipal, and commercial (including industrial)—same as above;
3. transport, including asset valuations, impacts on capes and cash flows, temporary or permanent impacts on revenues and earnings;
4. financial institutions, particularly potential adjustments to lending portfolios and the risk weightings of assets related to capital allocation processes;
5. insurance and re-insurance, particularly whether risk assessments were appropriate, and whether annuity schedules reflect the correct timing and scope of risk assessments and emergence;
6. utilities, primarily relating to asset valuations and potential stranded assets, and costs associated with the expected energy transition; and
7. supply chain impacts, largely relating to transportation costs and product or component availability.

(Note that categories 2 and 3 may be included in infrastructure.)

Since a considerable portion of humanity lives along the coast or the banks of rivers, and these are where significant global economic activity takes place, it would be cavalier to assume that the impacts of the manifestations of these risks will not be felt broadly. We note also that the increased emergence of physical risks will stimulate increased efforts at adaptation and mitigation. We will discuss both of these in Chapters 5 and 6.

Direct physical risks attendant to any particular property are probably restricted to only a few instruments and sectors—mortgage securities are the best example, but project finance sites will also have a specific geographic coordinate upon which estimates can be based. If the geographic coordinates of a property are known, inferences about possible risks can be based on what is known about acute and chronic events that correlate with that location. A company with a broad and diverse property portfolio, such as Siemens, may be facing multiple physical risks. But Siemens is a large, wealthy company whose valuation does not rely on its physical assets, even though it has a lot of them. Companies with relatively specific property portfolios, however, such as mall developers or railroads, will likely find that some of their property assets are more vulnerable than others. More broadly, the insurance industry, and the financial sector in general, appear to have potentially wide exposure here, although this exposure is perhaps not generally appreciated.

More generally, stranded assets are a significant concern for investors and lenders. There is a wide range of cost estimates for the process of actually stranding assets, but recent work has suggested that this value could exceed US $1 trillion for the fossil fuel industry alone.[82] Granted, this is a large, apparently financially strong industry at the moment, in spite a generally desired transition to a less carbon-intensive economy among public policymakers and investors. There was a time when this number would have been summarily dismissed, although we suspect this is no longer the case. According to the authors of the relevant research, the bulk of this asset destruction would fall on financial organizations, primarily shareholders, but also other parties as well.

This is an example of a single-sector range of stranded asset risks. As is often the case, however, there is a variety of ways of looking at potential financial disruption. If we consider water risks, for example, we find a number of possible measures that could generate significant stranded asset risks. A recent report[83] from Planet Tracker and CDP identified four critical areas:

1. physical risks (of the sort discussed here),
2. regulatory risks,
3. reputational and market risks, and
4. technological risks.

We discuss these in Chapter 7. However, the point to be made here is that a single risk driver—water—can generate a wide range of financial and policy implications. As mentioned previously, water risks span a range of potential firm risks.

This discussion raises some issues that investors and lenders need to resolve in the course of any analysis of physical risks. The first is whether valuation of the firm is directly dependent on the valuation of its physical assets; this will, of course, eventually lead to a discussion of the potential for stranded assets (which we discuss later).

Most industrial firms are not dependent on a single physical asset. However, there are sectors where there is a rationale for a particular physical location or a concentration of them. For example, ports, by definition, are located adjacent to bodies of water, and utilities typically are too. Mines need to be located where the resources are located; the same is true for the forestry industry. In this way, it is possible that physical assets in the aggregate may present risks that, individually, would be immaterial as a single property. The same will be true for property portfolios: single property risks may be small, but in the aggregate, these risks can become material.

While asset value implications may appear straightforward, implications for other financial measures, particularly revenues, and margins, and cash flow availability, may be more complex. This derives from the simple reason that transition measures, both adaptation and mitigation transitions, will reflect to a considerable extent developments in public policy over the next decade or two. Much may depend on potential increases in CAPEX to fund potentially ambitious adaptation measures, for example.

Even though the classification of physical risks is relatively straightforward, there are nonetheless a number of issues that make modeling these risks a complex process. This situation reflects issues already associated with the scenario analysis and modeling, which generally lie outside the scope of this book. There is considerable uncertainty associated with many of these models,[84] although the models themselves are improving regularly.

One potential complication of any modeling or scenario analysis exercise, already mentioned, is that the extent to which feedback loops need to be included in any sort of modeling may be significant. Scenarios for physical risk models attempt to link probabilistic assessments of the frequency and severity of climate- and weather-related events at future time points to an impact assessment of economic damages. This is especially the case in systems where the interaction of climate risks produces a cascade effect of the sort described by Verisk Maplecroft in its *Environmental Risk Outlook 2022* publication.[85] Of particular concern is the potential for these risks to cascade sufficiently so as to destabilize countries. While sovereign outlooks are not the subject of this book, there is certainly overlap in the model envisioned by Maplecroft and the range of potential risks applicable to firms.

NOTES

1. Bank of England. *A Framework for Assessing Financial Impacts of Physical Climate Change: A Practitioner's Guide for the General Insurance Sector,* May 17, 2019.

2. Moody's Investor Service. *Carbon Transition and Physical Climate Risks Shape Corporates' Credit Profiles,* October 3, 2022.

3. World Meteorological Organization. *Water-related Hazards Dominate Disasters in the Past 50 Years,* July 23, 2021.

4. Gleick, Peter and Heather Cooley. Freshwater Scarcity. *Annual Review of Environment and Resources* 46: 319–348, October 2021.

5. Bevere, Lucia and Federica Remondi. *Natural Catastrophes in 2021: The Floodgates Are Open—Losses from Floods Have Been on an Upward Trend Globally.* Zurich: Sigma, Swiss Re Institute, 2022.

6. Bloomberg News. *World's Food Supplies Get Slammed by Drought, Floods and Frost.* Bloomberg UK, July 24, 2021.

7. Moody's Investors Service. *How Moody's Assesses the Physical Effects of Climate Change on Sovereign Issuers,* November 7, 2016.

8. For example, Cambridge Institute for Sustainability Leadership. *ClimateWise Transition Risk Framework: Managing the Impacts of the Low Carbon Transition on Infrastructure Investments,* February 2019; *ClimateWise Physical Risk Framework: Understanding the Impacts of Climate Change on Real Estate Lending and Investment Portfolios,* February 2019.

9. Moody's Analytics. *Uncovering Climate Hazard Concentrations in Loan Portfolios: A Case Study,* November 2022.

10. Swiss Re sigma 2/2020. *Natural Catastrophes in Times of Economic Accumulation and Climate Change,* April 8, 2020.

11. Martin Kuebler. *How Climate Change Is Shifting the Water Cycle.* Flipboard, October 2022.

12 Damian Carrington. Himalayan Glacier Melting Doubled Since 2000, Spy Satellites Show. *The Guardian,* June 19, 2019.

13. Vano, Julie A. Implications of Losing Snowpack. *Nature Climate Change* 10(May): 386–391, 2020.

14. Baker, Mike. Amid Historic Drought, a New Water War in the West. *The New York Times,* June 1, 2021; Monroe, Rachel. The Water Wars Cone to the Suburbs. *The New Yorker,* June 29, 2022.

15. Famigletti, J. S. The Global Groundwater Crisis. *Nature Climate Change* 4: 945–948, 2014; Brett Walton. *Groundwater Depletion Stresses Majority of World's Largest Aquifers.* Circle of Blue, June 2015; Bessire, Lucas. The Next Disaster Coming to the Great Plains. *The Atlantic,* December 2021.

16. Jasechko, Scott and Debra Perrone. Global Groundwater Wells at Risk of Running Dry. *Science* 372(6540): 418–421, 2021.

17. Gies, Erica. *Water Always Wins.* London: Head of Zeus Publishers, 2022; Judith K. Schwartz. *Water in Plain Sight.* White River Junction, VT: Chelsea Green, 2019.

18. World Resources Institute. *The New AQUEDUCT Water Risk Atlas: What's New & Why Does It Matter to You?* August, 2019.
19. Federal Register. Oil and Natural Gas Sector: Emission Standards for New, Reconstructed, and Modified. *Sources Review*, September 14, 2020; US Environmental Protection Agency.
20. *EPA Issues Supplemental Proposal to Reduce Methane and Other Harmful Pollution from Oil and Natural Gas Operations*, November 11, 2022.
21. In addition to its support for fracking, discussed in part here, the United States provides a range of producer subsidies to the fossil fuels industry, a subject we will be returning to.
22. Lall, Upmanu, Laureline Josset, and Tess Russo. A Snapshot of the World's Groundwater Challenges. *Annual Review of Environment and Resources*, 45: 7.1–7.24, 2020.
23. "The future is already here—it's just not evenly distributed"—William Gibson. *The Economist*, December 4, 2003.
24. IPCC. *Climate Change 2002: Mitigation of Climate Change—Summary for Policymakers*, 2002.
25. Raymond, Colin, Tom Matthews, and Radley M. Horton. The Emergence of Heat and Humidity Too Severe for Human Tolerance. *Science Advances*, May 8, 2020.
26. Butler, Ben. Economic Impact of Australia's Bushfires Set to Exceed $4.4bn Cost of Black Saturday. *The Guardian*, January 8, 2020; Reuters. US Wildfires Could Spark Financial Crisis, Advisory Panel Finds. *The Guardian*, September 10, 2020.
27. Penn, Ivan. PG&E's Bankruptcy Filing Creates 'A Real Mess' for Rival Interests. *The New York Times*, January 29, 2019.
28. Kahn, Deborah. California Continues to Face Wildfire Risks: Insurers Think They Have an Answer. *Politico*, December 30, 2021.
29. S&P Market Intelligence. The Growing Economic Cost of Wildfires. *S&P Global,* January 28, 2021.
30. Wang, Daoping et al. Economic Footprint of California Wildfires in 2018. *Nature Sustainability* 4: 252–260, 2021.
31. Borunda, Alejandra. "Zombie" Fires in the Arctic Are Linked to Climate Change. *National Geographic*, May 19, 2021.
32. McGivney, Annette. Megadrought in the American Southwest: A Climate Disaster Unseen in 1,200 Years. *The Guardian*, September 12, 2022; Williams, A. Park et al. Rapid Intensification of the Emerging Southwestern North American Megadrought in 2020–2021. *Nature Climate Change* 12: 232–234, 2022; Sullivan, Brian K. Megadrought Plaguing Western U.S. Is the Worst in 1,200 Years. *Bloomberg News*, February 14, 2022.
33. Marvel, K. et al. Twentieth-century Hydroclimate Changes Consistent with Human Influence. *Nature* 569: 59–65, 2019.
34. For example, Europe, where drought impacts are likely to be significant: see Naumann, G. et al. Increased Economic Drought Impacts in Europe with Anthropogenic Warming. *Nature Climate Change* 11: 485–491, 2021.

35. Data.worldbank.org. *Employment in Agriculture—Guatemala*, 2016. Online. Available at: https://data.worldbank.org/indicator/SL.AGR.EMPL.ZS?-locations=GT

36. Food and Agriculture Organization of the United Nations. *Central America Dry Corridor Report*, 2016. Available at: https://reliefweb.int/report/guatemala/central-america-dry-corridor-situation-report-june-2016

37. Data.worldbank.org. *Forest Area—Guatemala*, 2015. Online. Available at: https://data.worldbank.org/indicator/AG.LND.FRST.ZS?locations=GT

38. Ortiz-Bobea, Ariel et al. Anthropogenic Climate Change Has Slowed Global Agricultural Productivity Growth. *Nature Climate Change* 11(April): 306–312, 2021.

39. Gerber, Nicolas and Alisher Mirzabaev. *Benefits of Action and Costs of Inaction: Drought Mitigation and Preparedness—A Literature Review.* Integrated Drought Management Programme Working Paper No. 1, World Meteorological Organization, 2017.

40. Adaawen, Stephen and Benjamin Schraven. The Challenges of "Drought Migration." *The Current Column*, German Development Institute / Deutsches Institut für Entwicklungspolitik, 2019.

41. Kummu, Matti et al. Climate Change Risks Pushing One-third of Global Food Production Outside the Safe Climatic Space. *Science Direct, One Earth* 4(5): 720–729, 2021. We discuss the notion of a "safe operating space" in Chapter 7.

42. IPCC. *Summary for Policymakers*, 2013

43. Barber, Gregory. The Wetlands Are Drowning. *Wired Magazine*, May 23, 2022.

44. Rawlence, Ben. *The Treeline: The Last Forest and the Future of Life on Earth.* London: Jonathan Cape, 2022.

45. Enríquez, Alejandra R. et al. Spatial Footprints of Storm Surges along the Global Coastlines. *Journal of Geophysical Research: Oceans* 125(9), 2020.

46. Note that river flooding may be an even greater risk in various parts of the world, especially those with significant riverine deltas such as Bangladesh, Vietnam, and Louisiana in the United States—we discuss this in greater detail in our discussion of extreme precipitation risks.

47. Rush, Elizabeth. *Rising: Dispatches from the New American Shore.* New York: Milkweed Editions, 2018.

48. Gies, Erica. *Water Always Wins.* London: Head of Zeus, 2020.

49. Van Engelen, Joeri, G. H. P. Oude Essink, and Marc Bierkens. Sustainability of Fresh Groundwater Resources in Fifteen Major Deltas around the World. *Environmental Research Letters* 17: 125001, 2022.

50. The World Bank. *Bangladesh: Economics of Adaptation to Climate Change*, 2010; Norwegian Institute of Bioeconomy Research, *Food Security Threatened by Sea Level Rise*, 2017. Available at: https://www.nibio.no/nyheter/food-security-threatened-by-sea-level-rise

51. Fountain, Henry. The World Can Make Water from the Sea, but at What Cost? *The New York Times*, October 22, 2019.

52. Including, for example, the fact that there are areas of the earth's surface that are still rising from the retreat of Northern glaciers.

53. Snider, Laura. *A Subtle Effect of Climate Change: Uneven Sea Level Rise.* NASA Earth Data, December 18, 2018.
54. Moody's Investors Service. *Sea Level Rise Increases Credit Risk for Coastal States and Local Governments*, September 17, 2020.
55. Gies, Erica. *Water Always Wins.* London: Head of Zeus, 2020.
56. Sreenath, A. V. et al. West Coast India's Rainfall Is becoming More Convective. *npj Climate and Atmospheric Science* 5(1): 36, 2022.
57. Payne, Ashley E. et al. Responses and Impacts of Atmospheric Rivers to Climate Change. *Nature Reviews: Earth & Environment*, March 2020; Corringham, T. W. et al. Climate Change Contributions to Future Atmospheric River Flood Damages in the Western United States. *Scientific Reports* 12: 13747, 2022.
58. Dunne, Daisy. Africa's Unreported Extreme Weather in 2022 and Climate Change. *Carbon Brief*, October 26, 2022.
59. Neslen, Arthur. Flooding and Heavy Rains Rise 50% Worldwide in a Decade, Figures Show. *The Guardian*, March 21, 2018.
60. Jongman, Brenden, Philip J. Ward, and Jeroen C. J. H. Aerts, Global Exposure to River and Coastal Flooding: Long-term Trends and Changes. *Global Environmental Change* 22(4): 823–835, 2012; Willner, S. N., C. Otto, and A. Levermann. Global Economic Response to River Floods. *Nature Climate Change* 8: 594–598, 2018.
61. Edmonds, Douglas et al. A Global Analysis of Human Habitation on River Deltas. *Astrophysics Data System*, April 2017.
62. Watts, Jonathan. Climate Scientists Shocked by Scale of Floods in Germany. *The Guardian*, July 16, 2021.
63. World Meteorological Organization. *Weather-related Disasters Increase Over Past 50 Years, Causing More Damage but Fewer Deaths*, August 31, 2021.
64. Calma, Justine. A Nasa Scientist Explains Why Weather Is Getting More Extreme. *The Verge*, August 10, 2021; Krebs, John and Julia Brown. Britain's Weather Is Becoming Ever More Extreme. Why Are We Failing to Prepare? *The Guardian*, February 28, 2022.
65. Kossin, J. P. A Global Slowdown of Tropical Cyclone Translation Speed. *Nature* 228: 104–107, 2018.
66. Carbon Brief. *Mapped: How Climate Change Affects Extreme Weather Around the World.* August 4, 2022
67 Guzman, Oscar et al. Global Increase in Tropical Cyclone Rain Rate. *Nature Communications* 13:7325, 2021.
68. Berardelli, Jeff. How Climate Change Is Making Hurricanes More Dangerous. *Yale Climate Connections*, July 8, 2019; DATU Research and Environmental Defense Fund, *Climate Change-induced Weather Disasters: Costs to State and Local Economies*, Summer 2020.
69. National Centers for Environmental Information. National Oceanic and Atmospheric Administration, *October 2022 Tropical Cyclones Report*, November 2022.
70. Mangi, Faseeh. Pakistan's Catastrophic Flood Damage Estimated to Cost $40 Billion: Officials. *Insurance Journal*, October 30, 2022.

71. World Meteorological Organization. *WMO Atlas of Mortality and Economic Losses from Weather, Climate and Water Extremes (1970–2019)*, 2021.

72. Hook, Leslie, Christian Shepherd, and Nastassia Astrasheuskaya. Extreme Weather Takes Climate Change Models "Off the Scale." *The Financial Times*, July 24, 2021.

73. Vince, Gaia. *Nomad Century*. London: Allen Lane, 2022.

74. Lustgarten, Abraham. How Climate Migration Will Reshape America. *The New York Times Magazine*, September, 2020.

75. McKinsey Global Institute. *Climate Risk and Response*, January, 2020.

76. International Union for the Conservation of Nature. *Ocean Warming*, IUCN Issues Brief, September, 2017.

77. Bojanowski, Axel. *Melting Glaciers Transform Alpine Landscape*. Spiegel International, April 26, 2013.

78. Rouquette, Pauline. *World's Glaciers Are Melting Faster than Expected, with Visible Consequences*. France24, July 31, 2022.

79. Khan, S. A. et al. Centennial Response of Greenland's Three Largest Outlet Glaciers. *Nature Communications* 11: 5718, 2020.

80. Water doesn't go away—it simply changes its state.

81. Milner, Alexander M. et al. Glacier Shrinkage Driving Global Changes in Downstream Systems. *Proceedings of the National Academy of Sciences* 114(37): 9770–9778, 2017.

82. Semieniuk, G. et al. Stranded Fossil-fuel Assets Translate to Major Losses for Investors in Advanced Economies. *Nature Climate Change* 12: 532–538, 2022.

83. Planet Tracker and CDP. *High and Dry: How Water Issues Are Stranding Assets: A Report Commissioned by the Swiss Federal Office for the Environment*, May 2022.

84. The literature on macroeconomic or sector impacts of potential climate risks is fairly broad—see, for example, the scenario discussion in *Climate Change 2022 Mitigation of Climate Change*, Working Group III Contribution to the Sixth Assessment Report of the Intergovernmental Panel on Climate Change Summary for Policymakers. However, firm-specific modeling of climate risks is remarkably sparse, at least until recently, reflecting the influence of the increasing demand for climate risk disclosure by firms.

85. Nicholls, Will. *Environmental Risk Outlook 2022*. Verisk Maplecroft, July, 2022.

CHAPTER 5

Adaptation Risks

The physical changes expected to emerge from climate change are well identified and it follows, therefore, that many of the measures for adapting to these changes are also reasonably well developed. Indeed, the IPCC definition of adaptation is elegantly straightforward:

> In *human systems*, the process of adjustment to actual or expected *climate* and its effects, in order to moderate harm or exploit beneficial opportunities. In natural systems, the process of adjustment to actual climate and its effects; human intervention may facilitate adjustment to expected climate and its effects.[1]

The risks involved in adapting to the diverse consequences of climate change are treated fairly uniformly across taxonomies. We continue this trend in that most of the specific potential risks outlined here derive directly from risk indicators used in traditional financial analysis. Note that our taxonomy designates adaptation risk as a type of *transition risk*, in addition to the traditional perception of adaptation risk as more closely associated with physical risks. Figure 5.1 presents the proposed adaptation risk categories.

It is important to specify what we actually mean by adaptation. We believe there are several broad categories for implementing, or even commenting on, adaptation as a climate-related issue:

1. Adaptation as a response to specific physical climate risks, such as flooding in urban areas.
2. Adaptation defined by the type of infrastructure being addressed; both gray (human-constructed) and green (wetlands) infrastructure can be affected.

3. Adaptation strategies, which are generally categorized as resistance, accommodation, avoidance, and retreat.[2]
4. There are also broader multicategory systems such as agriculture, complex aggregated systems such as supply chains, areas of public policy such as transportation, and steps leading to implementation of a circular economy. Many of these also present transition issues that transcend specific physical risks, or involve multiple categories of risk.

Note also that there are significant differences in the abilities of developed countries, compared with developing countries, to develop effective adaptation measures that are not necessarily captured in these categories, although it is a difference that public policymakers and international debt providers are acutely aware of. These differences between developed and developing markets are currently widening, and these are likely to continue to do so.

Note that point 3 above (adaption strategies) is critical for potential risk assessment, since these reflect the specific public policy responses to adaptation risks in whatever form—either in terms of the type of risk, or the infrastructure potentially affected. These four responses can be organized as follows: [3]

1. Resistance—erecting barriers such as seawalls to eliminate, or at least reduce, the physical risks in question.
2. Accommodation—allowing the physical changes to occur, but accommodating these changes through changes in, for example, construction methods.
3. Avoidance—don't build in the potentially affected area—wetlands, for example—in the first place.
4. Retreat (generally referred to as managed retreat)—transporting potentially affected communities away from potential harm, such as receding coastlines. This is now the preferred strategy for coastal problems adopted by the US Federal Emergency Management Agency (FEMA) and other branches of the US government.[4] Costs for this process are largely funded by governments and the affected parties.

There is actually a further option, one that has been proven effective throughout human history: abandonment. This will likely be the strategy (if strategy is indeed what it is) with the most significant potential economic costs.[5]

ADAPTATION TO PHYSICAL CLIMATE RISKS

Following the above, we suggest that these potential risks can be organized by three category specific frameworks previously indicated:

1. the specific physical risk driving the adaptation policy or project;
2. the type of infrastructure being addressed; and
3. the adaptation response: resistance, accommodation, avoidance, advance, and retreat.

These are categories of projects and project spending that may often overlap—these are unlikely to be orthogonal categories. Of the categories put forward, we suspect most adaptation projects globally will occur in the context of points 2 (specific infrastructure projects) and 4 (broader systems such as agriculture) for example, irrespective of their wide geographic diversity. The difference between numbers 1 and 2 is really one of perspective, and one would expect significant classification overlaps here. However, we believe there is merit to granulating these classifications, primarily as a heuristic for determining what areas of interest are receiving the most funding currently, and what areas are most in need of funds going forward. We note that since many, probably a majority, of adaptation projects are likely to be publicly funded, these categorizations are really also public policy choices.

The most general statement that can be made is that adaptation is a response to an existing or potential physical threat to infrastructure or activity in relation to some desired (or at least targeted) resilience state. The other categories are ways of categorizing modes of response. Overall, however, *the overriding motivation behind adaptation is to reduce risk.*[6] As we will see, risk targets here can be broader than physical risks, although they will clearly be the main focus.

In the model shown in Figure 5.1, we have used adaptation to specific physical risks as our baseline framework. However, it is clear that a range of approaches may be undertaken in determining the most appropriate framework for adaptation risk assessment.

We note that much of the work done here naturally tends to fall into some easily identifiable categories of financial risk, similar to the approach we take to mitigation risks outlined in Chapter 6. All five of our indicative categories—asset valuation risks, operational impairments, cost of business adjustments, regulatory changes, and subsidy loss risks—are categories assessed in the normal course of assessing credit risk of most investment, for example. We have chosen these as being the areas where specific potential risks relating to adaptation efforts are most likely to manifest themselves, with our specific indicative examples in the right-hand column. Note that

FIGURE 5.1 Proposed adaptation risk taxonomy.
Source: Green Planet Consulting Ltd. *What is Climate Risk? A Field Guide for Investors, Lenders and Regulators.* London: Centre for Climate Finance and Investment, Imperial College Business School, February 2022.

these examples are just that—examples. Each category contains multiple potential risks.

Significantly, as has been noted elsewhere, adaptation efforts in which risk assessment is a critical component, is an iterative process:

> Iterative risk management emphasizes that the process of anticipating and responding to climate change does not constitute a single set of judgments at any point in time; rather, it is an ongoing cycle of assessment, action, reassessment, learning, and response. In the adaptation context, public- and private-sector actors manage climate risk using three types of actions: reducing exposure, reducing sensitivity, and increasing adaptive capacity.[7]

This means that the risk assessment process will be iterative as well. Note also that two of the adaptation risk categories—subsidy loss risk, and asset valuation risk—appear more than once in the overall taxonomy. This has been a recurring issue—specific risks can result from more than one potential climate impact.

WHAT SORT OF INFRASTRUCTURE ARE WE TALKING ABOUT?

It is important to recognize a distinction between "gray" infrastructure and "green" infrastructure. *Gray* infrastructure refers to the built environment, ranging from private residences to the more established categories that we usually think of as infrastructure, which generally include:[8]

1. energy,
2. transportation (rail, maritime shipping, vehicular, air),

3. building and housing stock,
4. telecommunications and technology, and
5. water and waste management.

This list is not exhaustive but it does contain the major categories of gray infrastructure.[9] Interestingly, a number of these categories contain sectors that are capable of generating cash flows in their own right, which is of critical interest for investors, and which may facilitate these sectors in developing their own adaptation projects. These sectors include (but again, are not limited to):

- water supply;
- wastewater treatment and waste management;
- energy infrastructure;
- rail (both freight and passenger);
- ports and airports;
- bridges, tunnels, and roads;
- telecoms and other technology-related infrastructure; and
- building and housing stock.

These infrastructures are of interest because of their financial risk-mitigation potential. To the extent that there are infrastructure generated cash flows, these may be used to reduce the potential financial risks that arise in specific circumstances.

In contrast, *green* infrastructure involves using natural landscape features to adapt to or mitigate climate impacts. The largest segment of existing or proposed green infrastructure projects involves water issues, including water purification, water depletion concerns, waste management, reduction of flooding risks (both coastal and river), and storm surge defenses.[10] There are areas where nature-based solutions involving green infrastructure, or nature-based infrastructure (NBI), can play a role.[11] We will expand on this point in the Natural Capital chapter.

ADAPTATION, RESILIENCE, AND SUSTAINABILITY—SOME DEFINITIONAL ISSUES

The issue of what some organizations or situation should be *adapted to* has been a lively topic for years, especially among, for example, urban planners whose task is to anticipate climate impacts.[12] This process involves designing and implementing systems resilient enough to accommodate a wide range of risks. This should (although it does not always appear to) provide a rationale for including some criteria for what represents a "resilient" system—or, as is often the case, a "sustainable" system. However, we think there has been considerable confusion over these terms.

Arguments over the Oxford comma have nothing on arguments over the meaning of "Sustainability," for example. For such a commonly used word, one would think there would be some relatively reasonable and granulated definition that everyone was happy with. But it seems as if we have progressed little from the Brundtland Commission's definition from way back in 1987 in the context of development:

> Sustainable development is development that meets the needs of the present without compromising the ability of future generations to meet their own needs.

This was a pretty good general concept, but hardly an operational definition. It has, however, proved to be sufficiently vague so as to capture a wide range of meanings.

There seems to be a certain degree of fuzziness with which these terms are used. In particular, we note that the term "sustainability" is often misused, when what is meant is "resilience"—and vice versa. Our view is straightforward: resilience is a systems characteristic, be it ecological, infrastructure-related, or financial. Properly, resilience should define the extent to which any system can recover from events back to its initial (or at least targeted) state, either fully or partially.[13] Sustainability, on the other hand, should be regarded as a set of tools for achieving a desired level of resilience. These do not mean the same thing.

One approach here is to develop, as suggested in 2016 by ClimateWise, an association of insurers based at the Cambridge Institute for Sustainable Leadership, a system of "resilience ratings."[14] This is a concept that emanates from the insurance industry and if anyone has a good measure of the resilience of, say, property to weather events associated with global heating, it's going to be this industry. They have already got the numbers. For this sector, resilience is indeed a quantifiable characteristic—they do it all the time.

In fact, we believe that "resilience" could be thought of as a good substitute word for "green." Surely something more is conveyed by *green* than simply referring to, say, just GHG reductions. It's also accommodating water depletion and allocation issues. It means preserving natural capital in forests and fisheries. It means waste reduction and a more circular economy. It means reducing topsoil loss, which is occurring on a global basis and may even be a more imminent systemic challenge than global heating. In fact, there is a whole range of "green" issues that we can easily subsume under the concept of resilience.[15] And the fact that there is much about the concept of resilience and the particular domains it can apply to that is quantifiable is a point in its favor.

Adaptation Risks

Though we concede that adaptation risks are inescapably derivative of physical risks, we classify them as transition risks for two reasons. First, adaptation to some physical impact is likely to be a process—sometimes a very long one. Moreover, adaptation measures (like mitigation measures) will always cost someone money, meaning that governments, insurers, and even firms themselves may be exposed to a wide and perhaps daunting range of costs.

There has been significant interest in this transition because of the pressure on traditional business models, for fossil fuel companies in particular. Much of the focus here has been on what strategies oil majors, including state-owned companies, for example, will need to adapt.[16] In contrast, the adaptation and mitigation response costs that are likely to arise for all industries where carbon intensity is a factor (e.g., steel, chemicals, and cement) have received far less attention, although this currently seems to be changing as a result of increased decarbonization measures and proposals (often in the context of achieving net-zero emissions).[17] Replacing carbon-intensive sourcing, manufacturing, and distribution in existing infrastructure with lower-carbon intensity practices is likely to be an expensive process—as is constructing new infrastructure and processes.

More broadly, it seems clear that in general adaptation efforts tend to be local, with little broader integration, with some degree of uncertainty as to whether existing measures are actually reducing adaptation risks.[18] Note that adaptation measures may not be possible in some locations, and even if they are, they may prove quite costly to implement. Ports, which are generally found at sea level (excepting inland ports like those on large lakes) may well be able to physically adapt to rising sea levels and increased storm surges. But the costs of doing so may be quite high, especially for port-related infrastructure such as transportation networks, although in many cases these costs can be amortized over a considerable length of time. This aspect is, in fact, a general characterization of many adaptation costs: *lead times may be quite long*, which can allow for the timely implementation of specific adaptation measures and for the costs to be spread out over an extended period of time. Nonetheless, these are costs with some degree of uncertainty attached to them at present, so they pose potential risks to the financial measures that we have previously indicated. Similarly, as S&P recently noted, physical risks—wildfires, storms, and water-related events— are now driving continued increases in adaptation and mitigation spending by utilities, for example.[19]

In addition, it is now generally recognized that coastal property values might be strongly impacted by rising sea levels,[20] and that large portions of current coastal property may be so negatively affected that they are essentially worthless, say, by the end of the century. But this is a long time from an investing horizon. Thus, this prospect is highly unlikely to affect rating agencies', investors', or lenders' assessments of likely corporate financial risk changes over the next three to five years (although, as S&P noted in a recent discussion of flooding risks in the United Kingdom much depends on potential changes in rainfall amounts).[21] For that matter, this horizon does not necessarily provide a near-term constraint on REIT composition at present (although REITs with significant urban Florida coastal exposure may wish to increase their monitoring of Miami's increasing flooding problems[22]). Hence, while pointing out this potential development might seem to be stating the obvious, it may not yet be particularly relevant for investors.[23] Further, it is worth noting that adaptation measures may differ in both cost and scope depending on whether the physical risk being addressed (i.e., adapted to) is acute or chronic. Measures designed for ocean flooding will be quite different if they are aimed at adapting to increased storm frequency versus general sea level rise.

Adaptation spending is ultimately a public good. Thus, as is the case for many public goods, we believe it should in turn benefit from public funding. This is indeed generally the case in the United States, where municipal (state and local) infrastructure spending represents about 75% of all infrastructure spending, with the balance being provided by federal and private financing. And of this municipal spending, some 80% is directly funded through the municipal bond market. At the risk of overgeneralizing, this suggests that comparable municipal borrowings in other countries could eventually represent the majority of funding for adaptation projects in affected countries if developed for adaptation funding purposes.[24] The UK's National Adaptation Programme, for example, currently embodies a federalist approach to adaptation spending, which involves funding decisions largely being made at the sovereign treasury level—even, in many cases, for local spending.

We note that there has been considerable discussion over the past several decades of a broader implementation of the concept of adaptation, particularly with reference to limits, reflecting potentially necessary changes to existing broader aspects of the modern economy.[25] These will generally involve discussion of potential public policy options relating to specific categories of public and private goods. The following areas are often used as examples of broader economic or financial systems whose current operational frameworks may be, and in fact need to be, adapted to a more resource-constrained and climate-risky world (this is an indicative, not an exhaustive, list):

1. agriculture,
2. water,
3. transportation,
4. supply chain issues, and
5. circular economy issues.

Notably, all of these sectors are the subjects of considerable focus in discussions of a *transition economy*. Such discussions inescapably involve considerations of sustainability and resilience.[26]

TARGETING ADAPTATION COSTS

This category refers to a broad range of potential costs, perhaps over a long time period, relating to addressing the impacts of climate change. Rising ocean levels and increased flooding will pose risks—to coastal areas, for example, including port facilities, railroads, and associated infrastructure, not to mention residential housing. If these risks are left unmanaged, they have the potential to produce potentially significant stranded assets, or at least substantial asset devaluations (and, in some cases, improved valuations for inland locations). These also have the potential to dramatically increase capital spending to accommodate whatever adaptation measures may be adopted—for example, in the transportation sector.[27] Moreover, climate-related disruptions to capital projects also have the potential to affect overall costs of capital for organizations.

Currently, these costs are generally being borne by governments and insurance companies. For instance, New York City has undertaken an aggressive $20 billion program[28] to try to avoid a repeat of the flooding conditions that prevailed during Hurricane Sandy in 2012. Some other major storms, such as Hurricane Katrina in 2005, have also generated physical responses, although the degree to which these programs actually reduce physical risks remains uncertain. Over the longer term, these costs have the potential to be significant, and certainly have the potential to create stranded assets on a broad scale. Moving a building's contents from a coastal location to higher ground is one thing; moving an entire railroad line is considerably more complex. As another example, the costs associated with repairing the damage caused by the 2021 flooding in British Columbia are likely to be considerable—perhaps as high as US $9 billion. When the potential scope of all such flooding incidents, even on an annual basis, gets aggregated on a global basis, we are actually talking about hundreds of billions of potential damages.[29]

The US Gulf Coast offers a salutary lesson on adaptation costs. It is the heart of the country's energy complex, and also the mouth of the Mississippi River, which is fundamental as a transport link to many parts of the US economy. However, as the events of Hurricanes Katrina and Harvey indicated, it is also vulnerable to the effects of extreme weather. The economic consequences of Hurricane Katrina were significant because of multiple effects: disruption of traffic on the Mississippi River (a major transit conduit for the mid-American economy), the impact on US and chemical energy infrastructure, and the devastation of a major US city's infrastructure.[30] Further, the US Gulf Coast is just one area among many globally where significant assets are based on coasts or rivers. Adaptation measures in these areas are likely to be substantial, if not necessarily imminent.

The more recent damage caused by Hurricane Ian in Florida, which was mostly residential and commercial (and not industrial) nonetheless created the largest storm-related economic damage of any event in Florida's history—insured losses may be as high as US $67 billion.[31] This figure does not include uninsured flood losses. Moreover, in this case, much of the residential housing was uninsured for flood damage, which is a problem, since most of the damage resulted from storm-surge generated flooding. The rebuilding process here will be a lengthy one.

We observe that the concerns in this regard will be for assets in general, and not necessarily stranded assets. In some cases of longer-term adaptation risks, the assets in question may already have been fully depreciated so that the risk of stranded assets may be relatively minor, or indeed nonexistent. This does not, however, mean that asset risks in general are modest. Replacing assets at any time has the potential to be costly, irrespective of asset values in financial statements; this may be especially true in the case of infrastructure affected by global heating risks, particularly transportation infrastructure such as railroads, ports, and some airports.

WHAT WILL ADAPTATION MEASURES ACTUALLY COST?

As Figures 5.2 and 5.3 from the Climate Policy Initiative[32] suggest, at present, adaptation spending is very much the "poor cousin" of mitigation spending. Moreover, it is not clear what will change this dynamic in the near future, although the need for such change is significant and apparent.

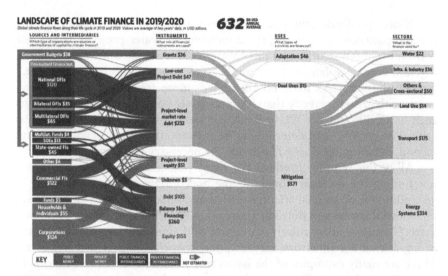

FIGURE 5.2 Climate flow of funds 2019/2020.
Source: Climate Policy Initiative. *Global Landscape of Climate Finance 2021,*
December 2021.

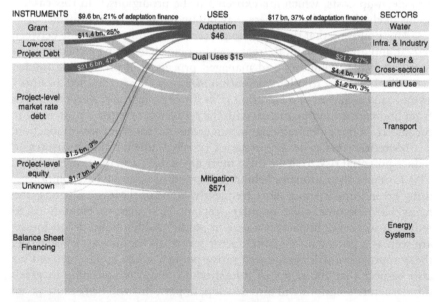

FIGURE 5.3 Adaptation flow of funds 2019/2020.
Source: Climate Policy Initiative. *Global Landscape of Climate Finance 2021,*
December 2021.

More specifically, the funding flows within adaptation manifest some specific patterns—principally, the dominance of water projects. Given our constant reiteration of the scope of water risks associated with global heating, and even in isolation as a natural capital concern, this is unsurprising.

As physical risks manifest themselves more frequently and, in many cases, with greater severity than has previously been the case, organizations such as UNEP and the World Bank are seeking to accomplish two major critical objectives: first, determining what adaptation projects will cost; and second, determining who will provide the necessary financing.

All of this requires funding. For many potential adaptation situations, not finding the necessary funds or the appropriate strategy will result in an additional option: abandonment. Abandonment brings a different set of financial issues and outright risks, often encompassed by the "stranded assets" concept—particularly valuation and financial losses, which may be significant for investors, insurers, and property lenders in particular.[33] There are many examples of the issues surrounding abandonment, notably in the Pacific Islands. There are also examples closer to home; Fairbourne, in Wales, looks set to hold the title of the UK's first climate refugee town.[34] Another example is the current rate of abandonment of fracking sites in the United States by operators unable to pay the often-expensive restoration and clean-up costs, which are expected to be prodigious.[35] In this case, it seems likely that the burden here may fall on municipal governments.

This points up that there is an important distinction to be made between retreat and abandonment. Retreat may involve abandoning a specific location, but it is a voluntary and managed process, and presumably funded accordingly, similar to other adaptation measures. There are, then, basically two broad categories of adaptation risks for organizations: those that stem from finding the funding to deal with the problems, or those that stem from the uncertain but potentially significant economic consequences of inaction.

Moreover, this raises the issue of possible amelioration measures to reduce potential risk to make them more amenable to adaptation measures. This is one of the rationales behind the notion of nature-based solutions—using green infrastructure more frequently. Some of these are obvious, and many have become quite popular—replanting mangrove plantations to reduce storm-surge impacts is a case in point.[36] Additionally, urban forests are seen as a potential mitigating factor for urban heat impacts. We expect these approaches will continue to prove popular when applicable, and we also suspect that the range of infrastructure projects amenable to green infrastructure solutions will also develop. In part, this will be because green infrastructure projects can be, in general, less costly than gray infrastructure projects.[37]

We note also that public policy changes have been shown to have a positive impact on addressing climate risks. For example, even though the US southwest has been in the midst of a long-term drought, several cities, including San Diego and Phoenix, have undertaken various adaptation measures that ensure better water supplies than might otherwise be the case.[38] As we mention elsewhere, there is a variety of proposed measures to improve water access in the face of escalating global drought conditions—we discuss some of these in the Natural Capital discussion.

WHAT SORT OF FUNDING REQUIREMENTS ARE WE TALKING ABOUT, AND WHO IS AT RISK?

Since adaptation is a response to the impacts of a wide potential range of physical risks, there are several considerations that must be specified to discuss adaptation funding requirements:

1. What is the physical risk being reduced?
2. What is the type of infrastructure affected?
   a. Gray (buildings, transportation, energy, ICT, etc.)
   b. Green (forests, wetlands, etc.)
3. Is the ownership public or private? Different countries have different ownership models. How does this affect adaptation financing prospects and, perhaps more critically, sources?
4. If the infrastructure is publicly owned, what level of government is involved (national vs. local planning; most Conference of the Parties (COP) signatories have developed national adaptation plans)?
5. If the infrastructure is privately owned, do the benefits of any interventions extend to private companies as well (e.g., a government-funded flood protection scheme)?

As a result of these diverse considerations, adaptation policies and programs have the potential to be considerably more fragmented than mitigation policies, which tend to cluster around a well-specified set of targets, including energy transition and decarbonization, that most countries have agreed to adhere to. To some extent, this disconnection is reflected in the lack of unified or, in most cases, sufficient attention to adaptation needs. It also means that there has been insufficient commitment to providing sufficient funds for adaptation programs and their implementation, as suggested by the previous figures. This latter point has contributed to what is referred to as the "adaptation financing gap"—the gap between estimated adaptation financial needs, and what actually has been committed by governments and other potentially affected parties. This issue is so significant that UNEP publishes an annual report on the status of this gap.[39]

The numbers around adaptation funding and needs are quite high and quite variable, depending on the source. UNEP has estimated that overall adaptation spending requirements are expected to be in the range of $180 billion annually through 2030 (by comparison, total climate spending could reach $4.5 trillion annually) and even higher between 2030 and 2050.[40] The 2021 UNEP report notes that "the pace of adaptation financing is indeed rising, but it continues to be outpaced by rapidly increasing adaptation costs." Moreover, and alarmingly, "[a]nnual adaptation costs in *developing countries* are estimated at USD 70 billion. This figure is expected to reach USD 140–300 billion in 2030 and USD 280–500 billion in 2050." These are the countries that are receiving more than their fair share of climate-related impacts, despite having contributed little to the problems generating global heating historically.[41] Note that this does not include estimates for new and replacement gray (built) infrastructure across all markets—which could total US $4.29 trillion annually for the next twenty years, according to one estimate.[42]

These are global figures, as indicated. Unsurprisingly, there is a wide range of estimated national costs. As a result of discussions and the ratification of the Cancun Adaptation Framework at COP16 and in Cancun in 2011, signatory countries agreed to develop national adaptation plans, and many of these are now in effect. The UK's National Adaptation Programme, for example, details a series of targets to be achieved (including net-zero targets) by a specified date and a set of recommendations on how to achieve them.[43] As might be expected, wealthier nations in the Global North have a significant advantage in developing such plans—not only in terms of the infrastructure framework to be addressed, but also in terms of the potential for governments to fund a portion (potentially a significant one) of the necessary spending. At time of writing, thirty-eight less-developed countries (LDCs) have submitted national adaptation plans to the UN; funding availability in much of the Global South appears to be considerably more uncertain.[44]

Disappointingly, but perhaps not surprisingly, reports from various government agencies and NGOs in general reflect a remarkable lack of specificity in terms of financing sources. These reports generally assume that someone, and presumably governments, will be the default funder. However, given the potential scope of what adaptation funding might entail, this is an issue that needs more specific resolution, and soon.

ASSET VALUATION RISKS

Asset impairments can occur in the normal course of business for any number of reasons, most of which, frankly, are wholly unrelated to climate or natural capital issues. Any time the market value of an asset is less than the recorded value in a company's accounts, an impairment may result (although there is often some discretion allowed in making this call). Hence, an established accounting and financial process exists for dealing with such events. Asset values change over time in any event, and this is usually accommodated for through amortization and depreciation schedules.

However, climate and natural capital risks add a level of complexity to this process; this is because we may know that some assets, such as coastal infrastructure, are exposed, but the scope and timing of their potential impairment is uncertain. Such uncertainly is most likely for physical assets exposed to physical climate risks. Utilities need water for cooling purposes, and as a result are often located on coasts at sea level, or on rivers with potential flood risks. Mining companies also need water, although for different reasons, often in regions where water availability may be constrained. As noted elsewhere, given the amount of the world's population and economic activity located in coastal or riverine environments, the scope for potential asset impairments from physical risks is actually quite large. These risks will be exacerbated by global heating.[45]

This is in part something of a governance issue. Is management aware of the potential long-term risks associated with some assets, and do they have a strategy for dealing with these at minimal cost? This will involve a monitoring process. Often managements will benefit from the often relatively long lead times associated with the physical risks and the adaptation response. It is also the case that adaptation measures may reduce the potential impacts of climate impacts on asset valuations. However, such measures are expected to be time consuming and costly.

Stranded asset risks represent a good example of how climate risks can be granulated to a level that fits a traditional approach to financial analysis. They are quantifiable and, if crystallized, can have potentially material impacts on asset valuations, earnings, and cash flows. As a result, asset impairments can have negative financial risk implications, including on credit ratings—as many European utilities discovered in 2013,[46] and as a number of oil majors discovered in 2020.[47]

Carbon-based assets appear to be particularly vulnerable, and as we point out throughout this report, there is a wide range of industries where such assets may present potential risks to various financial instruments. In their report on carbon asset risk,[48] the WRI and UNEP provide an example

Category	Example Sectors	Principal Types of Risk Facing the Category	Typical Financial Asset Classes
1. Fossil-fuel assets	Coal mining; oil and gas production	Policy; technology market and economic; reputational	Equities; bonds; corporate lending
2. Fossil-fuel dependent-infrastructure	Oil and gas pipelines; rail lines (for example, those shipping coal)	Policy; market and economic; reputational	Bonds; project finance
3. High-carbon assets facing shift to low-carbon technologies	Fossil fuel–fired power plants	Policy; technology market and economic	Equities; bonds; corporate lending
4. High-carbon assets without low-carbon competitors	Cement; steel; glass	Policy; technology market and economic	Equities; bonds; corporate lending

FIGURE 5.4 Summary of typical risk types and asset classes associated with each category of assets.
Source: World Resources Institute and UNEP Finance Initiative. *Carbon Asset Risk: Discussion Framework*, 2022.

of sectors and instruments that are likely to be vulnerable, as shown in Figure 5.4.

While the list in Figure 5.4 is not necessarily intended to be exhaustive, it is a fairly representative listing of carbon-intensive industries and some suggested risks associated with each. Note also that it is intentionally vague both in terms of the scale of the potential impacts in these categories, as well as the timing of potential manifestation of financial impacts. In addition, the example sectors all seem to be corporate in terms of ownership. There is also a whole range of assets owned by noncorporate entities—often infrastructure owned and operated by municipalities and regional and national governments (such as rail systems in most countries),[49] but these are generally outside our scope here. However, many of the physical and adaptation risks discussed herein are also likely to be applicable to state-owned infrastructure.

The recent impacts of COVID-19 on the global economy, something not predictable in any taxonomy, have affected a range of industries. The fossil fuel industries were hit especially hard in 2020, with highly leveraged operators in the United States seeking bankruptcy protection at very high levels and major oil companies indicating possible (and considerable, even for large oil companies) ranges of financial impacts on assets. In connection with this development, a number of oil majors—including Shell, BP, Total, and ExxonMobil—had to take material charges to reflect potential stranded asset risk. As a result, the stranded assets issue for the fossil fuel industry again received some attention. The relevant questions are now: (1) whether various stranded asset risks (and risks of asset value deterioration in general) will crystallize, and (2) if so, when. Just because value has been impaired, this doesn't automatically result in an immediate adjustment to valuations, or in classification as a stranded asset. Note that given the recent spike in fossil fuel pricing, these discussions have seemed to have gone away. We are confident they will return.

We have previously suggested[50] that the likely generators of asset risks with potential impact for material financial profile alterations could include, but are not limited to:

1. regulatory compliance risks,
2. carbon pricing risks,
3. reputational and license to operate risks,
4. physical adaptation risks,
5. increased likelihood of weather-related event risks,
6. depletion risks,
7. global warming impacts on natural resources (e.g., agriculture, oceans, forests), and
8. subsidy loss risks.

For some sectors, such as coal mining and utilities, financial analysts have already pointed to myriad vulnerabilities to risks emanating from current regulatory or physical climate risks. We have seen credit rating downgrades in both sectors as a result of these concerns. Moreover, as noted elsewhere, we are seeing increased negative credit ratings pressure in a number of sectors because of many of these concerns.

OPERATIONAL IMPAIRMENTS

The issue of operational impairments[51] seems like a relatively obvious risk candidate, and we would fully expect it to be part of the traditional risk assessment of an investment. External (and occasionally internal) factors can regularly have an impact on operating measures such as revenues, earnings, and margins. Climate factors, particularly regulatory changes relating to GHG reduction, have the potential to contribute to uncertainty surrounding any assessment of these factors' trajectories, as we discuss in more detail in Chapter 6.

Note that operational impairments alone do not necessarily result in asset impairments per se, although they may contribute to such. For example, while the US coal industry presented a raft of issues to investors and regulators in the past decade, it was ultimately its declining margins that were cited as being a key factor in credit agency downgrades. This financial impact, which eventually led to a series of bankruptcy filings in the industry, were chiefly driven by adaptation and mitigation efforts in its largest customer base—utilities that were reducing their coal dependency on climate grounds. In lower-margin businesses such as fracking, physical constraints (possibly driven by state or increased federal regulation) necessitating adaptation measures, mainly related to water consumption and wastewater disposal concerns in regions of increasing water scarcity, are likely to be felt more broadly than in a higher-margin industry such as specialty chemicals.

The key issue here is likely to be adaptation costs, since these will affect earnings and margins, rather than outright revenue decreases, as was the case in the coal industry. This issue raises an interesting distinction that investors and lenders should keep in mind: sometimes adaptation cost impacts are the result of company measures and sometimes they are the result of upstream or downstream entities, in the latter case, principally customers—as was the case of coal companies and the utilities that comprised their traditional customer base. It is essential to consider both.

A further complication when assessing the impacts of adaptation costs is that changes to these costs may well be stimulated by regulatory factors. Transition risks such as reducing GHG generation, for example, or reducing wastewater discharge in water-stressed areas, tends to be expensive, involving significant capital expenditures, with potential impacts on both margins and cash flows. This is even more true in the case of potential adaptation measures. As regulations trend toward becoming more onerous in a number of regions, particularly in terms of, for example, property resilience measures, it is likely that their effects on cost structures will become more material. On the other hand, as in other factors, these regulatory changes may often involve a long lead time for project execution, providing companies with some flexibility to manage the process more efficiently.

COST OF BUSINESS ADJUSTMENTS

The costs of business adjustments, which include relocation, insurance, and decommissioning, among others, may prove to be among the most significant that companies and sectors may bear. There are several reasons for this.

First, to the extent that operating facilities need to be moved because of a physical risk such as increased storm surge, this process will inevitably be expensive. Both the cost of new facilities and the cost of reducing exposure to the affected facility are likely to be onerous, even for large organizations— especially if there are significant clean-up costs associated with closing a facility. Moreover, in many sectors there are regulatory and/or legal require- ments for clean-up following a facility's closure; this is particularly true in the US fossil fuel industry, for example, where there are (widely varying) requirements for post-closure clean-up (even though, apparently, these are not always enforced). These clean-up requirements represent a general trend and one that a number of industries have acclimated to over the years.

However, climate risks are likely to increase in some sectors, acceler- ating the closure of facilities (as in the case of fracking wells in the United States at present that require post-closure clean-ups).[52] In some cases, com- panies are declaring bankruptcy before these costs can be allocated, basi- cally socializing those costs to taxpayers. State and local US governments are aware of these developments, but with limited powers to control this trend. Even without this regulatory aspect, it is likely that the closure of many plants and utilities will accelerate because of climate considerations.

Second, insurance costs seem destined to increase as climate risks become more prevalent. Such increases have already occurred in property insurance along coastlines and are currently occurring in areas affected by wildfires in California and Australia. In addition, given the expected increases in extreme weather, it is likely that the insurance industry will come under significant pressure, particularly in terms of constraints on the industry's actions to price insurance in terms of relevant potential costs. This issue has been a recurring one in Florida for a number of years; it is now becoming an issue in insurance pricing for wildfire damages. There may be adaptation costs that are simply uninsurable.

The third reason why business adjustments costs can be significant is one that we see little coverage of: the costs associated with relocating infra- structure associated with larger systems. In some cases, this process will be expensive, but straightforward. The actual footprint of most plants, includ- ing utilities and petrochemical facilities, for example, is generally relatively small. In other cases, however, the requirements are industry specific, and pose particular siting complexities. Railroads are a case in point. Most rail infrastructure is fully depreciated, so stranded asset risks to balance sheets are, in many cases, probably minimal. But where entire sections of line must be replaced (e.g., as might be the case for railroads with significant coastal or riverine placement) several issues can arise. First, where might an alterna- tive route be sited? Often, location is dependent on policies and land avail- ability constraints from a century or more ago, when eminent domain was frequently used as an inexpensive source of land for track. Further, in many of these cases, it is unclear where a new replacement rail could be placed, given likely demographic changes from when the track was first sited. Many of these same concerns arise with reference to airports as well, given their relatively large footprints. Predicting potential adaptation costs in these circumstances could prove particularly difficult.

This infrastructure relocation cost is not limited to private companies. Municipalities, regional governments, and national governments will all face similar issues relating to, for example, highways or public transportation (particularly underground transportation). Again, predicting costs here is a highly speculative enterprise. Nonetheless, estimates have been put forward: McKinsey, citing the World Bank, notes,

> Infrastructure is expected to bear the brunt of expected climate change adaptation costs, typically estimated to be between 60 and 80 percent of total climate change adaptation spending globally, which could average $150 billion to $450 billion per year on infrastructure in 2050.[53]

Note that infrastructure is not just roads and power grids—it also includes telecommunications networks and server farms, for example.

It also may include entire communities. The potential physical and economic impact of storm surge and flooding in Miami, Florida, is well known. Less well known is the flooding caused by water rising up through limestone when storms produce heavy rainfall—and rainfall keeps getting heavier all the time. But to date the State of Florida and a range of local municipal governments have not yet achieved unity on any sort of remediation plan.[54] Similar problems have arisen in Germany, with plans to dredge portions of the Rhine river to reduce the impacts of drought on waterway availability during drier than average summers, such as that of 2022. The project has generated considerable controversy, given its location in the middle of a World Heritage site.[55] Projects such as this are likely to receive more attention as more countries encounter more frequent and severe droughts. In this case, the project is to be funded by government agencies—but given the critical importance of the Rhine to the German economy, there is considerable interest across a range of firms in Germany that rely on the Rhine for transport of parts and/or finished goods. The major risk to firms here—business interruption—is similar to technology firms dependent on extended supply lines for the timely movement of goods. In this case, the risk is not the occasional semiconductor plant fire, but the expected increase in difficulties in getting goods to market form an increased physical risk—drought.

Finally, it is clear that there will be considerable disruption at municipal and regional levels, and that addressing this disruption will cost significant amounts of money. Given the sheer number of coastal communities that are exposed to increasing climate risks, one would expect these costs to be high. How high is suggested by the recent experience of the Quinault Nation in Washington state, which has decided it needs to move a half-mile inland to avoid the worsening impacts of global heating on their shoreline community. The proposal is to move the entire town. The estimated cost is $150 million.[56] Scale this up to the number of communities that might be interested in a similar action, saying that costs may be considerable is probably an understatement.

REGULATORY CHANGES (LAND USE AND ZONING)

As more land along coasts or in fire-prone forest areas becomes unavailable for use, we are likely to see increased pressure to control the allowable uses or zoning of such land. In areas where it is primarily residences and residential communities that are affected, there will be financial losses, including by insurance companies, but the overall economic impacts likely will vary by locale. However, for coastal areas where there is a significant concentration of economic wealth, the picture is less clear. In a recent report on US municipalities,[57] Moody's noted the following:

- By 2040, rising sea levels and greater risk of frequent flooding will affect most states' coastal counties, including more than 110 cities with a population greater than 50,000.
- Economic weakening, higher maintenance costs and lost tax revenue are particular credit risks for state and local governments over the next several decades.

These trends are likely to produce limitations on the potential availability of coastal areas for the development of properties and commercial uses. Municipalities and zoning authorities will be increasingly reluctant to allow the siting of enterprises that will entail high costs in the future. Since these uses may represent substantial property tax revenues for municipalities, the economic impact on these may be significant.[58] The impact of these limitations on property companies and insurers and investors in such companies could be even more problematic.[59]

In addition, there will be increased pressure to deal with the current siting of vulnerable industries, such as petrochemicals and other industries that require coastal locations. For example, does the petrochemical complex in the Gulf of Mexico present a near-term climate risk for investors and lenders? Should new facilities be allowed to be developed in regions where increases in physical risks are expected? Are the capital costs associated with either alternative—remaining in a vulnerable location, or moving elsewhere—affordable, and if so, through what mechanism—more borrowing or more equity? Investors and lenders will be increasingly interested in how such questions are decided upon and implemented.

LOSS OF SUBSIDY RISKS

Subsidy risks actually span three of the risk categories being discussed here: adaptation, mitigation, and natural capital risks. Subsidies generally enable economic producers and consumers to avoid paying the genuine economic costs of the extraction and usage of various resources. That's the actual point of subsidies, after all. To the extent that subsidies contribute to financial indicators of interest to investors and lenders (earnings and cash flows in particular), any loss of these subsidies could prove financially impactful, and perhaps even punitive. In some sectors, this result could negatively affect the ability and the speed with which firms may be able to undertake adaptation efforts.

It should be noted that subsidies of various forms—below market financing, for example—are not necessarily bad things. There are times when enabling firms to avoid some range of potential costs may be deemed a public policy good. This is often the argument made in support of agricultural subsidies, and also was the argument made in support of renewable energy sources. And it proved to be an effective argument—renewables are now more than competitive as electricity sources. We note that in many jurisdictions these subsidies are being phased out—although in many of those same jurisdictions, ironically, fossil fuel subsidies are not.

For example, one recent assessment, published by the International Monetary Fund, suggests that global energy subsidies (on a post-tax basis, reflecting environmental externalities associated with fossil fuels) ran as high as US $4.7 trillion in 2015,[60] a figure that rose to US $5.2 trillion in 2017 and US $5.9 trillion in 2020.[61] However, it is important to note that different organizations use widely different methodologies in calculating this figure. A recent estimate from the Organization for Economic Co-operation and Development/IEA dates from 2019 and estimated that energy subsidies for forty-four OECD and G20 countries will total US $178 billion—a considerably smaller, but nonetheless still material, number.[62] Notably, the latter figure represents a rise in subsidies after several years of decline. One issue for this industry, then, is whether such subsidies will continue, or whether their being phased out will compound or limit potential adaptation efforts. Given the speed with which renewables pricing became eminently affordable for utilities, this question becomes even more important as the industry deals outright with a number of transition issues.

These trends are not limited to the fossil fuel industry, although reliable recent data on other sectors is hard to come by. The Worldwatch Institute has estimated that global agricultural subsidies in 2012 totaled about US $486 billion, with OECD countries and seven others (Brazil, China, Indonesia, Kazakhstan, Russia, South Africa, and Ukraine) representing about 80% of the total.[63] Within the OECD, agricultural subsidies totaled about US $257 billion in 2012. More recent estimates, including from the OECD, have placed this figure at about US $700–750 billion.[64] Other recent estimates are high as well—the UN in 2021 estimated that annual agricultural subsidies ran at about US $543 billion (and suggested that most of these were harmful as well).[65] Thus, the trend in increased agricultural subsidies appears to be undiminished.[66]

Similarly, such subsidies are not confined to big, obvious targets such as fossil fuels and agriculture. The steel industry in China[67] continues to receive generous subsidies from the Chinese government (though this is not an unusual situation in China, admittedly, and even though this led to such global overcapacity that the Chines government had to reduce steel production sharply in 2021). The Australian mining industry,[68] particularly coal, benefited significantly from government largesse. The Carmichael mine, which has generated considerable controversy, apparently received more than AU $4.4 billion in direct and indirect subsidies from the Australian government as of 2019.[69]

The OECD recently compiled a review of 306 firms in 13 manufacturing sectors, all of which received some support through below-market financing from 2014 to 2018—a preferred form of government subsidy.[70] Notably, and presumably intentionally, this form of support tended to benefit older companies that financed with debt rather than younger firms that tended to use equity for fundraising. OECD does point out that firms that received below-market financing tend to be less productive, a conclusion perhaps related to another finding that firms that receive such financing (as opposed to outright government grants) generally add manufacturing capacity. As the China's steel debacle described previously shows, too much of an increase in manufacturing capacity can have significant negative impacts. Figure 5.5 shows the range of firms receiving subsidies from the governments in question. We provide this simply as an example of the potential range of industries actively receiving subsidies of some sort—below-market financing, government grants, or tax concessions in particular—and the range of governments providing such subsidies.

If governments are forced to become more aggressive in addressing anthropogenic climate change, as they may well be going forward, they will

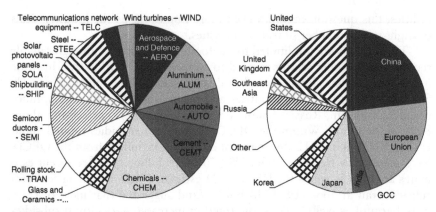

FIGURE 5.5   Sectors and countries represented in the OECD subsidy analysis.
Source: OECD. *Measuring Distortions in International markets: Below-market Finance.* OECD Trade Policy Paper 247, May 2021. https://www.climatepolicy initiative.org/publication/global-landscape-of-climate-finance-2021/

likely come under increasing pressure to remove a range of fossil fuel subsidies. In fact, as we note elsewhere, this process has theoretically already begun, albeit very slowly. There were a number of promises made about cutting fossil fuel subsidies as part of the Paris agreement—to date, execution has been disappointing. The announcement by President Biden regarding eliminating a number of fossil fuel subsidies, if enacted, may accelerate the process. But Congressional enactment has proved difficult, and may not happen.[71] A similar concern can be raised about agricultural subsidies in areas where water depletion risks are increasing. However, these risks may be so broad based and diffuse as to not have a particular impact on food producers directly.

Potential loss of subsidies has the clear potential to create stranded assets. We believe the energy and utility industries remain high on the potential list of candidate industries for stranded assets. This has the consequence of highlighting the potential risks to a number of bond issuers.

IMPLICATIONS FOR SELECT SECTORS

There are a number of industries that have exposure to adaptation issues, particularly coastal or riverine issues. These include ports (obviously), rail transport, refineries, cement manufacturers, and other manufacturers in a wide range of industries that depend on proximity to transit hubs. Of course, potential exposure will vary by country and by sector. In addition, industries with significant and occasionally complicated supply chains may also be vulnerable to adaptation risks. A series of reports from the IPCC[72] provides extensive discussion of climate hazards and impacts, including an analysis by economic sector. The thirteen sectors covered in the OECD report are representative of a broader range of firms that have some exposure to potential risks. We outline some of the specific risks to particularly vulnerable industries.

Utilities and Energy

Most utility infrastructure is coastal or river-based because industrial plants need a regular supply of water for steam generation and for cooling, and, historically, for coal shipments (which is still the cheapest way to move coal around inside a country). In the United States alone, for example, nearly 300 electric facilities (both power plants and substations) are located within four feet of high tide (see Figure 5.6), according to a report from Climate Central;[73] this includes over 100 nuclear power plants. This geographic coastal concentration poses obvious risks as sea levels rise, both from the ocean rise itself and from increased coastal flooding events. However, we note that the general shift to renewable energy sources in the United States may mitigate some of the riskier aspects of traditional utility plant siting. However, since steam turbines are likely to remain as a principal source of electricity, irrespective of energy source, we do not see the collective sea level rise as being quickly solved by moving to renewables as a source of power.

River flooding has also become an increasingly visible concern, and such flooding is a regular event in countries such as India, Bangladesh, and Pakistan, not to mention the United States in areas surrounding, say, the Mississippi river. Balancing these risks is the fact that managers of these facilities are unlikely to be surprised about potential adaptation costs. We previously mentioned the recent report from S&P Global Ratings on physical risk concerns for the US utility industry. Likewise, water utilities face similar risks. Moody's has recently published a report in which they cite the dangers of climate change to the US nuclear industry, including flooding risk and rising sea levels—risks that are likely to materialize over the next twenty years because of the plants' proximity to water.[74] Moreover, as the utility industry migrates to more renewable sources of energy, the need for existing facilities may decline.

We note that pipelines are also vulnerable assets, especially in the event that current flow levels for gas and other fossil fuel products may decline. The above figure does not reflect the US (or Canada's) pipeline exposure, but it is significant. It's a big country, and natural gas and oil are not always located where people live or where economic activity takes place. Pipelines

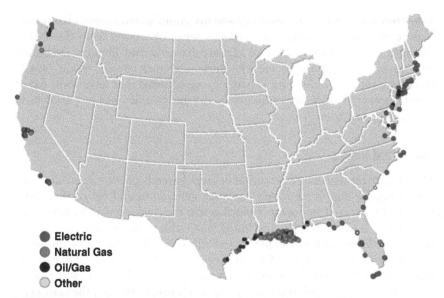

● Electric
● Natural Gas
● Oil/Gas
○ Other

FIGURE 5.6   US electricity facilities less than four feet above local high tide.
Source: Strauss, Ben and Remik Ziemlinski, *Sea Level Rise Threats to Energy Infra-structure.* Climate Central, April 19, 2012.

are a critical component of the US energy infrastructure, and these represent significant assets. This is true in Europe as well, but less so in Asia and Africa. Energy assets may be affected by other events as well. For instance, Tokyo Electric Power Company's (TEPCO) nuclear power plant issues deriving from the 2012 tsunami in Japan, which remain unresolved, are a pointed example of catastrophe risk that appears unrelated to climate factors but might emerge because of coastal locations. As noted, Moody's has recently discussed the potential risks to the nuclear power industry in the United States, finding them to be potentially significant but currently manageable.

Note that this overall energy sector classification is usually considerably more granulated than that which we have presented here. This customarily would be oil majors, refining and marketing companies, independent E&P companies, midstream energy companies, oilfield service companies, and coal mining and terminal companies. Each of these will have its own set of firm-specific risks, but the general patterns likely will be those discussed here. The major adaptation risk for the sector, aside from water concerns, remains being replaced by alternative fuel sources for both energy and transportation. While not specifically an adaptation concern, there is some likelihood that adaptation processes could be affected by the energy transition (which we discuss in Chapter 6).

Property and Real Estate

While it is difficult to paint the adaptation risks to property and real estate with a broad brush, the fact that substantial assets are located along coastlines should generate some interest. There are now fairly accurate models of these implications of coastal flooding in some areas. For example, as noted, flooding in Miami is occurring at such regular intervals as a result of higher tides overwhelming the city's storm drains that it is no longer regarded as abnormal. However, the increased frequency of these events has the potential to generate substantial regional stranded assets. REIT composition will become a more interesting exercise going forward as portfolio managers try to assess the increasing risks associated with owning coastal exposure.

As discussed elsewhere in this report, a number of global regions (e.g., Bangladesh, Pakistan) are already experiencing negative impacts of higher water levels. Again, the counterweight to these risks is that they appear to be longer-term risks in most cases, potentially giving governments enough time to develop mitigation and adaptation responses that will incur lower costs than the costs of doing nothing.[75] Miami and South Florida generally offer prime examples of the political difficulties that coastal communities may face over the near term in developing such adaptation plans.[76] However, we also note that these risks seem to be materializing more rapidly than expected just a few years ago, and this may raise some uncertainty regarding exactly how much lead time firm managers and public policy officials actually have.

Note that we are including all sorts of property in this grouping— residential, municipal, and commercial, including industrial. This is simply because most global economic activity occurs on the world's coasts, and it is coastal property that is at greatest risk from sea level rise and potential extreme weather and precipitation.

Agriculture

Lloyd's has tested a draconian but entirely plausible scenario that attempts to determine the extent of potential catastrophe risk to the global food system in the event of a single scenario: an El Niño event worse than those up to 2015.[77] As the report laconically states, under this scenario, "quadrupled commodity prices and commodity stock fluctuations, coupled with civil unrest, result in significant negative humanitarian consequences and major financial losses worldwide." These financial losses emanate from a variety of factors: the cessation of agricultural exports and the impact upon the global agricultural supply chain; interrupted trade flows and their impact not only on the agricultural sector, but also on the maritime and aviation shipping sectors; the overwhelming of rail and other land transport systems following the significant flooding of, and lack of access to, traditional river transport systems; and others. The impairment of both agricultural land and businesses throughout the agricultural supply chain becomes an inevitable result of such a scenario. We note that, although the COVID-19 pandemic clearly strained the global food system, it has not produced this sort of response. However, the disruption to distribution channels was notable, and a more severe pandemic could prove materially worse.

Transportation

We have discussed the problems that railroads and airports in particular may experience as a result of adaptation risks. In this regard, increased event risks simply compress the time frame for potential asset destruction. These have often been unpredictable events in the past, but perhaps not that unpredictable; that hurricane landfalls may indeed be difficult to pinpoint as coastal areas bear greater risks than mountains and plains regions seems straightforward. We note that in general there is no economic substitute for transportation networks, unlike, say, fossil fuels for energy use. Transportation firms may lack a discretion that other sectors may enjoy—and the CAPEX required for whatever adaptation responses are being made will be nondiscretionary as well.

Transportation infrastructure, particularly along coasts, appears especially vulnerable, although not necessarily in the near term. At the same time, the impact of England's coastal storms on some rail lines may be telling. This flooding was caused by excessive rainfall and increased precipitation that is one of the likely consequences of global warming. As others have noted, a number of US airports[78] have potential exposure to storm risks as well,[79] particularly those essentially at sea level such as those in Boston or San Francisco. There is, in many cases, considerable lead time in which the adaptation response can be managed. However, it is important to remember that the physical impacts of global heating are approaching faster, and with greater impact, than expected even a decade ago. Heat can have devastating effects on transportation infrastructure as recent events in a number of countries have shown.[80]

Ports

We treat ports as a separate category from transportation because they are traditionally government owned, and therefore embody municipal risks. However, there is now a mix of public and private ownership of ports globally, with the number of privately owned and operated ports increasing over the past two decades. Ports, by definition, are generally found at sea level. The port of New Orleans suffered significant damage from Hurricane Katrina and did not reopen for a number of weeks, costing the US economy several billion dollars. We note that for ports, at least, the lead time for adaptation measures is relatively long. We further note that adaptation measures here would apply not only to the ports themselves but also to the transportation infrastructure running in and out of ports, including land transportation aspects such as railroads, and that these transport links may be owned by other parties.

Mining

Mining companies have some particular vulnerability simply because they are very water-dependent firms, but often need to operate in areas of some degree of water stress. As indicated earlier, it is highly likely that areas of water stress will continue to increase. Companies such as Rio Tinto and Barrick Gold have had increasingly contentious issues with local populations regarding water availability over the past decade, and these are expected to continue. Partly this is because ore often does not have the same quality as in years past, and lower grade ore, as in the case of copper, requires more water. The more relevant reason, however, is that water is often farther away from mining activity. Since a mine cannot operate without water, this presents logistical problems for firms to solve—often by constructing water pipelines to the targeted area. In a 2019 report,[81] Moody's discussed the fact that an increasing number of countries where mining was a critical industry were also experiencing increased water stress. This list includes Peru, Chile, Australia, South Africa, and Mongolia, all countries where water withdrawals are expected to increase. This is especially problematic when the water in question is groundwater, for reasons discussed earlier. In some cases, the industry has turned to desalinization for better quality water, but this is an expensive option, and it's unclear whether this potential offset can be applied at scale. As a result, it is reasonable to assume that water-related capital expenditures will continue to increase, with likely cash flow and margin impacts.

We note that the chemicals industry shares many of the characteristics of the mining industry in terms of water requirements. While there is clearly more flexibility in terms of the siting of economic activity, many of the mining industry concerns—particularly availability and disposal frameworks—are critical to plant siting. Chemical plants are big and expensive to build, often requiring accessing capital markets. Getting water requirements right is an essential part of the process, and of increased interest to lenders and investors.

Sovereign Governments

In a number of publications, the three major rating agencies have addressed climate change's potential impact on a range of emerging market sovereigns—particularly those with a high dependence on natural resource or agricultural exports. These are sectors where the impacts are generally expected to be negative. The focus of these past analyses was on natural catastrophes and the possible mitigating impact of insurance. Rating agencies are mindful of the potential impacts of an array of physical phenomena (e.g., changing rainfall patterns) and are beginning to factor these issues into their analysis.[82] S&P, for example, has provided an extended discussion of environmental and climate issues relating to sovereign credit.[83] In a separate publication, Buhr and Volz offered a more detailed assessment of climate vulnerable countries' ability to finance adaptation and mitigation measures and a discussion of the difficulties such countries are facing,[84] even in a generally low interest rate environment. Volz has recently updated this work.[85]

In summary, while nearly every industrial and consumer-related sector is likely to be affected by the need to adapt to physical climate risks, it is clear that some industries are more vulnerable than others to these risks. Lastly, while we acknowledge that lead times are sufficient in many cases to adequately deal with a range of climate impacts and risks, this does not mean that the costs of doing so will not be formidable.

Sector Offsets to Adaptation Risks

If it is indeed the case that there may be trillions of dollars of infrastructure that needs to be replaced globally, it follows (or should, anyway) that this infrastructure is going to be replaced by newer, better located, and more sustainable and resilient infrastructure. Much of this will generally remain local—even if you're planning on moving an entire town, there are some limits that will constrain how far an actual town can be moved, cost probably being the principal one. These same constraints probably apply to systems of infrastructure such as rail lines. Moreover, much of this new gray infrastructure will continue to be constructed out of the materials that constructed the infrastructure being replaced—steel, for both buildings and transportation networks; construction materials such as cement and aggregate; timber and other forest products. And this is just for basic physical infrastructure—anything new will also need to be fitted out for 21st-century information and communication networks.

The new infrastructure will need to be made from something, and someone will actually have to construct it. We are reluctant to talk about climate change "opportunities," which sounds entirely too mercenary considering the human suffering climate change is already causing. Nonetheless, it remains the case that there are firms for whom business prospects may remain robust. We imagine equity and bond analysts who follow, say, the construction equipment industry, for example, or the forest products industry are already assessing potential demand trend changes, either positive or negative, reflecting the above. In addition, to the extent that the above may require major capital expenditures, often in excess of annual maintenance CAPEX levels, a not unlikely scenario, there will be demand for financial institutions to provide or arrange for that capital financing, a development that will inevitably involve lenders and investors.

NOTES

1. IPCC, Summary for Policymakers. In *IPCC Special Report on the Ocean and Cryosphere in a Changing Climate*. Edited by H-O. Pörtner et al. 2019. Available at: https://www.ipcc.ch/srocc/
2. Mach, Katherine and A. R Siders. Reframing Strategic, Managed Retreat for Transformative Climate Adaptation. *Science* 372(6548): 1294–1299, 2021.
3. ibid.
4. A. R. Siders. Managed Retreat in the United States. *One Earth* October 25, 2019.
5. Abandonment can perhaps be thought of as retreat without compensation.
6. Lempert, R. et al. Reducing Risks Through Adaptation *Actions*. In *Impacts, Risks, and Adaptation in the United States: Fourth National Climate Assessment, Volume II*. Edited by D. R. Reidmiller et al. U.S. Global Change Research Program, Washington, DC: 1309–1345, 2018. In fact, there is a significant literature.
7. Lempert, R. et al. Reducing Risks Through Adaptation *Actions*. In *Impacts, Risks, and Adaptation in the United States: Fourth National Climate Assessment, Volume II*. Edited by D. R. Reidmiller et al. U.S. Global Change Research Program, Washington, DC: 1309–1345, 2018.
8. This tabulation represents a distillation of a number of categorizations of infrastructure, which vary widely in number—it is not unusual to find frameworks that have as many as ten granulated categories. From a project management viewpoint, this may make sense. For present purposes, we believe this distillation will suffice.

9. The EU Green Taxonomy Group provided extensive discussion of some of these categories, particularly those related to energy and power, transport, and water, see *EU Technical Expert Group on Sustainable Finance, Financing a Sustainable European Economy Taxonomy Report: Technical Annex*, March 2020.

10. Note that in most countries, water is usually a government responsibility at some level—but not all. Water services in the United Kingdom are privately provided.

11. Holtedahl, Pernille, Alex Koberle, and Michael Wilkinson, *Future of Foods Part 3: Can Markets Save Nature? Investing in Nature to Help Tackle Biodiversity Loss and Enhance Food Security*, forthcoming.

12. In fact, there is a significant literature on resilience in the urban planning literature that could profitably inform some of the discussions on resilience that emerge in the climate investing community. Much of this literature concerns redesigning both gray and green infrastructure for urban environments, where climate impacts are expected to be most severe. See, for example, Amy Sherman, *The Heat Is On*, Planning August/September 2020.

13. Note that finding consistency among definitions of resilience even in the planning literature can be difficult—see Meerow, Sara, Joshua P. Newell, and Meilissa Stuits. Defining Urban Resilience: A Review. *Landscape and Urban Planning* 147:38–49, 2016.

14. Cambridge Institute for Sustainability Leadership, *Investing for Resilience*. Cambridge, December 2016.

15. The Global Center on Adaptation does an excellent job of tying together the Green Bond concept and climate resilience, which should guide much of the discussion going forward. See *Green Bonds for Climate Resilience: State of Play and Roadmap to Scale*. Global Center on Adaptation, 2022.

16. See, for example, Fattouh, Bassam, Rahmat Pouydineh, and Rob West, *The Rise of Renewables and Energy Transition: What Adaptation Strategy for Oil Companies and Oil-exporting Countries?* OIES paper: MEP 19, Oxford Institute for Energy Studies, May 2018.

17. McKinsey & Company, *Decarbonization of Industrial Sectors: The Next Frontier*, June 2018.

18. Berrang-Ford, L. et al. A Systematic Global Stocktake of Evidence on Human Adaptation to Climate Change. *Nature Climate Change* 11: 989–1000, 2021.

19. Lord, Rick and Steven Bullock. *Keeping the Lights On: US Utilities Exposure to Physical Climate Risks*, S&P Global Ratings, September 16, 2021.

20. Union of Concerned Scientists, *When Rising Seas Hit Home: Hard Choices Ahead for Hundreds of US Coastal Communities*, July 5, 2017; *Underwater: Rising Seas, Chronic Floods, and the Implications for US Coastal Real Estate*, June 18, 2018; Climate Central and Zillow Associates, *Ocean at the Door: New Homes and the Rising Sea*, July 30, 2019; Clayton, J. et al. *Climate Risk and Commercial Property Values: A Review and Analysis of the Literature.* UNEP FI, 2021.

21. Checconi, Arnaud. *Future Flooding Represents a Low Risk for UK RMBS Ratings.* S&P Global Ratings, March 19, 2020. S&P has done a similar analysis

of US CMBS exposure to a range of physical risks: see Lord, Rick and Steven Bullock. *Damage Limitation: Using Enhanced Physical Climate Risk Analytics in the US CMBS Sector*. S&P Global Ratings, February 19, 2021.

22. Goodell, Jeff. Goodbye, Miami. *Rolling Stone*, June 20, 2013; Elizabeth Kolbert, The Siege of Miami. *The New Yorker*, December 21, 2015.

23. We note that most research on this issue has focused on US property markets, but we suspect similar trends are at work elsewhere in the world.

24. Buhr, Bob. *Adaptation Bonds: Lessons from the US Municipal Bond Market to Help Close the Adaptation Financing Gap*. London: Centre for Climate Finance and Investment, Imperial College Business School, September 2022.

25. Daly, Herman E. and Kenneth N. Townsend. *Valuing the Earth: Economics, Ecology, Ethics*. Cambridge, MA: MIT Press, 1993; Adair Turner. *Just Capital: The Liberal Economy*. London: Macmillan, 2001; Dieter Helm. *Natural Capital: Valuing the Planet*. London: Yale University Press, 2015. Andreas Malm, *Fossil Capital: The Rise of Steam Power and the Roots of Global Warming*. London: Verso Books, 2016; Kate Raworth. *Doughnut Economics*. London: Random House Business Books, 2017.

26. There is a substantial and still-growing literature on resilience and sustainability as factors to be integrated into economic and financial analysis of firms. While this is an important—indeed critical—discussion to be having, we do not intend to add to it here.

27. OECD. *The Potential Effects of Climate Change on Transport Infrastructure*. 2016; European Commission. *Climate Change Adaptation of Major Infrastructure Projects, 2018*.

28. Feuer, Alan. Building for the Next Big Storm. *New York Times*, October 25, 2014.

29. Hunter, Justine. Cost of Rebuilding B.C. After Flooding Nears $9 Billion. *The Globe and Mail*, February 19, 2022.

30. Englund, Michael. Katrina's "Unique" Economic Impact. *Bloomberg Businessweek*, September 6, 2005.

31. RMS. *RMS Estimates US$67 Billion in Insured Losses from Hurricane Ian*, October 7, 2022.

32. Climate Policy Initiative, *Global Landscape of Climate Finance 2021*, December 2021.

33. Brodie, Boland et al. *Climate Risk and the Opportunity for Real Estate*, McKinsey & Company, February 2022.

34. https://www.bbc.com/future/article/20220506-the-uk-climate-refugees-who-wont-leave; see also Elizabeth Rush's *Rising* (Minneapolis: Milkweed, 2018) and Nathaniel Rich's *Second Nature* (London: Picador, 2021), both of which discuss in some detail issues surrounding the potential retreat from and abandonment of land in southern Louisiana as a result of Gulf of Mexico encroachment.

35. Mikulka, Justin. *Will the Public End Up Paying to Clean Up the Fracking Boom?* DeSmog International, October 18, 2019.

36. Not removing them in the first place would have been a better idea.

37. Bassi, Andrea, Emma Cutler, Ronja Bechauf, and Liesbeth Casier. *How Can Investment in Nature Close the Infrastructure Gap?* International Institute for Sustainable Development, October 2021.

38. Robbins, Jim. A Quiet Revolution: Southwest Cities Learn to Thrive Amid Drought. *Yale Environment 360,* April 26, 2022.

39. The most recent being *The Gathering Storm: Adapting to Climate Change in a Post-pandemic World.* Adaptation Gap Report 2021, United Nations Environmental Program.

40. *The Gathering Storm: Adapting to Climate Change in a Post-pandemic World.* Adaptation Gap Report 2021, United Nations Environmental Program.

41. There has been considerable work on the extent to which developing nations are at risk; see, for example, Buhr, Bob and Ulrich Volz. *Climate Change and the Cost of Capital in Developing Nations: Assessing the Impact of Climate Risks on Sovereign Borrowing Costs.* London: Centre for Climate Finance and Investment and SOAS University, 2018; Volz, Ulrich et al. *Climate Change and Sovereign Risk,* SOAS Centre for Sustainable Finance, ADBI Institute, WWF, 427, and *Inspire,* October 2020; S&P Global Ratings; *Weather Warning: Assessing Countries' Vulnerability to Economic Losses from Physical Climate Risks,* April 2022.

42. International Institute for Sustainable Development report, *How Can Investment in Nature Close the Infrastructure Gap? 2021*—derived from a survey of national and regional plans. Note that as is often the case in this field, this estimate is just one of a number of estimates, all of which are large, but which vary widely.

43. The target dates for the second iteration of this plan are 2018–2023; for further information, see Department for Farming and Rural Affairs. *The National Adaptation Programme and the Third Strategy for Climate Adaptation Reporting,* July 2018.

44. It is unclear whether the loss and damage agreement agreed to at COP 27 will be sufficient to meet developing nations' needs. See, for example, Harvey, Fiona et al. COP27 Agrees Historic "Loss and Damage" Fund for Climate Impact in Developing Countries. *The Guardian,* November 20, 2022.

45. Analysis of these trends may also be complicated by the significant shift by utilities, increasingly on a global basis, from traditional energy sources to renewable sources.

46. Ernst & Young. *Benchmarking European Power and Utility Asset Impairments; Impairments at a High in 2013 as Utility Sector Transforms,* 2014.

47. Raval, Anjli. Oil Majors Face Up to Plunging Asset Values. *Financial Times,* July 2, 2020; Eaton, Collin and Sarah McFarlane. 2020 Was One of the Worst-ever Years for Oil Write-downs. *The Wall Street Journal,* December 27, 2020.

48. World Resources Institute and UNEP Finance Initiative. *Carbon Asset Risk: Discussion Framework,* 2020.

49. McKinsey Global Institute. *Will Infrastructure Bend or Break Under Climate Stress?* Case study, June 2020.

50. Buhr, Bob. *Should Credit Investors Be Worried About Stranded Assets?* Société Générale, April 11, 2016.

51. Note that our usage of the term "operational" is not the same as that employed by the Basel framework.

52. Mikulka, Justin. *Will the Public End up Paying to Clean up the Fracking Boom?* DeSmog, October 18, 2019. Available at: https://www.desmogblog .com/2019/10/18/public-paying-cleanup-fracking-boom-oil-gas-bonds; Carbon Tracker. *It's Closing Time: The Huge Bill to Abandon Oilfields Comes Early,* June 18, 2020; *Billion Dollar Orphans: Why Millions of Oil and Gas Wells Could Become Wards of the State,* September 2020.

53. McKinsey Global Institute. *Will Infrastructure Bend or Break Under Climate Stress?* Case study, June 2020. Note that infrastructure Is not just roads and power grids; it also includes, for instance, telecommunications networks and server farms.

54. Lexington. Miami's Submarine Future: American Government Is No Match for Global Warming. *The Economist,* June 9, 2022.

55. Muller, Natalie and Neil King. Plans to "Deepen" Rhine River Hit Resistance. *Deutsche Welle,* October 7, 2022.

56. Tomassoni, Teresa. The Rising Pacific Forces a Native Village to Move. Who Will Pay? Bloomberg News, November 5, 2021.

57. Moody's Investors Service, *Rising Sea Level Signals Need for US State and Local Governments to Address Growing Climate Risks,* September 17, 2020.

58. Kusnetz, Nicholas. Coastal Flooding Is Erasing Billions in Property Value as Sea Level Rises. That's Bad News for Cities. *Inside Climate News,* February 28, 2019.

59. Urban Land Institute. *Future-proofing Real Estate from Climate Risks,* April 2019.

60. Coady, David, Ian Parry, Nghia-piotr Le, and Baoping Shang. *Global Fossil Fuel Subsidies Remain Large: An Update Based on Country-Level Estimates.* Washington, DC: International Monetary Fund, May 2, 2019.

61. Parry, Ian W. H., Simon Black, and Nate Vernon. *Still Not Getting Energy Prices Right: A Global and Country Update of Fossil Fuel Subsidies,* Working Paper. Washington, DC: International Monetary Fund, September 24, 2021.

62. OECD. *Rising Fossil Fuel Support Poses a Threat to Building a Healthier and Climate-safe Future,* September 2020.

63. Potter, Grant. Agricultural Subsidies Remain a Staple in the Industrial World. Environmental News Network, March 12, 2014.

64. The Food and Land Use Coalition. *Growing Better: Ten Critical Transitions to Transform Food and Land Use,* September 2019. Available at: https:// www.foodandlandusecoalition.org/wp-content/uploads/2019/09/FOLU-GrowingBetter-GlobalReport.pdf; OECD. *Agricultural Policy Monitoring and Evaluation 2020.* Paris: OECD Publishing, 2020.

65. FAO, UNDP, and UNEP. *A Multi-billion-dollar Opportunity—Repurposing Agricultural Support to Transform Food Systems.* Rome: FAO, 2021.

66. Calder, Alice. Agricultural Subsidies: Everybody's Doing It. Trade Vistas, October 15, 2020. Available at: https://www.wita.org/blogs/agricultural-subsidies/

67. Wong, Fayen. Steel Industry on Subsidy Life-support as Chinese Economy Slows. *Reuters,* September 18, 2014.

68. Grunhoff, Matt. Pouring More Fuel on the Fire; The Nature and Extent of Federal Government Subsidies to the Mining Industry. The Australia Institute, Policy Brief No. 52, June 2013.

69. Smee, Ben. Adani Mine Would be "Unviable" Without $4.4bn in Subsidies, Report Finds. *The Guardian*, August 29, 2019.

70. OECD. Measuring Distortions in International Markets: Below-market Finance. OECD Trade Policy Paper 247, May 2021

71. Timberley, Jocelyn. Why Fossil Fuel Subsidies Are So Hard to Kill. *Nature*, October 20, 2021.

72. Intergovernmental Panel on Climate Change. *Fifth Assessment Report: Climate Change 2014: Impacts, Adaptation and Vulnerability*, 2014; *Global Warming of 1.5°C, Summary for Policymakers*, 2018.

73. Strauss, Ben and Remik Ziemlinski. *Sea Level Rise Threats to Energy Infrastructure*. Climate Central, April 19, 2012; Union of Concerned Scientists. *Power Failure: How Climate Change Puts Our Electricity at Risk*, April 22, 2014.

74. Moody's Investors Service. *Nuclear Operators Face Increasing Climate Risks, but Resiliency Investments Mitigate Impact*, August 18, 2020.

75. The Economist Intelligence Unit. *The Cost of Inaction: Recognizing the Value at Risk from Climate Change*, 2015. Available at: https://impact.economist.com/perspectives/sites/default/files/The%20cost%20of%20inaction_0.pdf

76. Mazzei, Patricia. A 20-foot Sea Wall? Miami Faces the Hard Choices of Climate Change. *The New York Times*, June 2, 22021.

77. Lloyd's Emerging Risk Report. *Food System Shock—The Insurance Impacts of Acute Disruption to Global Food Supply*, 2015.

78. Lord, Rick and Steven Bullock. *Scenario Analysis Shines a Light on Climate Exposure: Focus on Major Airports*. S&P Global Ratings, November 5, 2020.

79. Schroeer, Lisa R. *Extreme Weather Events: How We Evaluate the Credit Impacts in US Public Finance*. S&P Global Ratings, November 2, 2020.

80. Varga, Liz. Wildfires: A Rising Hazard for Infrastructure Resilience. *Journal of Civil Engineering and Environmental Sciences*, October 14, 2022.

81. Cowan, Carol. *Metals & Mining—Cross Region: Water Availability Poses Risks to the Global Mining Industry*. Moody's Investors Service, September 26, 2019.

82. November 2016; Moody's Investors Service. *How Moody's Assesses the Physical Effects of Climate Change on Sovereign Issuers*, November 7, 2016; S&P Global Ratings. *Sovereign Postcard: ESG and Sovereign Ratings*, February 7, 2018.

83. Mrsnik, Marko. The Heat Is On: Climate Change and Sovereign Ratings. In *Climate Risk: Rising Tides Raise the Stakes*. Standard & Poor's Rating Services, December 2015; Moody's Investors Service. *Understanding the Impact of Natural Disasters: Exposure to Direct Damages Across Countries*, 28. Available at: https://legacy-assets.eenews.net/open_files/assets/2016/11/30/document_cw_01.pdf

84. Buhr, Bob and Ulrich Volz. *Climate Change and the Cost of Capital in Developing Nations: Assessing the Impact of Climate Risks on Sovereign Borrowing Costs*. London: Centre for Climate Finance and Investment and SOAS University, 2018.

85. Ulrich Volz et al. *Climate Change and Sovereign Risk*. London: SOAS Centre for Sustainable Finance, ADBI Institute, WWF, 427, and Inspire, October 2020.

CHAPTER 6

Mitigation Risks

The mitigation category is the climate risk category that has the least amount of external climate-related validation, if that means aligning with other taxonomies. This is simply because there are no publicly available external taxonomies where these potential risks are articulated,[1] with the possible exception of the area of the "energy transition,"[2] where many of these potential risks have received varying degrees of attention.[3]

Mitigating the physical effects of climate change, like adapting to them, will inevitably involve a range of potential transition risks and associated costs for firms. It will also cost a lot of money—to take just one estimate, between US $30 trillion and US $40 trillion, according to Wood McKenzie—and there will be active discussion over time as to where those funds should come from.[4] As mentioned previously, mitigation risks are the most contingent of the risks categories assessed here, in that the extent of riskiness will depend directly on public policy measures adopted by legislatures and regulatory organizations—many of which have not yet been adopted. Unlike physical and adaptation risks, many mitigation risks are largely contingent on public policy decisions. For example, a number of industries face regulatory compliance costs that may increase in the future as a result of mitigation efforts relating to carbon pricing.

Such costs are usually the result of public policy decisions adopted by governments, and these can change as well. For instance, several years ago, Australia repealed its carbon tax when global trends seemed to favor developing a more effective global carbon pricing mechanism.[5] Meanwhile, the EU has considerably revised its carbon pricing mechanism in recent years, and has now laid out an ambitious program relating to achieving a zero-carbon economy that will have significant costs attached.[6] Both of these developments represent the kinds of political and policy decisions that can have real-world regulatory compliance cost impacts. We expect that these will become a more significant factor in industry and company costs going forward, especially in resource-dependent industries.[7] Of considerable interest to investors and lenders is whether firms will be able to pass on such regulatory-driven potential cost increases to customers.

It must be noted that most of the existing discussions on efforts to mitigate climate change have focused on the energy sector and, more specifically, reflected measures designed to reduce GHG generation as opposed to adapting to it. We agree that reducing GHG output is a wholly appropriate and absolutely necessary objective. Thus, although we contend that the concept of "transition" needs to be broader in scope than just energy (e.g., changes in land use should receive considerably more attention than they have from policymakers to date),[8] we follow this larger trend by highlighting the energy transition here as well.

As in the case of adaptation risks, we have generally adopted indicators of potential risk from more traditional credit analysis—again, there turn out to be a number of potential climate impacts that can be expected to manifest themselves in these various categories. Technology risks, regulatory risks, and going-concern risks, for example, are an integral part of traditional analysis—we have highlighted them here simply because they currently have some climate-specific impacts with potentially material financial implications above and beyond normative operational levels.

The IPCC's definition of climate mitigation, as presented in its land use report previously cited, is straightforward:

> A human intervention to reduce the sources or enhance the sinks of greenhouse gases. This report also assesses human interventions to reduce the sources of other substances which may contribute directly or indirectly to limiting climate change, including, for example, the reduction of particulate matter emissions that can directly alter the radiation balance (e.g., black carbon) or measures that control emissions of carbon monoxide, nitrogen oxides, Volatile Organic Compounds and other pollutants that can alter the concentration of tropospheric ozone which has an indirect effect on the climate.

Note that this focuses mitigation efforts on those designed to *reduce* GHG gas generation, for example, as opposed to adapting to them. While this group represents the most diverse collection of specific risks of the whole taxonomy, the recurring theme of these specific risk indicators is that their potential impact is directly derivative of human activity *in response* to potential climate impacts. Of considerable relevance in this context are current measures to achieve net-zero carbon generation at some point in the future (usually 2050) by firms and by sovereign governments. We will discuss issues associated with net-zero throughout this chapter.

THE MITIGATION RISK TAXONOMY

The mitigation taxonomy offered in Figure 6.1 is clearly the most complex of any that we are proposing; this is simply because the range of potential risks to investments or loans at the firm level is greater, with a greater degree of potential uncertainty (and therefore complexity) than that posed by physical and adaptation risks. Importantly, this complexity does not mean that the costs associated with ameliorating mitigation risks will be comparable to or higher than others. Indeed, in many cases, the potential costs of addressing these risks may be lower.

Each of the risk instantiations in the right-hand column has the potential to have a financial impact on a firm. The relevant analytical process here is to determine which financial measures are likely to be affected. There are

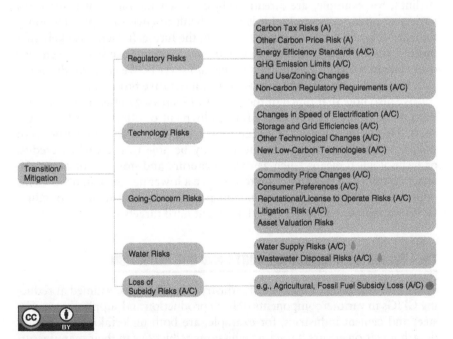

FIGURE 6.1 Proposed mitigation risk taxonomy.
Source: Green Planet Consulting Ltd. *What Is Climate Risk? A Field Guide for Investors, Lenders and Regulators.* London: Centre for Climate Finance and Investment, Imperial College Business School, February 2022.

a number of industries where regulatory compliance costs may increase in the future, adding to costs and having an impact on margins, for example—and perhaps some where these will decrease, often as the result of temporary subsidies (renewables). We note, again, that such costs are usually the result of public policy decisions adopted by governments, and that these can change as well. For example, several years ago, Australia repealed its carbon tax.[9] Meanwhile, the EU considerably revised its carbon pricing mechanism. Both are the kinds of political and policy decisions that can have real-world regulatory compliance cost impacts. We believe that these will become a more significant factor in industry and company costs going forward, especially in resource-dependent industries, for reasons outlined in our discussion of natural capital risks.

We note that at present there is a broad range of potential mitigation efforts being considered at various government levels, and some are even being implemented. As a result, we leave open the possibility that other mitigation costs, including tax measures and insurance costs, will become increasingly used policy options. Some of these may be industry specific. Airlines, for example, are already subject to a wide range of taxes for a variety of policy reasons, and it is not difficult to envision that such policy measures may be used more aggressively in the future. In fact, it is likely that most of the risks encapsulated in the above taxonomy are likely to change over time in terms of likelihood, timing, and severity. We envision this analysis, like traditional credit analysis, to be an iterative process.

We also note that much of the impact of increased mitigation costs may be contingent on a firm's successful employment of offsets to reduce these costs. This is the core of the arguments in support of developing net-zero policies—that firms (or governments) may be able to use carbon credits, or technological means (such as carbon capture and storage), or other offsets, to balance GHG generation to produce a lower net-zero number.[10] This approach would, as has been repeatedly pointed out,[11] allow firms to reduce GHG emissions at a slower rate than might hard targets.

THE LINK BETWEEN MITIGATION COSTS AND GHG REDUCTION

There are, at present, a number of industry-specific projects aimed at reducing GHGs in various components of both production and supply chains. The steel and cement industries, for example, are both undertaking significant decarbonization efforts, targeting emissions reductions in their manufacturing processes—but these are different products, and firms can be expected to develop sector-specific approaches, even though these may overlap on occasion.[12] In fact, it is likely that most of the risks encapsulated in the risk taxonomy as currently conceived are likely to change over time in terms of likelihood, timing, and severity, and to vary somewhat by sector. We envision this analysis, like traditional credit analysis, to be an iterative process.

As the costs of mitigation are related to transitioning away from GHGs, understanding exactly where GHGs come from can serve as a useful first step in transition risk assessment. Even though this breakdown may not necessarily reflect how transition costs will be allocated over time, it's not a bad place to start, either. In fact, there is some evidence that higher emissions are associated with higher credit rating risk.[13] As of 2018, it was possible to identify, by industrial sector, the principal contributors to GHG generation, as shown in Figure 6.2. We expect current emissions outputs to resemble those in this figure.

Note that this is not the only way to organize the framework of how to assess firm risk. GHG emissions are clearly an important metric, and adhering to stronger GHG requirements is necessary going forward. However, an alternative metric for looking at firm carbon exposures is not which GHGs

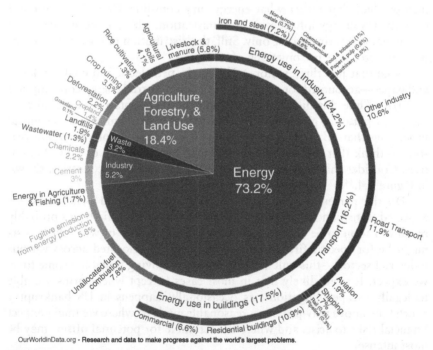

OurWorldinData.org - **Research and data to make progress against the world's largest problems.**

FIGURE 6.2   Greenhouse gas emissions by sector, 2016.
Source: Climate Watch, The World Resources Institute, 2020. Our World in Data. https://ourworldindata.org/emissions-by-sector / last accessed December 12, 2022. / CC BY 4.0

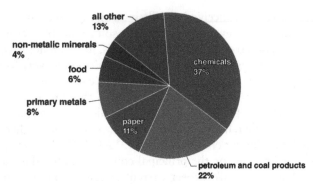

total = 19.44 quadrillion British thermal units

FIGURE 6.3   US manufacturing energy consumption by sector.
Source: US Energy Information Administration. https://www.eia.gov/energy
explained/use-of-energy/industry.php. Last accessed December 12, 2022.

they produce, but rather what energy they consume. Consider Figure 6.3 from the US Energy Information Administration, which looks at energy use in the manufacturing sector only. Still, the distribution of energy consumption by sector may be something of a surprise.

Note that just three sectors—chemicals, petroleum and coal products, and paper—accounted for over two-thirds of industrial energy consumption in 2018. While this distribution may not be representative of global consumption patterns, given the high amount of petrochemical and chemical processing that takes place in the United States for export, there are reasons to think that this distribution is fairly representative of OECD countries. Consider this distribution from 2009 in the EU-27 countries, shown in Figure 6.4.[14]

Do the percentages in Figure 6.2 constitute a good benchmark for expected transition spending? It may appear that way initially. It's probably much too soon to be able to provide reliable estimates of what these costs might be for specific firms, and how they will be allocated across various industrial sectors—this will actually remain a moving target for some time, we expect. It seems likely that in most cases (except where firms are able to legally escape obligations, as occasionally happens in US bankruptcy courts) the above may provide a reasonable guide to where we might expect financial risks to arise, and where the scramble for potential offsets may be most intense.

Granulating by energy consumption is probably not an identical industrial breakdown as is by GHG emission. However, it's probably not a bad substitute, for one critical reason—it's an obvious target for firms looking to

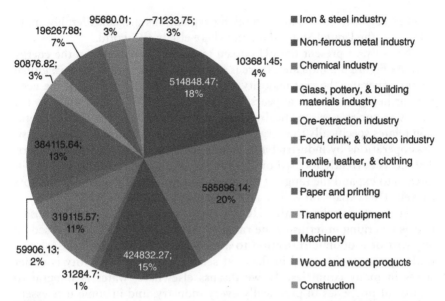

FIGURE 6.4   Final energy consumption of the industry in EU-27 in different industry sectors.
Source: Eurostat—European Commission. Energy Balance Sheets—2008–2009, Publications Office of the European Union, Luxembourg, 2011.

reduce GHG emissions, especially those industries in which process heating is essential to manufacturing activity.[15] Process heating refers to the need to generate high amounts of heat as part of the industrial process in making the product in question—be it fertilizer, steel, or cement. Since generating high amounts of heat is tremendously energy consumptive, these are industries where additional carbon costs feeding through energy pricing could have a material impact. And these are industries where a financial analyst might expect managements to be pursing strategies to increase efficiencies in heat production—which is exactly what's happening, as we will discuss later.

More broadly, we suspect that the correlation between GHG generation and financial risk is much more complex than it first appears. For one thing, industries do not produce GHGs in an economic vacuum. In many cases, industrial production is heavily subsidized by governments, and these subsidies may vary considerably by country. Litigation issues may also be more of a concern than is currently recognized—in certain sectors (e.g., tobacco and pharmaceuticals), litigation expenses are a given in the assessment of industry valuations, and this practice may become more important in some of these industries potentially affected here. Again, this may vary across borders. Likewise, regulatory standards can vary significantly across countries or even regions; for instance, fracking regulations are considerably more relaxed in the United States than anywhere else in the world.

Notably, at present the EU's green taxonomy is focused on the energy area. As Figure 6.2 indicates, there is a fairly obvious reason for this: global energy generates the vast majority of GHGs. However, even here, the need for further granulation appears obvious. Some GHG generation in the energy sector relates specifically to energy production; other GHG generation relates specifically to energy consumption in the course of normal business operations by industrial and commercial interests, and by consumers. The EU is currently focused on the former, but it also has indicated that it intends to expand the range of the green taxonomy to include other sectors as well. This expansion will be an ongoing and iterative process.

The cost of dealing with GHG production is just one part of the mosaic that is emerging in terms of the range of issues that must be addressed by any sort of economic transition to a zero-carbon world. In terms of natural capital (as discussed in the next section), water availability is under stress in many countries. As we discuss elsewhere, water is integral to industrial processes in practically every industry, and in some it is essential—no water, no anything. Other renewable resources are also being depleted more rapidly than they are being replenished—topsoil being the most dramatic example, largely through contemporary agricultural processes.[16] Transportation infrastructure needs to be redesigned to be more energy efficient. Thus, there will be myriad mitigation efforts that will need to be undertaken and many of these—transitioning transport systems to lower carbon generation, for example—will be large, expensive infrastructure projects that may take considerable time. For some of these sectors, the transition appears straightforward but expensive. However, for certain issues, such as topsoil depletion, the means of addressing them efficiently at scale remain unclear.

There are also a number of possible scenarios under which these efforts will be undertaken. These generally encompass (a) possible policy options, in terms of how significant these should be and (b) the timing of implementing these options. These scenarios, which vary widely by the options being assessed (timing, for example) are well discussed in much of the recent modeling literature, and will not be considered further here.

REGULATORY RISKS

There are numerous industrial sectors where the current regulatory structure is likely to become more stringent in terms of developments such as carbon pricing or mandated GHG reductions. Such restrictions will, in turn, increase regulatory and perhaps litigation risks for those industries that currently generate high levels of GHGs. Industries that are extremely energy consumptive (e.g., energy and power, transportation, maritime shipping, airlines, chemicals, cement, and metals and mining) are especially vulnerable to aggressive regulatory action and thus more exposed to the costs of an energy transition. Further, industries that receive generous government subsidies (most industries, in fact, but particularly fossil fuels and agriculture) may see them reduced or even eliminated. This broad range of potential risks leaves financial institutions, in general, broadly exposed.

GHG Emission Limits

GHGs are gases that essentially trap heat in the earth's atmosphere—a process known as the greenhouse effect. This is because they are "transparent" to short-wave solar radiation, but "opaque" to long-wave infrared energy, effectively preventing some energy from leaving the earth's atmosphere. This effect results in an increase in temperature on a global basis, with some regional variations. Much of this increase is absorbed by the oceans, but there may be a limit to the rate of oceanic absorption. This analysis is complicated by the wide variability in annual absorption patterns, reflective of both human activity and natural events such as volcanos.[17]

The principal GHGs are water vapor, carbon dioxide (CO_2), methane (CH_4), nitrous oxide (N_2O), hydrofluorocarbons (HFCs), perfluorocarbons (PFCs), and sulfur hexafluoride (SF_6). Some of these gases have a greater potential for causing the greenhouse effect than others. Methane, for example, is a stronger greenhouse gas than CO_2, but is present in much smaller quantities and has a shorter life in the atmosphere, so its overall contribution to global warming was thought for some time be lower. At present, uncertainty over this issue prevails, since it appears that methane generation over the past several decades has in fact been higher than previous estimates would suggest.[18] Moreover, while methane has a shorter lifespan in the atmosphere, it is significantly more potent a GHG than is CO_2.

In general, GHGs have actually had a positive impact on life on Earth, in that the Earth's temperature is higher than it would be without them. As such, GHGs have contributed to the Holocene, the current geological epoch supportive to the development of human civilizations.[19] It is the accelerating growth in the production of CO_2 in particular during the past century that appears to be the major contributory factor to anthropogenic warming.[20] The bulk of CO_2 discharge by firms, which accounts for about two-thirds of total GHG production, is accounted for by a relatively small number of firms in a few large industries—primarily agriculture, chemicals, energy, materials, and utilities.[21] Figure 6.5 indicates the major categories of GHG emissions.

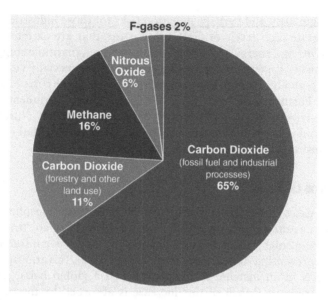

FIGURE 6.5 Global greenhouse emissions by gas.
Source: IPCC, 2014.

This trend in accelerating emissions growth is not only unfavorable, but is also expected to remain strong for some time until effective mitigation efforts are implemented. It seems very likely then that governments will continue to undertake some more aggressive regulations to control GHG generation directly from its numerous sources, although, as the recent COP26 meetings indicated, this progression will not be smooth, and as is often the case in a range of countries, there is often significant political opposition to the adoption of such regulations. Since CO_2 derives from a range of industrial and consumer actions, each of these regulations may not have a material impact individually, but in the aggregate they might. Of concern for investors and lenders is the fact that whatever physical mechanisms are involved, they will likely increase product manufacturing costs. For some products (e.g., automobiles) they will also increase product costs.

Methane Methane is a significantly more powerful GHG than CO_2 but its survival in the atmosphere is considerably shorter. Industrial beef production and the global dairy industry have become frequent targets of concern over methane levels. Although it may be worth noting that the claims regarding methane production by the beef industry appear to be confined to

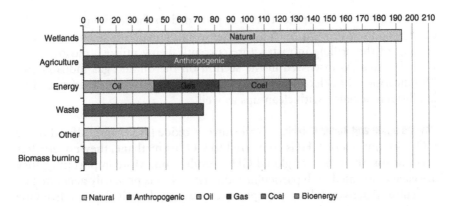

FIGURE 6.6 Global methane emissions by source.
Source: International Energy Agency, 2021, https://www.iea.org/reports/global-methane-tracker-2022/methane-and-climate-change#abstract. Last accessed December 12, 2022 / CC BY 4.0.

the impacts of modern industrial beef agriculture,[22] the amounts produced are significant. In the United States, for example, agriculture accounted for nearly 8.4% of GHG production in 2017, according to the US Environmental Protection Agency.[23] In less industrialized countries, this figure would likely be higher.

Figure 6.6 presents the IEA's assessment of methane sources. Two areas—wetlands and other—are not under human control. All of the other sources are, and these are the areas where more aggressive regulatory actions might be expected.

Recent findings have suggested that CH_4 releases during fossil fuel production have been materially higher than expected,[24] or than previously assessed by the US Environmental Protection Agency. These results may expedite methane regulation process further, although they have not done so yet (it is unclear whether the IEA assessment in Figure 6.6 reflects these changes). The Biden administration has proposed some limitations on CH_4 production, but these have yet to be Congressionally finalized. However, it is almost certain that increased regulations (and enforcement of them) of CH_4 discharge from oil and gas wells are likely to generate sufficient, albeit currently uncertain, costs to impact marginal drillers.[25] In this way, the adoption of various environmental and health regulations could have the effect of changing the cost dynamic of horizontal fracturing to such an extent that fracking may become unprofitable again. This scenario would be particularly likely if Congress were to reverse the 2005 exemption from the federal Clean Water Act that was provided to the fracking industry by the Bush administration. Such a reversal would potentially strand some percentage of the drilling infrastructure currently being utilized, mostly in the United States. As discussed in the section on the oil and gas industry (see "Implications for Select Sectors"), there is the potential threat of stranding liabilities associated with clean-ups as well.

Nitrous Oxide and Sulfur Dioxide   While nitrous oxide (N_2O) and sulfur dioxide (SO_2) are not major GHGs compared to CO_2 or methane, they nonetheless account for about 8% of global GHG production. More importantly, they are each associated with particular industries. N_2O is primarily generated by agricultural activity (along with phosphate waste), largely deriving from the use of nitrogen-based fertilizers; this is a particularly hard problem to solve, since modern industrial agriculture relies heavily on such fertilizers. Other sources of N_2O generation (particularly fossil fuel combustions) seem more amenable to measures designed to reduce its generation.

Sulfur dioxide is also associated with fossil fuel (mainly coal) combustion. The other major industry associated with SO_2 generation is the maritime shipping industry. Like the global airline industry, the shipping industry is not regulated at the country level, but by the International Maritime Organization. After a number of years, this organization has recently introduced more aggressive guidelines for reducing CO_2 generation, and, from January 1, 2020, reduced sulfur usage by using only lower-sulfur fuels.[26] These changes are expected to have a substantial impact on SO_2 generation, but will likely add to global shipping costs. However, it is not clear whether these proposals will be sufficient to meet Paris goals for the industry.[27] At the same time, a variety of desulfurization technologies are being developed, with varying degrees of success.

Hydrofluorocarbons   HFCs have been widely used as refrigerants since the Montreal Protocol in the 1980s, which was designed to reduce and eventually eliminate the chlorofluorocarbons (CFCs) that were implicated in creating the now-famous "ozone hole" over Antarctica. Although HFCs replaced these chemicals, which solved the ozone depletion problem, they are powerful GHGs themselves—considerably more so than CO_2. In 2019, the Kigali Amendment became operative, which requires users of HFCs to reduce their use by 80% over the next thirty years. Notably, there are in fact substitute refrigerant chemicals.

Carbon Pricing Mechanisms

Control of carbon emissions has been a regulatory goal for some time now, but there is a significant lack of agreement regarding the most efficient means to achieve this. One way to do it is via putting a price on emissions as an externality, a Pigouvian tax, and making the emitters pay. Carbon pricing mechanisms include the risks posed by national, regional, and perhaps global attempts to price carbon, how these may evolve, and the differential effects such policies may have on different industrial sectors. *We believe that this risk category is the most serious potential near-term climate risk facing a number of sectors.* This is the prime example of a regulatory risk with a potentially significant financial impact, particularly on operating margins and asset valuations.

It has been proposed among the scientific community that carbon emissions—particularly CO_2 and methane CH_4—must be not only reduced, or targeted to net zero, but ideally eliminated entirely.[28] The extent to which this is possible is an open question. However, the need for action is best demonstrated by looking at the historical generation of CO_2, the principal GHG (see Figure 6.7).

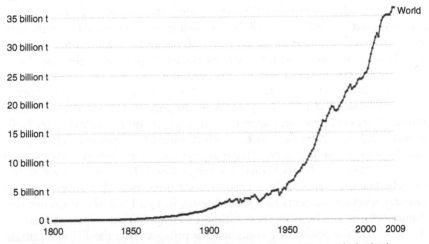

Note: Carbon dioxide (CO_2) emissions from the burning of fossil fuels for energy and cement production. Land use change is not included.
CO_2 emissions are measured on a production basis, meaning they do not correct for emissions embedded in traded goods. OurWorldInData.org/co2-and-other-greenhouse-gas-emissions/ • CC BY

FIGURE 6.7   Annual CO_2 emissions, 1800–2019.
Source: Our World in Data. https://ourworldindata.org/co2-emissions. Last accessed December 12, 2022 / CC BY 4.0.

At present, carbon pricing, which many believe is the most desirable mechanism from a market perspective, has achieved little in the way of actual global carbon reduction.[29] Rather, it has evolved into an inconsistent mix of national policies that are often disconnected from each other. In at least one case—the EU's Emissions Trading System (ETS) program—there appears to be evidence that the scheme does indeed reduce emissions intensity, although whether it is actual ETS carbon pricing, or rather the threat of higher pricing in the future, that achieves the necessary objective is at present unresolved.[30] The price of emissions-related carbon varies widely around the world, and the impact on specific industries can also vary widely. In fact, recent research suggests that on a global bases, carbon pricing remains entirely too low—$4.42 per ton in 2021—and certainly is not high enough to spur significant corporate action.[31]

At the same time, there are signs that this situation is improving,[32] although whether this progress will lead to global carbon regulation remains to be seen. An increasing push is under way to move toward regulating carbon on a global basis, although not necessarily with a uniform global price. The World Bank has noted that, as of 2022, about sixty-seven countries have carbon pricing mechanisms, either in the form of a carbon tax, or through some sort of ETS framework.[33] In fact, this is consistent with the recommendations of the Paris COP21 negotiators, and that agreement provided countries with a degree of flexibility regarding meeting its carbon reduction goals without the apparent need for a uniform global carbon price.

An even broader and more stringent carbon price in a globalized carbon market could also have a significant impact on a number of industries in addition to the energy industry. Any industry that is highly energy intensive—one that relies on process heating in its industrial processes—could see its cost dynamics altered enough to potentially strand older facilities, though it is clear that such an effort would be expensive. These firms could also see significant negative margin impacts as carbon costs escalate CGS numbers. The International Monetary Fund (IMF), in a recent note[34] on whether there should be a carbon price floor, provided an estimate of country-level adjustments that would result from a US $50 carbon tax (see Figure 6.8); as can be seen, these estimated cost additions are not trivial. There is also the potentially complicating prospect that the EU will initiate a cross-border carbon tax, the Carbon Border Adjustment Mechanism,[35] which would tax imports from countries with less stringent carbon pricing mechanisms. This proposal has generated some strong pushback from many of the EU's trade partners. However, we suspect it will go into effect as planned in 2023.

Country	Coal Baseline Price, $/GJ	Coal Price Increase	Natural gas Baseline Price, $/GJ	Natural gas Price Increase	Electricity Baseline Price, $/kWh	Electricity Price Increase	Gasoline Baseline Price, $/Liter	Gasoline Price Increase
Argentina	2.9	172%	3.7	86%	0.08	18%	1.14	13%
Australia	3.4	154%	7.9	37%	0.12	25%	1.13	12%
Brazil	4.4	122%	9.2	34%	0.07	7%	1.23	8%
Canada	2.6	209%	4.2	69%	0.08	10%	1.14	11%
China	4.4	114%	10.5	25%	0.05	46%	1.13	12%
France	6.2	94%	15.8	18%	0.13	2%	1.77	9%
Germany	5.8	91%	12.4	23%	0.17	9%	1.74	8%
India	5.0	99%	3.5	98%	0.06	47%	1.12	12%
Indonesia	2.7	187%	5.7	44%	0.08	57%	0.45	31%
Italy	4.6	116%	15.4	24%	0.12	11%	1.90	8%
Japan	3.7	132%	11.1	24%	0.12	24%	1.37	10%
Mexico	1.8	284%	3.0	91%	0.09	26%	0.97	14%
Russia	2.2	209%	2.7	95%	0.08	36%	0.73	18%
Saudi Arabia			3.9	69%	0.10	33%	0.27	45%
South Africa	1.6	285%	3.7	62%	0.05	66%	1.16	10%
Korea	4.7	103%	11.4	25%	0.08	37%	1.46	8%
Turkey	1.4	421%	7.6	41%	0.06	59%	1.40	10%
United Kingdom	6.9	74%	11.5	27%	0.12	9%	1.72	8%
United States	2.4	220%	4.4	69%	0.07	23%	0.83	16%
Simple Average	3.7	171%	7.8	51%	0.11	39%	1.19	14%

FIGURE 6.8 Illustrative energy price impacts for a US $50 carbon tax p/tCO$_2$e by 2030.

Source: IMF: https://www.imf.org/en/Publications/staff-climate-notes/Issues/2021/06/15/Proposal-for-an-International-Carbon-Price-Floor-Among-Large-Emitters-460468. Last accessed December 12, 2022.

Notes: Baseline prices are retail prices updated from Coady and others (2019) and include preexisting energy taxes. Baseline prices for coal and natural gas are based on regional reference prices. Baseline prices for electricity and gasoline are from cross-country databases. Impacts of carbon taxes on electricity prices depend on the emissions intensity of power generation. Carbon tax prices are per ton. GJ = gigajoule; kWh = Kilowatt-hour. All prices are stated in real 2018 terms.

Carbon Tax Risks

There are a number of arguments that a carbon tax is the most straightforward method of pricing carbon appropriately.[36] Such a tax has been mooted for several decades, but significant political and business opposition has prevented the idea from taking hold in any meaningful way globally, although there are numerous country-specific schemes. Nonetheless, the notion has a direct appeal, since its impact would be immediate. The tax itself would be imposed at the source of carbon generation—in most cases, a power plant or an industrial plant generating CO_2. Energy transport would be the most directly affected sector and would presumably try to pass the additional costs on to purchasers, who might often end up being consumers. However, events of 2022 in response to the sharp increase of costs of natural gas emanating from problems with Russian gas availability point up how politically complex passing on such costs may be.[37] Even leaving aside the potential inflationary impact of a carbon tax, it is easy to see why governments have been reluctant to impose such taxes outside special industries, such as airlines.

Yet, imposition of a carbon tax in itself would provide a measure of certainty to markets, even if the tax is draconian—say, on the order of US $100 per ton (or even, as has been suggested, as high as US $160 per ton).[38] It would therefore allow firms to price input costs, including energy costs, in such a way as to capture externalities and to facilitate an energy transition. Thus, there are considerable advantages to the notion of an outright carbon tax.[39] However, there would also be significant penalties to a range of industries in the event of a material tax like that suggested earlier. For many sectors, energy costs are already a considerable portion of overall costs, and the impact of a significant carbon tax would exacerbate those costs, with a resulting margin impact.

In any event, carbon taxes introduced to date appear unlikely to achieve one of their targeted objectives on their own: meeting various governments' commitments under the Paris Accord. Figure 6.9 presents a representative list of countries (as of 2019) according to their ambition and whether those ambitions and pledges are being achieved (as suggested by the IMF).

Figure 6.9 suggests that more ambitious measures will be necessary to achieve these targets. Moreover, it is not unreasonable to expect these efforts to gather momentum over the next year or two, given the severity of climate-related impacts that increasingly dominate the global news flow. However, it is not necessarily clear that the results of COP27 advanced these objectives.[40]

Tracking reductions

Countries such as Canada, France, Mexico, and Saudi Arabia made ambitious CO_2 reduction pledges under the Paris Agreement. Even with a $70 a ton carbon tax, these countries will fall short in achieving their pledged CO_2 reductions.

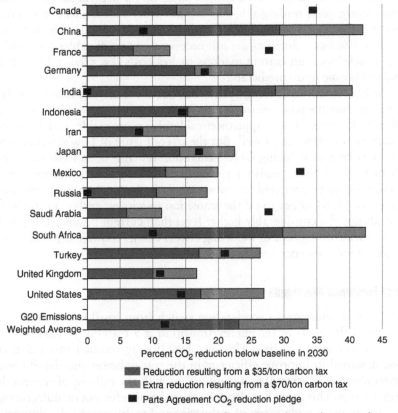

Note: For countries such as China, India, and South Africa that are heavy coal users, even a $35/ton carbon tax is extremely effective in reducing overall emissions.

FIGURE 6.9 Tracking countries' goals versus actual reductions.
Source: International Monetary Fund, June 2019. https://www.imf.org/external/pubs/ft/fandd/2019/06/pdf/what-is-carbon-taxation-basics.pdf

Other Carbon Pricing Risk

The main alternative to a government-mandated carbon tax is to allow the market to determine the price of carbon through an open trading system. In line with this latter approach, emissions trading schemes have emerged in a number of areas, particularly the EU. In this system, a government (or a consortium of governments) sells permits to allow a certain level of emissions, and these are traded in open markets. While this system is not a direct tax, prices are determined by the market based on the decarbonization costs. Consequently, such trading schemes are not truly independent from government influence. Note that while carbon taxes are predictable in terms of costs, emissions reductions are not necessarily as predictable; conversely, an approach based on carbon markets makes costs less predictable, while emission become more predictable.[41]

The EU Emissions Trading System has had a checkered history of volatile pricing over the past several decades. Since a repricing several years ago by the EU, the market now appears considerably more stable, and, by some accounts, more effective as well. But the overall issue of how effective this system has been at reducing GHG generation remains open to debate. The Bank of England has recently suggested that banks, and by inference everyone else, should be prepared for substantially higher carbon costs, perhaps in excess of US $100 per ton if the transition to a lower-carbon energy system is abrupt,[42] a considerably higher level than current pricing. That said, there is a wide divergence of modeling effects being reported at present and substantial inconsistency among models.

Energy Efficiency Standards

In addition to spurring an accelerating switch from fossil fuels to renewables, one of the goals of the energy transition is a material increase in the more efficient use of energy. This aim has already resulted in regulatory action designed to improve efficiency in the transmission and distribution of energy, which is occurring in conjunction with the roll-out of renewable energy sources. This trend has also encouraged more efficient manufacturing processes across a wide range of industries and is driving the development of new standards and technologies (e.g., those that increase the efficiency of consumer appliances). In some cases—automobile mileage and emission standards—these efficiency improvements were mandated by regulation, or in some cases by law.

Note that the reference to "efficiency" is in the broadest sense, and sometimes things don't go as planned. The UK government undertook an effort several years ago to insulate homes, in part because home insulation is a straightforward method to improve home heating efficiency. Taken in the aggregate across a nation's housing stock, these efficiency improvements can be quite material. Sadly, much of UK housing stock cannot be insulated in the traditional sense, and the program was abandoned. One of the reasons it

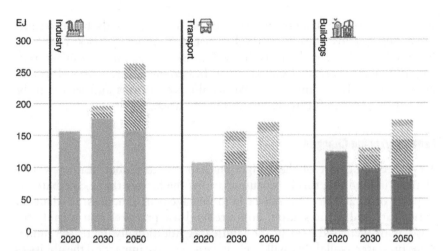

FIGURE 6.10 Energy efficiency milestones in the "Net Zero Emissions by 2050 Scenario," 2020–2050.
Source: International Energy Administration, 2021. https://www.iea.org/reports/ energy-efficiency-2021. Last accessed December 12, 2022 / CC BY 4.0.
Notes: EJ: exajoules.
Cross-hatched areas are those where "demand avoidance" will be generated by efficiencies, electrification, or behavior change.

was opposed was the expense that, while partially borne by the government, would still largely accrue to the property owner.

Nonetheless, we would expect efficiency improvements to continue to be a targeted policy option. There are a number of domains where such improvements may be generated in a fairly straightforward manner—in other domains, improvements may be a bit more achievable. The IEA has, in fact, detailed about forty target areas for improvements, in line with the EU's "Net Zero Emissions by 2050" Scenario. This breaks down into three broad areas: industry, transportation, and buildings.[43] The latter area is where such improvements will be most straightforward to achieve, although improvements in the industrial area are likely to have more impact, as indicated in Figure 6.10.

Note that it is perfectly justified to assume that manufacturing firms in all three areas will be targeted for efficiency improvements. We have already mentioned two principal areas in industrial process where we will undoubtedly see increased an efficiency focus: heat and water. Transport efficiencies will be largely gained through electrification of motor vehicles, although efficiencies in industries such as air and maritime transport will generally involve more efficient use of fuels. Improvements in building efficiencies will relate to several issues—improved construction methods, but also shifts in heating systems from gas and oil to electricity in many cases. These will be broad-based national efforts that will necessarily involve manufacturers. The IEA notes that, for example, over 120 countries are involved in efficiency standards for appliances. We would expect firms and sectors to be actively involved in future discussions in this area.

Land-use/Zoning Changes

We expect that part of the mitigation response to global heating will be changes in land use; this is because many of the factors that exacerbate the impacts of global heating reflect land-management practices, particularly agriculture and deforestation. Both are land use practices that amplify the impacts of increased heat in the landscape. Additionally, increased limitations on water availability will likely have a negative impact on the ability of firms in some sectors (e.g., mining) to continue to operate in certain regions. In this event, license-to-operate restrictions will become more common for both mining and forest companies.

Restrictions on agricultural land are increasingly likely as well, although these will likely run up against the need to increase agricultural production in general to feed a growing global population. Such restrictions will be due to a number of negative outcomes that industrial agriculture has caused in the past several decades, including increased runoff of agricultural chemicals in water supplies and increasing concerns about biodiversity loss because of mainstream agricultural practices. A number of governments have recently instituted a range of programs to regenerate polyculture agriculture, as well as meadows, hedgerows, and forests. These are all landforms that have a mitigative effect on temperature increases. Replacing forests with paved surfaces is generally going to create problems.

What this suggests is that, as we discussed elsewhere, land use in certain regions may become more constrained. This will have a particular impact on the three industries mentioned here—agriculture, mining, and forestry. Agriculture is a pretty diversified industry, and it is, frankly difficult to find concentrated impacts of sufficient materiality to affect investors, other than at agricultural product trading firms (although, as we have been constantly reminded over the past several years, the political costs of drought on food supplies can be considerable). On the other hand, the operating environment for mining and forestry companies may become more constrained.

At the same time, this trend will almost certainly be affected by increasing pressures for housing in and near urban centers. In particular, land currently devoted to transportation infrastructure, which in some countries is considerable, may be freed up as transportation modes change. For example, the long-term outlook for the airline industry because of global heating is not exactly clear; this may result in a surplus of airports, which tend to take up lots of land generally near urban centers.

Noncarbon Regulatory Requirements

Clearly, not all climate-related issues derive from carbon generation into the atmosphere. Thus, many climate-related activities do not involve carbon reduction. Much of the regional impact of global heating reflects land use changes, as mentioned. Some of these have resulted in significant deforestation, for example. There are several other factors that are also subject to potential constraints.

The most important of these potential risks is restrictions on water use. All industries use water. But some industries are "thirstier" than others and in many cases, these industries are already engaging with the issues that surround concerns about longer-term availability. The two industries currently dominating water consumption are energy and agriculture; for instance, electric power generation is the single largest industrial use of water. Other industries that are significant water consumers include metals and mining, the food and beverage industries (including both direct and indirect use), textiles, chemicals (especially agricultural chemicals), steel, automobile manufacturing, and paper. We would expect these industries to receive rapidly increasing attention from governments and regulators on water management issues going forward.

Moreover, we suspect that the siting of plants in the future, like residential developments, may be more constrained by water availability issues than they have been in the past. Various mining operations in different parts of the world are already increasingly affected by water availability and wastewater disposal issues, in some cases to the extent that projects have been canceled over local water concerns. In many cases, water extraction issues have become bound up with license-to-operate issues that many companies are facing.

TECHNOLOGY RISKS

While these risks do not represent the broad spectrum of technology risks that would be covered by traditional financial analysis, they do arise from climate risk considerations, since they represent technology developments specifically related to the energy transition to a zero-carbon economy—not just in terms of the generation and transmission of electricity, but in terms of the potential impacts on the existing energy infrastructure. These impacts are already being felt, as recent developments affecting the automobile and fossil fuel industries have demonstrated. More broadly, the utility industry is in the process of being transformed.

Changes in Speed of Electrification

Developments in electrification represent another trend that is moving much faster than anyone would have expected a decade ago. Electric car infrastructure, particularly charging points, are accelerating in most areas, especially in Europe and parts of Asia. Similarly, the speed with which electric grids are adapting to renewables, coupled with dealing with still somewhat erratic load factors, suggests that there is still a significant amount of work to do in many countries, especially those with a relatively low contribution from renewables. Nonetheless, the continued drop in the price of renewable energy kits, particularly solar panels, is having a transformative effect. This issue is of critical importance, given many of these countries' reliance on coal and natural gas as the primary energy source. We expect that governments will be encouraged to move more rapidly on electrification in those areas where there have previously been few incentives to do so. This will clearly have impacts, mostly broadly distributive, for energy networks, which will in many cases affect operating models in the energy and utility sectors.[44]

Storage and Grid Efficiencies

This area remains the next frontier—improvements in storage and distribution are essential to the speed with which fuller electrification can take place. Improving the efficiency of lithium-based batteries in particular remains an issue that is receiving intense focus. Likewise, there is intensive research under way to improve grid distribution. Much of this is geared to large power systems where there is a perceived need for full power availability in peak demand periods, which traditionally have led to concerns about the potential reliability of renewable sources during these periods.

Other Technological Changes

Given the abysmal track record of predictions regarding power and energy that were dominant a decade ago, it would be foolish to predict the emergence of technological developments over the next decade; this does not prevent such predictions from emerging, of course. At present, however, we assume that the general shape of how the global power industry is going to develop is generally understood, including those areas where significant breakthroughs are likely.

We note that there is currently considerable interest in using hydrogen in more interesting ways—generating green hydrogen, for example, would produce apparently significant carbon savings. However, as is the case with many such newer technologies, costs appear to be a potentially limiting issue—especially for storage. There are several areas—fusion energy has been one of these for decades, literally—where the technologies are appealing until the real-world instantiation is attempted.

New Low-carbon Technologies

Over the past two decades, we have seen the rapid development and deployment of lower-carbon energy sources, particularly solar and wind power. The speed with which the cost of these technologies has declined caught the entire energy industry unprepared, not to mention public policy makers and regulators. There is still great uncertainty about the potential scope of future cost reductions. It is unclear whether Moore's Law[45] is applicable to solar technologies, but it certainly seems as if it was for a limited period. Major utilities have already been hit by significant charges relating to write-downs on existing plants as a result of newer technologies dramatically altering the price function of energy sources. While this trend may have reached its endpoint, it remains a cautionary area for managements.

Achieving Net Zero

We note that achieving targeted net-zero goals relies on offsets of various forms. Some of these are less tangible than others—carbon credits available on exchanges, for example. However, others are definitely tangible. The first and most visible is CCS technology. Considerable importance (or outright hope) has been placed on CCS, which plays an important role in many firm net-zero strategies. Support for CCS comes from a wide range of entities, including the IPCC and the fossil fuel industry. Indeed, many estimates of the timing and intensity of climate impacts over the next century specifically rely on the success of CCS to reduce CO_2 levels in the atmosphere. Discussions of this problem usually point out that if this issue is not resolved, CO_2 levels will remain higher than many organizations expect, and this may have an impact on other efforts to reduce CO_2 generation.

However, the extent to which CCS technology will be operable at scale at reasonable costs remains to be seen. Moreover, whether CCS can achieve its carbon reduction targets also appears questionable. To date, most of these projects globally have either failed or been substantially less efficient than promised, according to a recent IEA report.[46] This is fundamentally a technological issue, of course. Whether the promised CCS efficiencies can be delivered remains somewhat speculative at present.

Second, and with perhaps more promise, are improved battery technologies. Longer-term storage is a critical component not only of achieving net zero, but also in the general plans of utilities as they replace and supplement existing grid structures with new ones that will accommodate renewable generation.

We note that achieving net zero is necessarily a combination of work in numerous areas. The obviously targeted area is emissions reduction, and many of the proposed offsets related to dealing with carbon in some form—transforming the energy system, in other words. Other options provide different opportunities, the principal one being changes in land use systems. This principally involves halting deforestation, particularly that associated with agriculture. While in many cases this is subsistence agriculture, in other cases it is simply soybeans for animal feed (and meatless meat increasingly). As we mention below, you can't discuss biodiversity loss without also considering land use changes and biogeochemical flows; achieving net zero requires including land use in the dynamic of whatever tools are being considered.

GOING-CONCERN RISKS

We make no claims of novelty about our catalogue of what we are referring to as "going-concern risks" (i.e., risks associated with the day-to-day running of the firm and staying out of trouble). Our focus here is on risks associated specifically with global heating and climate change that may have a negative impact on firms' ability to operate on a daily basis. Portfolio managers, analysts, lenders, and regulators will be familiar with most if not all of these categories, since many are an integral part of traditional financial risk analysis. However, these are still worth highlighting in this taxonomy because of the potentially unique problems posed by climate change risks.

Commodity Price Changes

Commodity prices, which declined during the 20th century,[47] have been rising in the 21st century. Moreover, commodity price volatility generally remains at historically high levels. As the physical impacts of climate change continue to affect available arable cropland, not to mention potential water supplies, there is every reason to think that agricultural commodity prices may well continue to increase[48] especially in those areas where transport costs may become increasingly unaffordable. Also, costs may well continue to rise in the metals and mining sectors generally, given water constraints caused by geographic difficulties of reaching relevant places and, eventually, also in the fossil fuel sector as exploration and production (E&P) activity becomes more expensive. We suspect that transport costs for commodities, which have generally been low over the past century, will rise, perhaps substantially, as a result of decarbonization measures, and expense, in the land-transport and maritime-shipping sectors.

Fossil Fuels We include fossil fuels in our commodity section because, even though they are a refined product, they are foundational to much of the economy, and fossil fuel costs are a critical element to issues of firm profitability in many sectors.

Largely because of the impact of fracking in the United States and the COVID-19 pandemic, oil prices are currently volatile, having recovered from significant lows at the time of writing, largely from Russia's invasion of Ukraine, which has wreaked havoc on global gas pricing.[49] The issue is whether levels will return to lower prices over the longer term relative to recent higher prices. Several major oil companies, including BP, Total, ExxonMobil, and Royal Dutch Shell, took significant impairment charges during 2020,[50] only to return to strong profitability in 2022.

Until recently, natural gas prices remained low, as they have been for most of the current decade, again because of US fracking activity. Whether the recent rise in gas prices will persist in the face of ongoing industry volatility remains unclear. Lower fossil fuel prices benefit a wide range of industries, including transportation, chemicals, utilities, and any industry involving the production of heat to generate a product (steel and cement, for example). In particular, a number of petrochemical sectors are currently enjoying relatively low input prices.

However, as we have noted elsewhere, the fossil fuel industry benefits considerably from government largesse in most countries and these subsidies take a variety of forms. While governments pledged to reduce subsidies at COP15 in Paris, government follow-up action has been very slow—close to nonexistent[51] (though the recent announcement by the US government of its intention to phase out a range of fossil fuel subsidies may help to accelerate the process globally). In addition, there is ample evidence that much fracking activity in the United States is currently occurring well below break-even levels, and bankruptcies in the sector continue to rise.[52] While it may be plausible to suggest that the return of higher prices, if it occurs, will spur on new fracking activity, it is likely that under a new administration, fracking activity in the United States (virtually the only place where it occurs at scale these days) may be more regulated than it has been in the past.

We defer the balance of our commodities concerns to our natural capital discussion in Chapter 7.

Consumer Preferences

Consumers change their preferences, and increasingly, they seem to be doing so on environmental/climate-related grounds. While these changes present opportunities to firms, they also present risks to revenues and earnings of established products, and perhaps stranded assets as well. Three product categories can serve as useful cases to illustrate this trend: electric cars, plastics, and meat.

Electric Cars   Although electric cars remain a very small part of the global auto fleet, it seems clear that a range of government policies are steering the industry in this direction. In particular, many governments (including the UK government) are legally mandating becoming carbon neutral by 2050, or in some cases even earlier.[53] A major component of the plans to achieve this policy is reducing, and eventually eliminating, the internal combustion engine automobile.

The large-scale use of electric cars will indeed have a positive impact of reducing emissions.[54] However, there are several aspects of risk to the expected transformation. First, the manufacturing of electric cars, while requiring fewer workers, will still involve very expensive modifications to manufacturing plants and workforces.[55] Second, the roll-out of charging facilities has been very uneven—nonexistent in many areas—and this roll-out is essential for the fleet of electric cars to expand successfully.[56] Finally, development of the electric car industry is critically tied to developments in battery storage technologies. Despite significant progress over the past two decades, battery-constrained mileage limitations still represent a possible impediment to successful penetration of the consumer market. Still, so far, consumers seem to be accepting this shift, if sales of electric cars are any indication. At the same time, there remains a high level of uncertainty regarding the potential costs of this transition, particularly for auto manufacturers.

Plastics   Recent years have seen a surge of consumer interest in problems associated with plastic pollution. It is difficult to open a magazine or newspaper these days without encountering a picture of a fish or sea turtle intertwined with some plastic product and the level of micro-plastics residue throughout the oceans is unexpectedly high—as is awareness of this fact.[57] Moreover, recycling plastics has proved largely ineffective; for example, it turns out that much of Europe's plastic has simply ended up in rivers in Malaysia.[58] Partially as a result of this high-profile media coverage, there is now increasing pressure to regulate or even ban single-use plastics, including plastic bags. If this trend becomes sufficiently strong, it is possible that the petrochemical industry, for which plastics have been a reliable profit generator for decades, may be pressured to find substitute products. However, it is unclear how consistent and durable consumer concerns about plastics will be. It is also unclear how the industry will respond. Until now, the trend has been to accentuate recyclability; whether this will be sufficient, or will even work, in the future remains uncertain. Nonetheless, given the success of consumer choices in redirecting other industries, the issues surrounding plastics seem likely to remain relatively high profile.

Meat   By far the most visible example of consumer choice having a material impact on an industry is the current controversy over meat production as a driver of climate change. There is now considerable publicly available information (some of it not necessarily factual) regarding the role of industrial meat production as one of the drivers of global heating[59] and the packaged food industry's relatively rapid response in the development of "nonmeat meat."[60] There is no question that industrial meat production on a global basis poses several climate risks—methane generation, water availability, and wastewater disposal being among the most important.[61] The consolidation of the global meat industry is largely responsible for the increase of these risks over the past two decades.[62] Whether this represents a rationale for moving toward dramatically reducing meat in people's diets or simply encouraging the growth of the grass-fed meat industry remains an open question.[63] Unsurprisingly, most packaged food companies and, indeed, meat producers are attempting to benefit from this trend. How extensive this benefit might be to anyone other than soybean farmers remains unclear.

Regardless, consumers have responded to meat substitutes enthusiastically, both in their grocery shopping and at chain restaurants. That all of this occurred in a relatively short time frame (four to five years or so) highlights just how rapidly consumer preferences can change and, likewise, how rapidly the food and restaurant industries can respond. These developments may represent a risk for large-scale industrial meat producers, which, incidentally, will also experience increasing pressure to upgrade facilities for health and safety as well as environmental purposes. Again, operating costs are likely to rise here.

Reputational/License-to-operate Risks

Reputational risk is something of an amorphous concept but an important and pervasive one, and a decided risk for companies in some sectors (e.g., the consumer and retail sectors). It is also a Pillar II risk under the Basel framework. A botched product recall, for example, can have significant if short-lived impacts, as auto manufacturers are constantly rediscovering. In some cases, it may be a business practice that has compromised reputations, as Nestle discovered with its ill-fated attempts to sell infant formula in Africa; despite having only a financial impact at the time, this decision was a risk that has persisted even to today. Similarly, some of Nestle's actions in the bottled-water market, where it is a significant player, have generated significant controversies.[64] In fact, it seems clear that many company managements are treating these issues seriously. According to a 2014 survey by Deloitte, 87% of CEOs surveyed felt that reputational risk was a "top strategic business risk" and 88% indicated that their companies were focusing on managing this risk.[65]

Thus, reputational risk is not a new concept for risk managers to consider. However, the issue it relates to, social license-to-operate risk, is becoming increasingly driven by climate concerns, especially when there is water involved. In some ways, this risk is a derivative of those same conditions that generate reputational risks. But there is a useful distinction to be made between areas where reputational risk may affect only the willingness of consumers to purchase a company's products (as in the case of automobiles and other consumer products) and those areas where corporate misbehavior may lead to the inability to conduct business that relies on regulatory or government approvals (as is the case in many extractive industries, particularly mining). The term "reputational risk" was originally coined for the mining industry, but is clearly broader in its applicability, and can apply to any resource-based business reliant on local or national permitting and authorization, including the oil and gas industry, agriculture, and forestry. These issues also arise for selected industries in some countries but not others. For example, meat processing is considerably more regulated in the EU than it is in the United States, largely because US companies have been able to overcome social license-to-operate issues—not always in a positive way.[66]

Both reputational and license-to-operate risks are derivative issues; however, they derive from other, more basic risks of the type we have described, risks generally relating to governance issues. Therefore, these two types of risk are probably more suitably treated as potential economic impacts of the risk categories listed earlier that can have further implications. In fact, there are several other possible economic impacts that are also derivative. Any of these can have a direct financial impact, whether on operating costs, cash flows, or indeed on assets as well. We note that litigation risk (discussed in the next section), which is a traditional risk category, can have clear knock-on effects in terms of both reputational and social license-to-operate risks. The same management failures that can lead to regulatory fines and other penalties can often result in litigation exposure.

While it is tempting to think that highly regulated industries, such as power and water utilities, might be more at risk from these concerns, we suspect this is not the case—they do, after all, usually provide a service for which substitutes are not available. For some other industries, however, life is not so simple. In particular, the mining industry has encountered a number of situations where license-to-operate concerns have arisen and in several cases have produced a result that involves a significant asset becoming stranded. These have usually involved water issues: either the availability of water in increasingly water-stressed areas, or the appropriate methods of wastewater disposal in certain regions. Moreover, this issue is starting to become more frequent in other extractive industries, particularly forestry.

Litigation Risks

The same management failures that can lead to regulatory fines and other penalties can often result in litigation exposures, which, as the pharmaceutical and tobacco industry can testify, can result in substantial judgments against companies. These judgments can often have severe impacts on companies' cash positions, cash flow, and provisions—and can sometimes lead to credit rating downgrades. In the case of the asbestos industry in the 1980s, these judgments resulted in wholesale bankruptcies of nearly an entire industry.

In terms of overall ESG criteria, we believe that nearly all social and governance categories, and many environmental categories as well, can be characterized as traditional business and financial risks. In our previous report of 2014,[67] for example, we highlighted a number of social risks relating to child labor, worker safety, union relations, and human rights. Indicators routinely tracked by socially responsible investing/ESG screening organizations (e.g., Asset4, MSCI, Sustainalytics) in the social category include the following issues (employed by Asset4): employment quality, health and safety, training and development, diversity, human rights, community, and product responsibility.

However, from the standpoint of outright investment and lending risks—that is, issues that could have a sufficiently negative impact on either the business or financial profile of a company to create a financial risk— this list is not particularly useful. Not being a signatory to the UN Global Compact is unlikely to be regarded by the rating agencies as a potential credit event. Only two of the categories being tracked are actually capable of generating sufficient risks to be of potential concern to rating agencies or investors: health and safety, and product responsibility. These are the areas where both regulatory risks and litigation risks are most likely to emerge, and the latter certainly can be a cause of rating agency downgrades, as seen in the pharmaceutical industry.

Importantly, climate litigation has been increasing in recent years. It has taken several forms, some of which have been successful and some less so. In general, such litigation has become a relatively high-profile event with considerable media coverage. It is premature to conjecture the extent to which firms themselves actually face some financial risk deriving from this litigation; the best that can be said is that such litigation shows no signs of going away. Most of these cases occur in either the United States or Australia.

There appear to be two major themes relating to climate litigation. The first theme involves seeking to force governments to take action. The most noteworthy case in this respect has been in The Netherlands, where in 2019 the Supreme Court ruled that the government had a legal requirement to take stronger measures to deal with climate change.[68] More recently, the Belgian Supreme Court issued a ruling very similar to that reached by the senior court in The Netherlands: the Belgian government's existing climate policies were insufficient.[69] This trend appears likely to continue. In the United Kingdom, the Supreme Court rules that the UK government was not meeting its legal responsibilities under its Climate Change legislation.[70] And in Germany, the German Federal Constitutional Court in 2021 ruled that the German government had a legal obligation to develop climate policies in line with the Paris Agreement. Given the broad constitutional breadth of the ruling, it is expected that this ruling will prove influential elsewhere.[71] There are similar cases in various stages of litigation proceeding in a number of countries. A recent case, which generated considerable media attention, was a purported class action against the Australian government for not disclosing climate risks in offering documents relating to sovereign debt issuance.[72] This case is unresolved as of the time of writing (2022).

The second theme reflected in much of the litigation involves seeking damages against major oil companies for knowing about, but not revealing publicly, the extent of potential climate change risk and damages. There have been several relatively high-profile cases here, and a major case was recently ruled in the defendant's favor. The case, brought by the New York State Attorney General, relied on a claim that oil companies had deliberately misled investors over the years—in other words, had committed fraud against investors. This case was dismissed by the judge, on the grounds that the state had actually not demonstrated securities fraud.[73] But a number of cases along similar lines are proceeding in the United States and elsewhere. Most recently, the City of New York has brought claims against a number of major oil companies over potential damages from global heating on the basis of "misrepresentation." However, this follows the city's attempt to force companies to pay damages from global warming impacts that was dismissed at the appellate court level. As Reuters noted,

> Earlier this month, the 2nd U.S. Circuit Court of Appeals in Manhattan ruled in a separate lawsuit in favor of BP, Chevron Corp (CVX.N), ConocoPhillips (COP.N), Exxon and Shell, and rejected the city's efforts to sue under state nuisance law for damages caused by the companies' "admittedly legal" production and sale of fossil fuels, and said the city's federal common law claims were displaced by the federal Clean Air Act.[74]

Again, we expect these cases to continue. In fact, a similar case is being pursued in Massachusetts in a case initiated in 2019.[75] Recent reports from The Geneva Association and the Climate Change Laws of the World project at the Grantham Research Institute on Climate Change provide a good summary of the current status of much of this litigation.[76]

In addition to the above cases, there is also increasing litigation surrounding various aspects of the natural gas business, particularly methane, in the United States. While the Trump administration decreased the federal government's involvement in regulating much of the oil and gas sector, the Biden administration has taken steps to reverse this process. In addition, a number of states have continued to pursue more stringent discharge penalties for pollutants, including CO_2 and CH_4, as well as wastewater from a range of plants, especially the mining and fracking industries.

Litigation risk has been a regular part of traditional firm risk analysis, and will undoubtedly remain so. Like reputational risk, it is a Pillar II risk under Basel, and there is little reason to think that will change. However, as those familiar with the litigation history of the asbestos industry in the United States will know, it is not unheard of for practically an entire industry to enter bankruptcy protection because of litigation risk. Moreover, those who have followed the tobacco industry litigation over the years (like the author) will recall that, although the industry prevailed in litigation for several decades, it took just one case to reverse that trend, with a significant rise in financial risks as a result.[77] The potential for financial mischief here may be high.[78]

SUPPLY CHAIN RISKS

Supply chains pose significant analytical issues for investors and lenders, not to mention regulators and company managements. In part, these issues stem from legislated, and often voluntary, tracking of GHG emissions across three categories.

1. Scope 1: Direct emissions from company-owned resources.
2. Scope 2: Indirect emissions, owned (generally from purchased energy).
3. Scope 3: Indirect emissions, not owned (all upstream and downstream emissions related to a company's business).

Companies that sign up to report their emissions under the GHG Protocols are required to report on scopes 1 and 2. Scope 3 reporting, at present, is largely voluntary. Nonetheless, many companies undertake to report all three levels because of the greater understanding of the internal workings of the business. Not reducing these risks, as reported through the Protocol, has been known to generate reputational issues. Moreover, investors and lenders are increasingly requiring scope 3 disclosures as part of normal financial reporting.

The other major reason to attend to supply chains is that they are inevitably vulnerable to events—both natural and manmade. In recent years, there have been numerous instances of supply chain disruptions in the automobile and technology industries following a single event, such as a warehouse fire or a tsunami,[79] and recovery can often take several months, or more. While many of these events appear to be caused by human activities (e.g., accidental fires) an increasing number of them seem to be related to extreme weather factors. The ongoing drought in Taiwan generated severe supply issues in the global semiconductor industry in 2021, for example.[80] This shortage continues to have significant supply impacts on myriad industries, including automobile manufacturing and mobile communications equipment. To take another example, water management risks—both insufficient supply, as in drought, or too much water, as in flooding—are becoming more critical in supply chain management as well.[81]

Moreover, global supply chains remain vulnerable to a range of disasters, including some that wouldn't necessarily be as familiar as drought and floods. In 2010, the eruption of Iceland's large volcano Eyjafjallajökull caused havoc, not just in the global airline system (which lost billions during this period) but on global, particularly European, supply lines:[82]

A century ago, even 30 years ago, an eruption from Iceland wouldn't have affected menus in Florence or auto assembly in Tennessee. But things have changed. The just-in-time mentality dictates that factories and retailers build superefficient, lengthy supply chains and keep as little capital and warehouse space as possible tied up in inventory. Globalization has meant that companies now source components and products from all over the world. The upshot: When there's a small disruption anywhere, the machinery of global capitalism slows down. And when there's a disruption in Europe, look out.

We would not expect such natural events to diminish in frequency or intensity in the future. In fact, with reference to climate-generated events, it should be clear that these will increase.

Pandemics, it turns out, can produce similar results. COVID pointed up, perhaps too easily, some of the deficiencies of the current supply chain model, which critically still depends in part on the JIT (Just-in-Time) model pioneered by Japanese industry in the 1960s and 1970s. This has proved to be a bonanza for management consulting firms. It has also highlighted the fact that some aspects of supply chains (maritime shipping) were relatively resilient, as were, unsurprisingly, life sciences companies such as pharmaceuticals. Notably, nearly all manufacturing industries were disrupted—in part because of staff availability challenges, but also because of the frequent and often complete shutdown of national transportation systems. Interestingly, McKinsey reported that most companies responded to supply chain challenges by building inventories[83]—exactly the sort of issue that JIT supply chains were intended to avoid. Overall, however, supply chains emerged from the pandemic with not much significantly changed, other than the speed with which materials flowed globally.

Whether future supply chain shocks will benefit from improved supply chain management remains to be seen. What seems clear is that as the risks of extreme weather appear to be increasing, as well as increased water-related events such as drought and flooding, supply chain shocks are also likely to continue.

WATER RISKS

As acknowledged at the beginning of this book, water risks are pervasive throughout this taxonomy. Most of our discussion treats water as a natural capital risk, specifically in terms of its depletion risks, and therefore, most of the discussion on water can be found in Chapter 7. Here we simply note that there is a wide range of mitigation considerations relating to water usage—especially in those industries where water is an integral part of the industrial process. What is emerging as a fundamental mitigation challenge for heavy water users is reducing consumption; this is particularly the case in energy (especially utilities), chemicals, mining, and other resource-based enterprises, and, above all, agriculture. While some of the risks currently characteristic of the energy industry may diminish as a result of the general move to renewables, this transition will take time, and will likely cost someone money.

There are, in fact, mitigation issues associated with both water availability and wastewater disposal; reducing both will be a critical element to the transition strategies of a number of industries. As a case in point, as mentioned, the mining industry is facing increasing challenges in siting mines in areas where water availability is a concern. In some cases, firms face the prospect of expensive transport infrastructure, as water is extremely heavy. In addition, the industry also faces increasingly stringent requirements for wastewater disposal, which gets more complicated as mines themselves move to more water-scarce areas, where disposal may be as complicated as availability. The ongoing decline of numerous aquifers on a worldwide basis is not likely to help this situation.[84] CDP has recently introduced Water Watch, a tool that evaluates the water consumption trends for over 200 industrial activities, with a ranking of relative criticality of water use for each. And as we mentioned elsewhere, avoidance of these obligations (often through bankruptcy filings) is becoming a more critical issue in a number of energy-related industries, particularly the US shale gas industry.

LOSS OF SUBSIDY RISKS

We have included loss of subsidy risk as a type of mitigation risk, as well as a type of adaptation risk and a type of natural capital risk, simply because whatever their other impacts, subsidies generally enable economic producers and consumers to avoid paying the genuine economic costs of the extraction and usage of various resources. To the extent that subsidies contribute to financial indicators of interest to lenders, investors, or regulators—earnings and cash flows in particular—loss of these subsidies could prove to be financially punitive. The fossil fuel industry, for example, benefits from a variety of subsidies on a global basis, particularly in the United States, and also (obviously) in countries with state-owned oil companies. The assessment of the value of these subsidies can vary, depending on where the assessment comes from.[85] We itemized a number of larger government subsidy areas earlier, noting that assessments of the value of these subsidies vary, depending on their source.[86] We itemized a number of larger government subsidy areas in our earlier discussion of adaptation risks (Chapter 5: see "Loss of Subsidy Risks").

If governments are forced to become more aggressive on anthropogenic climate change, as they may well be, they will likely come under increasing pressure to remove a range of fossil fuel subsidies of various kinds. This process, in fact, was to have begun more robustly in some regions, but in actuality appears to have stalled globally. In some major countries, subsidies have not been cut meaningfully—oil and gas companies in the United States continue to enjoy a whole range of subsidies from governments at the federal and state levels.

Recently the administration of President Joe Biden has indicated it will propose reducing or eliminating a range of fossil fuel subsidies in the United States.[87] We would expect that this attempt will meet significant resistance from representatives of states with a significant fossil fuel dependence for economic activity. Most of these subsidies seem to be related to tax accounting rather than direct subsidies, and there is still some uncertainty over which particular subsidies will be targeted. Nonetheless, this proposal delivers, or starts to deliver, on the United States' promises at the Paris 2015 COP meeting to reduce subsidies. We will follow this proposal with interest.

As with the aforementioned subsidies to the fossil fuel industry, concerns can be raised about agricultural subsidies in areas where water depletion risks are increasing. Major agricultural countries and regions, including the United States, Canada, and the EU, have provided generous subsidies to the farming and food industry for decades, ranging from direct benefits to producers to support for other points of the agricultural supply chain.[88] This scenario is increasingly the case in developing countries, where major funding organizations have often subsidized the development and growth of industrial agriculture in countries as a tool for debt repayment.

Fossil fuels and agriculture are simply the two largest industrial beneficiaries of global subsidies. The actual range of sectors receiving subsidies, often on a site-specific basis, is quite large. A number of new mining projects of the past two decades have relied on generous subsidies, often for water in water-scarce regions.[89] Forest companies frequently receive allocations for below-cost access to government lands, as is the case in the United States.[90] Likewise, plant construction in the United States is often a vigorous competition between municipalities over who can offer the most generous tax subsidies.[91]

All of these industries would be penalized by an outright loss of subsidies, especially if the loss was immediate. Even if the subsidy loss was phased in, there would still be economic damage to many of these firms. In these instances, asset valuations as well as operating metrics could be severely affected. We believe the energy, utility, and natural resource industries remain high on the potential list of candidate industries for stranded assets. This has the consequence of highlighting the potential risks to a number of lenders and bond issuers.

Loss of subsidies also has the clear potential to create stranded assets. We believe the energy, utility, and natural resource industries remain high on the list of candidate industries for stranded assets, highlighting the potential risks to a number of lenders and bond issuers. There are other industries that are also vulnerable. The global automotive industry has some potential risks in this regard but often as a secondary consequence; in any event, it appears to be transitioning at an accelerating pace to a lower-carbon future, primarily through electric cars. In fact, in many ways, automotive subsidies are moving in the direction of supporting the electrification of transportation, as indicated by the increasing prevalence of charging stations provided by local and regional governments.

Finally, it is worth mentioning that in many parts of the world, consumer subsidies are highly prevalent. These are usually to subsidize the purchase of fuel or food that might otherwise be unaffordable for a significant portion of a country's population.

POTENTIAL COST OFFSETS

Note that in the discussion of mitigation risks, we have considered only risk assessment, saying nothing yet about possible offsets to diminish the scale and scope of these risks. For instance, regulatory and litigation risks in the pharmaceutical and tobacco industries have been offset to a considerable extent by the strong cash flow characteristics and liquidity of companies in these respective industries. Further, each continues to have substantial market opportunities on a global basis, which has allowed each industry to demonstrate continued sales growth. In the case of the tobacco industry, this global sales growth has continued in spite of demographic and public policy changes in their traditional western markets, including significant reputational risk and license-to-operate issues that have led to restrictions on consumers (e.g., to smoke cigarettes in public places).

However, many other industries lack these robust cash flow characteristics, and, moreover, are considerably more capital intensive than either pharmaceuticals or tobacco. Extractive industries such as agriculture, chemicals, mining, and forestry are already receiving more attention from regulators and governments, particularly in countries with more resource-based economies. For mining companies, for example, worker fatalities have become a more meaningful metric for governments, and in some cases this issue has led to social license-to-operate concerns for governments; this suggests an area of possible offset in the potential for companies to improve their social license-to-operate profiles.

We assume that interested parties that take the time to develop risk assessments based on (or similar to) the above categorizations will also be mindful of the potential positive offsets, which, of course, will vary by sector. Sometimes this risk reduction takes the form of direct action within the scope of the industry. This is generally true for companies whose main business is natural resource extraction of some sort, and those industries where physical risks are manifest. As a result, most of the resiliency measures described next relate to actions that can be taken to offset physical risks. Resiliency measures that have the potential to reduce transition risks will be considered elsewhere.

Examples of resiliency offsets include: (1) afforestation and reforestation, increasingly in conjunction with indigenous practice methods,[92] mainly for the paper and forest products industry; (2) land restoration, mainly for the mining and agriculture industries, but also for the oil and gas exploration and development sectors, and for specialized situations (e.g., Superfund sites in the United States); and (3) wetland restoration, primarily for property developers, agriculture, and local and sovereign governments.

Decarbonization

Perhaps the best example of potential offsets comes from the growing efforts to decarbonize production practices. While this approach can include reducing the impact of, say, supply chain issues on scope 3 emissions, the primary focus in most firms and industries is actually reducing GHG generation in the production process, be it ammonia, steel, or cement. As we discussed earlier, firms that rely on process heating for production of product will be facing higher production costs as carbon costs increase, with clear potential impacts in the absence of corresponding price increases. Improving the efficiency of heat generation is a clear way to reduce that potential impact.

In fact, it has been pointed out that decarbonization, both in energy and in industrial processes, often involves decarbonization of heat.[93] There are a number of potential pathways to do this, some of which are industry specific:

1. zero-carbon fuels,
2. zero-carbon heat sources,
3. electrification of heat, and
4. better heat management.

Not all of these are uniformly applicable to all heat-consuming industries. In fact, there is a wide variation of potential impacts, unsurprisingly. An alternative framework, categorizing decarbonization methods by type of efficiency, may be of greater interest to financial analysts, since it is a potential framework for actions that managements will likely be undertaking:

1. energy efficiency,
2. material efficiency,
3. industry-specific efficiency, and
4. power grid efficiencies.

Figure 6.11 provides a clearer illustration of the various proposed efficiencies that can be gained by various decarbonization methods in eight targeted industries.[94]

As indicated, some industries already tend to be more energy efficient than others, whereas some have considerable opportunity to improve material efficiency. The authors of this report suggest that substantial industry-specific efficiency gain can be obtained through the broad application of these measures.

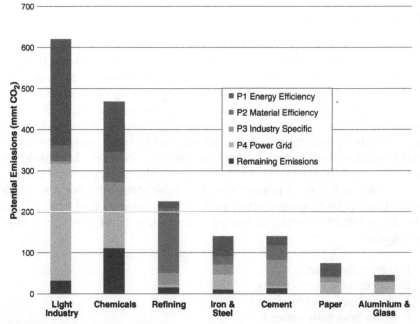

FIGURE 6.11 Industry-specific relative contributions to deep decarbonization of manufacturing (DDM) by type of industry action.
Source: Worrell et al., 2022 / Elsevier / CC BY 4.0.
Note: Remaining emissions in gray, reductions in color.

Note that will be a large and costly process for most firms in potentially affected industries. In some cases this will require significant capital expenditures, which may involve accessing capital markets. Cost estimates vary widely, of course, as do estimates of the relative efficiency of various approaches to decarbonization. Surprisingly, most of the literature on this subject is relatively sparse on cost estimates, although many of these come from firms themselves. A McKinsey estimate,[95] in the context of analyzing the cement, steel, ethylene, and ammonia sectors, concluded that:

> the investments needed to fully decarbonize the ammonia, cement, ethylene, and steel sectors will be substantial: $11 trillion to $21 trillion through 2050—0.4 to 0.8 percent of global GDP—depending on the price of zero-carbon electricity. Operating expenses constitute 50 to 60 percent of the cost, and capital expenditures, mainly for decarbonizing the cement sector, make up the rest.

There are, of course, a range of estimates for the potential costs of decarbonization, as well as the potential methods available to firms.

Note also that perhaps the most critical element of sector decarbonization will be the extent to which local energy and electricity costs are available. Since electricity consumption will increase strongly in any decarbonization scenario, this may require additional capacity to service this. If it's not available, it will need to be added to the energy infrastructure system. McKinsey has estimated that, depending on the decarbonization scenario being pursued by energy-intensive firms,

> An analysis of the effects of different electricity prices suggests that decarbonization would have an upward impact on the costs of the industrial products: cement doubling in price, ethylene seeing a price increase of ~40 to 50 percent, and steel and ammonia experiencing a ~5 to 35 percent increase in price.[96]

There is clearly much that is potentially adjustable in these numbers, but it does provide a framework for asking the relevant questions of whether this will involve new infrastructure at the electricity generators or at the consuming firms themselves, and whether these costs can be passed on to customers. The implication here is that moving to more carbon-efficient production systems in energy-intensive industries will clearly cost firms money. In all likelihood, for energy-intensive firms this will mainly manifest itself as higher running costs, particularly for power and electricity, and as necessary new plant, which would likely require capital markets access.

Carbon Capture and Storage and Bioenergy with Carbon Capture and Storage

We are not treating these processes as likely offsets in the near term, for several reasons. As discussed earlier, CCS and bioenergy with carbon capture and storage (BECCS) remain expensive and very energy intensive, and deployment on a large scale appears speculative at present. There are a number of practicalities that have yet to be resolved regarding their use, particularly near-term cost concerns.[97] We have discussed CCS in more detail earlier.

Enhanced Weathering

For some industries, enhanced weathering may provide some near-term protection against acute risks. For example, the world's largest petrochemical complex is located on the United States' southern coast in the Gulf of Mexico—Texas, Louisiana, and Mississippi. This is an area where hurricanes seem to be becoming more frequent and stronger, and the insurance industry has noticed this. Largely following the damage caused by Hurricane Katrina in 2005, the petrochemical industry has responded not by moving facilities elsewhere, which would be exorbitantly expensive, but by reinforcing the durability of the existing infrastructure. A number of US utilities located on shorelines have been pursuing similar efforts. We expect this will become a more common occurrence in areas prone to flooding as well, especially for larger infrastructure that will be difficult and expensive to move.

Business Profile Diversification

Business profile diversification is by far the resiliency measure with the broadest applicability: companies in virtually any industry can alter or modify their business profiles. We have seen a number of examples of this trend in the energy and utilities space over the past decade. For instance, utilities that used to rely on fossil fuels are increasingly expanding, usually by acquisition, into the renewable energy businesses. This trend is actually somewhat contrary to the overall trend of industry consolidation that has characterized business over the past several decades—certainly in the United States following the Reagan administration's relaxation of antitrust enforcement.[98] The net result of that change was to allow for much greater industry consolidation in industries ranging from telecommunications to food processing to steel production to chemicals. The entire range of US industry, in fact, has seen nonstop consolidation during this period.

However, a number of "brown" industries seem to be reconsidering this approach; it is not clear that being a large coal miner in this environment is necessarily a better option than being a small one. Likewise, being a large gas utility does not preclude being faced by the same regulatory and other issues that are being faced by smaller firms. Hence, two major US energy companies, Duke Energy and Dominion Energy, have announced plans to become carbon neutral by 2050,[99] following the cancellation of a major joint gas pipeline project. We expect more examples of this sort of corporate behavior. Pursuing zero-carbon policies is likely to have a positive impact on risk reduction for a number of industrial sectors, although it may have material near-term costs. It is also a popular strategy with investors.

As discussed previously, there is currently a lively discussion among regulators and investors, particularly in the EU, regarding whether the banking system should incorporate a "green supporting factor" or a "dirty penalizing factor." While such discussion lies outside the scope of this publication, we do note that the prospect of a wide range of incentives for mitigation efforts should not be discounted. The solar industry benefited from a range of subsidies for several years. The question of exactly what kinds of support should be available for companies engaged in transition efforts should receive more attention and research. In a similar vein, as noted earlier, the EU is actively considering developing applying a "green" tariff[100] for goods where non-EU producers gain some cost advantage by not having comparable climate regulations (and, by implication, costs) to those of the EU. The United States, among others, has pushed back on this proposal. Moreover, the recent "green" initiatives embodied in 2022's Inflation Reduction Act (IRA) in the United States present a clear challenge to the EU proposal, given the extent of subsidies the IRA encompasses. We expect this will become an increasingly lively topic of discussion going forward.

Implications for Select Sectors

It is difficult to envision an industry that will not be affected by mitigation efforts. However, not all industries will be comparably affected. The following summary of our mitigation risk discussion highlights some of the industries that might be most affected—the so-called "brown" industries. Many, but not all, are carbon intensive.[101] We anticipate that it is in these industries where scenario analysis will be most complicated and, perhaps, most urgent. These are also, incidentally, the sectors with the highest exposure to potential net-zero costs.

As a general rule of thumb, the issues here are straightforward. No matter what sort of risk we are assessing, the questions for investors and lenders are: (a) What will be the cost impacts of decarbonization measures and technologies? (b) How will they be paid for? and (c) Will those costs be passed on to customers?

Energy and Utilities

Oil and gas drilling continues to become increasingly problematic and occasionally more difficult, as evidenced by BP's loss (albeit short-lived) of its US offshore drilling permits following the Deepwater Horizon spill in 2010. A significant and increasing number of oil and gas exploration and distribution projects have been abandoned. Hydraulic fracturing, which has transformed the US oil and gas industry, has not been as warmly received elsewhere in the world—a number of countries (including France) have an outright ban on fracking, and wastewater concerns have been particularly problematic in many areas. Shell's ambitious attempts to drill in the Arctic seas never really garnered sufficient public (or government) support, leading the company to abandon the project after US $7 billion had been invested.[102] The potential for stranded assets here is considerable. Natural gas, like coal, now appears to be at increasing risk, with the potential for stranded assets from projects currently being planned to reach US $100 billion, according to a recent report.[103] Much of this has been elided by the recent strong performance of the industry following Russia's invasion of Ukraine; we would not expect this impact to be long-lived once the conflict is resolved.

In addition, may parts of the United States are now facing the potential for clean-ups of abandoned or expired oil and gas drilling sites. A recent report by Carbon Tracker has estimated that the costs of these clean-ups may be on the order of US $280 billion.[104] Clearly, these are costs that should be borne by the industry but in many cases may not be. Hence, we would expect considerable litigation over this issue.

On the one hand, the situations described above tend to apply only to large, well-capitalized global companies and there have been few specific credit rating downgrades, for example, as a result of any of these issues to date. On the other hand, some of these same companies have seen multiple credit downgrades over the past several years for a variety of reasons associated with commodity price volatility. We also note that although the social license-to-operate issue is most closely associated with extractive industries, it would not be surprising should highly water-intensive manufacturing industries need to address similar concerns. Previously mentioned reports from the TCFD have also discussed how some of the industry-specific financial impacts from climate change can be offset by what the TCFD refers to as "opportunities."[105]

We note that this heading encompasses a wide range of industries. Of particular interest are those sectors where the potential for stranded assets may increase. It is difficult to imagine that fossil fuel production will disappear, given its importance in the chemicals sector, even if its use in energy and transportation markets declines. However, a world with significantly lower fossil fuel volumes has the potential to create a surplus of infrastructure. In particular, pipeline companies appear to have some vulnerabilities in the event of declining volumes; for example, there may be too much pipeline capacity in the United States following a building boom in the late 2010s. If volumes will be declining longer term, some of this capacity will remain unused. Likewise, oilfield service companies may be facing a similar issue—if the number of producing wells declines over time, there will again be surplus capacity that will need to be taken out of the system somehow. All of this may be contingent on potential LNG exports from the United States, which are currently strong—the gas has to get to the terminal somehow. Europe, of course, has its own pipeline issues, although there are a lower number of pipelines (and increased political complexity, given the number of borders). Again, if volumes decline, there may be surplus capacity that will need to be taken out of the system.

There are, then, multiple areas where financial impacts may arise. First and foremost is the asset valuation issue—this is a sector with very significant prospects of stranded assets. In addition, the cost of funding the energy transition will be prodigious, and will entail significant accessing of capital markets (in the form of borrowing, or capital increases from additional equity). We suspect that traditional borrowing, through capital markets, may become more expensive for this sector, in part because of longer-term questions about credit trajectories, and in part because social license-to-operate concerns may reduce the range of potential buyers. Of possible concern for both investors and lenders is that much of what happens to this sector will be contingent on developments in renewable technologies, where costs have declined considerably more robustly than expected even five years ago. This problem creates some uncertainty about the length of lead times the fossil fuel industry in developed markets actually may have to manage an energy transition.

Note that this discussion mainly relates to fossil fuel use in energy and transportation sector. However, fossil fuels have a broad range of product categories, such as petrochemicals that provide a whole range of industrial and consumer products, many of which have no available substitute products at present. While we expect pressure on plastic demand to increase, we would not expect these markets to show comparable stress.

Note also that as power generation moves away from fossil fuels to more diverse and renewable (or low-emission) providers of power, mainly electricity, there will need to be very substantial investment in new facilities. This brings both stranded asset risks for existing facilities, and funding requirements for new plant, which may be considerable. This spending will encompass a range of subsectors: power generation, grid updating, and energy storage components of the system. It is difficult to envision this spending being funded from operating expenditures—we believe regular capital market access will be the preferred financing route here.

Transportation

Critically, both airlines and marine transport run entirely on fossil fuels and will therefore be exposed to eventual (and perhaps aggressive) regulation of CO_2 emissions. So far, neither of these industries has been addressing efficiency and emission standards congruent with a 2-degree climate goal. Airlines are at some risk here, depending on what sort of carbon tax or other regulation may be applied to the airline industry.[106] Like the maritime shipping and cruise industries, emissions are international, and are treated as such by the UN. In the aggregate, airlines actually generate less CO_2 than maritime shipping, although (prior to COVID-19, at any rate) air traffic is expected to grow robustly over the next several decades, according to both Boeing (+4.9% through 2034) and Airbus (+4.6% through 2034). However, fuel efficiency is increasing by only 1–2% annually. Nonetheless, we do not at present see significant stranded asset risk for airlines from increased carbon regulation, and in any event, the industry has been responding with more fuel-efficient aircraft and improved engine technology. Still, there is some risk here for additional carbon regulatory costs. We suspect at least some of this risk will be borne by the aircraft leasing companies. These companies own nearly half of the current operating fleet and may have little in the way of other assets. In the event of a significant deterioration of aircraft asset values resulting from more stringent carbon regulation, these firms may have some vulnerabilities. Airlines have the option of adjusting pricing (and thereby passing on increased regulatory costs to customers) more easily than aircraft leasing companies do. Further, although the aircraft industry has been engaged in an aggressive program to develop alternative aircraft fuels to reduce carbon emissions, these efforts have shown little success to date.

The global maritime shipping industry recently adopted a set of potentially significant emissions reduction targets. Maritime shipping, like the airline industry, is not domestically regulated, and generally adheres to regulations promulgated by the International Maritime Organization. The global shipping industry has for years been powered by bunker fuel, which is highly polluting, containing, among other things, high levels of sulfur.

Adopting the new regulations will be costly for most shippers. The International Maritime Organization (IMO) in 2020 passed regulations stipulating that ship fuel must contain no more than 0.5% sulfur. This is an important step, given the industry's track record of significant SO_2 emissions—and given the fact that it will increase fuel (and therefore overall shipping) costs. Once again, we find that environmentally and socially justifiable actions may inevitably have cost impacts—the result of internalizing what in the past were handled as externalities. More recently, Maersk, the world's largest shipper, announced a new fleet powered by biologically based methane, which it hopes will set the standard for the next generation of ships. Even if it does, this is a process that will likely take decades, and the size and scale required will be significant. While essential, this industry is likely to remain under cost pressure for a number of years.[107]

Rail transport remains the most efficient way to move goods around on land, and in some areas this applies to people as well.[108] The longer-term dynamics of the industry appear complicated. In the United States, for example, a very large country, while there are many products where land shipment by rail is by far the most economical, the industry has been losing share to the trucking industry for a number of years. In addition, there are some major mitigation and adaptation costs coming along. We discussed the industry's potential adaptation issues in Chapter 5 in terms of track location (and condition—hotter temperatures expand rails; in the United Kingdom, this has occasionally halted service). The main mitigation issue relates to engine efficiency—much of the global locomotive fleet needs upgrade or replacement, especially since much of the fleet remains diesel powered. Electrification of rail systems remains challenging because of the sheer length of potentially affected freight track. Urban electrification, where it has not already occurred, would appear to be straightforward, if somewhat costly for developing markets.

Automotive

The global automotive industry has some potential risks with respect to mitigation. The industry seems to be slowly transitioning to a lower-carbon future. The complexity of this transition will be significant in its own right,[109] irrespective of government actions, both to original equipment manufacturers and their suppliers all along the value chain. For one thing, many government policies will render much of the existing global manufacturing stock obsolete over the next several decades, to be replaced by electric vehicle manufacturing plants and equipment. This trend is highly likely to have significant balance sheet impacts for firms, although these will likely be stretched out over time. In addition, electric vehicles involve simpler assembly than that involved in internal combustion engine autos. While both electricity and labor costs can be expected to decline as this shift occurs, the issue of labor will remain high on everyone's agenda for the simple reason that fewer workers will be needed. This has the potential to be an expensive issue for the industry. However, the industry benefits from having a fairly clear idea of where it needs to get to—although the timing of reaching this objective still appears to be a moving target.

Not the least of the potential problems facing the industry is the fact that electric vehicles, while in theory are simpler to assemble, simply cost more to make and to buy, at present, and this is likely to remain the case for some time until a range of costs decline. Given the volatility of some critical raw materials—mainly cobalt, lithium, and nickel (some of which comes from Russia)—for batteries and electric motors, price stability may take some time to emerge.[110] Figure 6.12 presents cost data compiled by Oliver Wyman, comparing real 2020 costs with expected 2030 costs.

Thus, the more automakers electrify, the more they are increasing their own costs, which will need to be passed on to consumers. Consumers appear

VEHICLE COST DEVELOPMENT
Battery electric vehicles are expected to almost close the gap to internal combustion engine powered vehicles by 2030

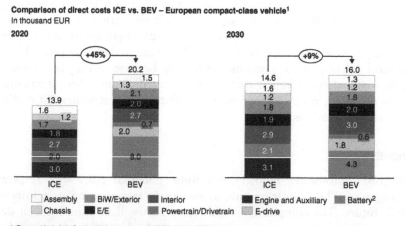

Comparison of direct costs ICE vs. BEV – European compact-class vehicle[1]
In thousand EUR

1. Does not include indirect costs (e.g. ramp-up, CAPEX, relative SG&A etc.)
2. Equals a 50 kw/h battery with 160 €/kWh in 2020 and Equals with 85 €/kWh in 2030

FIGURE 6.12   Electric car costs will not fall in line with combustion engines until 2030. *Source:* INSIDEEVs, September 2020. https://insideevs.com/news/444542/evs-45-percent-more-expensive-make-ice/.

willing to accept these higher costs because of expected low operating costs (assuming sufficient charging availability). But the industry may have to adjust to a different cost structure over the next decade.

As we mentioned previously, there are a number of potentially interesting supply chain risks deriving from climate impacts. The auto industry is one of the best examples of this complexity[111]—the supply chain here is prodigiously complicated, with significant manufacturers throughout. This means there are significant potential exposures all along the supply chain as well, including to climate-exacerbated natural events such as extreme weather and flooding.

Chemicals

As one of the world's largest industries, it is not surprising that decarbonization issues in this sector are complicated.[112] For one thing, this is the industry that has brought us plastics, which have generated their own kind of problems for society—plastic appears to be everywhere, including the deepest part of the oceans, the Marianas Trench,[113] and the long-term health and environmental impacts here are still not well understood. There are a number of factors at play here, including the fact that there are a range of chemicals necessary for the processing of materials essential to renewable power sources.

There are, we believe, three general areas of climate risks relevant to the chemicals industry. First is the fact that, like many other manufactured materials, chemicals are often subject to processing constraints. Moreover, these will largely be determined by the overall types of chemicals at issue. The organic/inorganic distinction may be overly general, but it fits. About 50% of chemical products are derived from petroleum, mainly from processing of the ethylene chain, from which we derive a wide range of necessary products. But processing methods may vary widely, although virtually all of them involve process heating as part of the production equation.

And there is a *lot* of processing—chemical production represents the largest use of energy in the industrial sector, so a critical issue for the industry is decarbonization. In fact, the chemicals industry generates more GHG than the transportation or buildings sectors. The carbon footprint here is, as a consequence, major, and has been decades in the making. While natural gas (in the United States, at least) remains at low prices, regulatory costs remain manageable in many chemical sectors in the United States. However, the costs of processing various products are likely to increase and the regulatory infrastructure becomes more complicated, especially if carbon pricing measures are more robustly implemented.

There are a range of technological solutions proffered on this subject, particularly relating to feedstock substitution and recycling at the production level, but these appear to have had only a moderate impact at best in terms of GHG reduction. Altering chemical production methods is not at all straightforward. More relevant have been energy efficiency gains in production processes, where the industry has, overall, been effective—particularly in regulated markets such as the EU and the United States. In fact, GHG reductions in the EU have been so robust—a 58% decline from 1990 to 2017, according to the European Environment Agency—that continued efficiency improvements are likely to be at a slower pace. Nonetheless, we would expect that the industry will remain under regulatory pressure to continue to monitor and address GHG emissions, particularly Level 3 emissions, which can be significant. While this pressure is already significant in the United States and the EU, we would expect more rapid adoption of stringent regulations in other parts of the world—India and China in particular—that will likely affect global pricing of a range of chemical commodities. This will be especially true in regions that continue to rely heavily on coal for energy production.

Second, the chemical industry is already heavily regulated as a result of the potential (and all too frequently, actual) range of potential discharge of harmful products into the environment. In the United States, the Clean Air Act, and Clean Water Act, created and passed in the 1960s and 1970s were the direct results of chemical pollution, particularly of waterways. While these problems have largely diminished, they have not disappeared completely, particularly in developing markets. Since chemical waste disposal almost inevitably involves water, water constraints may become an increasing concern—especially in areas where competition for water resources is increasing.

Moreover, the physical location of the plants themselves can generate its own set of risks. Chemical plants use lots of water in the production of materials, so there is a natural trend to site these along sources of water—much as the utility industry has traditionally done. Additionally, this siting trend often leads to exposure to extreme weather impacts—it has been noted that there are nearly 900 chemical facilities of some sort within 50 miles of the US Gulf Coast. This has led to concerns over the potential vulnerabilities of these plants to extreme weather. Chemical plants are not the only issue of concern. These concerns also include the status of numerous hazardous waste sites in the United States and Europe, which all too often were conveniently located in coastal regions such as wetlands. Potential costs in dealing with these issues and extreme weather becomes more certain but unclear, but, like other climate-related costs that will be coming along, these may be significant. The main issue is who will bear those costs.

Third, there are some product categories that may be at outright risk. As mentioned earlier (and discussed in more detail in Chapter 7) agricultural chemicals pose some particular risks.[114] These are widely used globally, transforming global agriculture. From an investor point of view, there are two potential risk issues of concern. First, manufacturing ammonia, the primary ingredient of agricultural fertilizer, involves prodigious amounts of both heat and water. Second, it is becoming increasingly clear that agricultural chemicals are heavily implicated in biodiversity loss, among other negative environmental effects. As concerns about biodiversity increase (as we discuss in Chapter 7) we suspect these concerns will become of greater interest to investors and lenders, to say nothing of public policy makers. Whether this puts an entire category of chemical products at risk is arguable, but at the very least there are likely to be some cost implications in the sector in response to potentially increased regulatory pressure.

We noted earlier that litigation related to climate factors is increasing. We see no reason why the chemicals industry should be insulated from this trend—there is already litigation on the books relating to plastic pollution, and the failure of the industry to develop targeted and effective recycling measures. We also expect targeted consumer behavior. No one is likely to be boycotting ethylene, but plastic bags, for example, and consumer packaging already are easy targets. Many retailers have shifted to paper bags as a result, and consumer products companies have made significant changes to product packaging.

Building Products

Cement is problematic.[115] The cement industry generates anywhere from 4% to 7% of global GHG emissions, depending on what source you use. And like other industries that rely on process heating for manufacturing the product in question, this alone contributes significant amounts of CO_2. However, the cement industry faces an additional problem. This is the fact that the very chemical process that produces cement in and of itself—the clinker process, that combines limestone with silicates—generates CO_2 as a byproduct. There is no substitute for this process in the manufacturing of cement. As a result, the challenge facing the industry is twofold—reducing GHG associated with the production process itself, and reducing GHG deriving from the energy consumed in making the product.

The complexity of this process can be best understood in the context of a visualization of how cement is manufactured, helpfully provided by

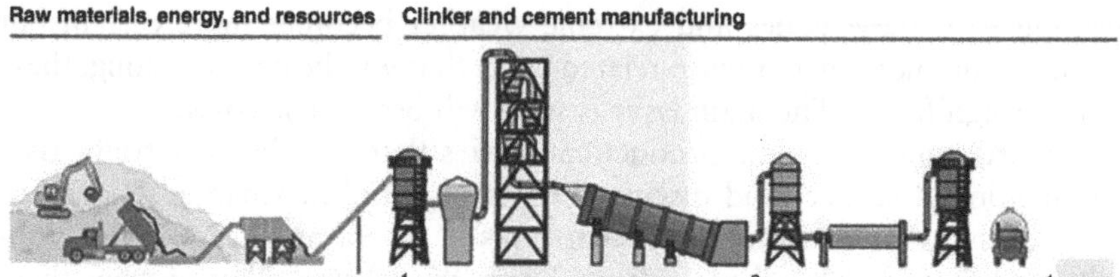

Raw materials, energy, and resources   Clinker and cement manufacturing

	Quarry	Crusher	Transport[1]	Raw mill	kiln and preheater/ precalcinator[2]		Cooler[3]	Cement mill	Logistics[4]	Total
Energy, megajoule/ton	40	5	40	100	3,150		160	285	115	3,895
CO_2, kilogram/ton	3	1	7	17	479 Calcination process	319 Fossil fuels	28	49	22	925

[1]Assumed with 1KWh/t/100m.
[2]Assumed global average, data from the Global Cement and Concrete Association, Getting the Numbers Right 2017.
[3]Assumed reciprocating grate cooler with 5kWh/t clinker.
[4]Assumed lorry transportation for average 200km.

FIGURE 6.13   How we get cement.
Source: Czigler, Thomas et al. *Laying the Foundation for Zero-carbon Cement,* McKinsey & Company, May 2020.

McKinsey in a recent report.[116] It is often easy to generalize about the ease with which carbon reductions can be achieved. In the cement industry, unsurprisingly, this process is complicated by the number of steps in the process, as shown in Figure 6.13.

Note that by far the most energy-intensive part of this process is in the clinker process. This is the part of the process that is the most resistant to outright improvement, although proposals for altering the raw material mix are presently receiving considerable attention.

The industry has made some progress in both of the aforementioned areas, but overall CO_2 levels have not declined. In part this reflects the fact that overall cement consumption continues to rise, especially in Asia. One issue appears to be that there are limits to the extent to which the clinker process itself can be economized. There are other approaches that are all being investigated at present: alternative fuel mixes (from increasing municipal waste, for example). It should be noted that cement is an industry where CCS is often trotted out as a potential offset and a way for dealing with these significant amounts of CO_2. The problem here is cost, as the authors of a recent study report:[117]

> The main limitation of the implementation of CCS is its very high cost. The cost of investment is 2 times higher than that of a new cement plant (approx. 150 Mio € for 1 million tonne annual capacity). If these technologies are to be applied at a large scale, the power consumption

would increase drastically. The requirement for high amounts of electrical energy also has implications for both the cost and CO_2 mitigation potential as it heavily depends on the decarbonisation of electricity.

As a result, there are several initiatives under way that are investigating decarbonization without CCS as an integral component, but results here are preliminary at best. This is a good caveat to CCS proposals in many other industries as well—reducing the cost of heat is critical. Cement, like steel, is manufactured globally—and generally tends to rely on external power sources. Given the global distribution of cement plants, ensuring comparability in the decline of process costs may be challenging.

This raises a further concern with regards to the global cement industry. Overall demand trends have been strong for decades, and these would appear to be set to remain so for the foreseeable future. However, as we have mentioned repeatedly, the extent to which land use changes have contributed to global heating has generally been unaddressed in favor of GHG reduction policies—but this appears to be changing. And one impact of this expansion of emphasis has to do with land use changes themselves—in particular, how much land has been covered over by a range of materials, principally cement.

While the overall land surface that has been covered by cement and other materials is relatively small—probably less than 1% of the total land mass—paving represents a significant heat enhancer in urban environments, which are mostly paved by something. Aside from deforestation for agriculture, such paving activity has often been a significant contributor to global heating in select areas, mainly urban environments—the heat island effect that raises local temperatures significantly higher than in surrounding regions. Since urban areas are where most of humanity is increasingly living, there are meaningful consequences for human health as global heating continues. In addition, roads are a major use of cement (often in the form of concrete), and motor transportation looks set to continue, even if the fleet is electrified. These trends will be an area of interest to policymakers, especially in light of increasing concerns over biodiversity loss.

Climate risks in the forest products industry are a bit simpler. First, as we discuss in Chapter 7, deforestation continues to occur in a number of areas. While afforestation efforts have had some meaningful local impacts, from an industry perspective these have been insufficient for replacing lost forest (and with negative biodiversity impacts to boot). Moreover, paper and forest products in general, including some important for the construction industry, need some degree of treatment and processing, which means water—many such plants are located on sources of water, needed for both supply and disposal. While it has generally been true that forests are generally found in northern and temperate regions where water availability traditionally has been a concern, this shows signs of changing through deforestation impacts and the gradual shift of the temperature zone northwards, both of which may exacerbate competition for water resources in regions where such competition is likely to increase. Note that increased deforestation generally leads to higher temperatures in deforested regions. The way to forestall this is to stop deforestation. There are a number of proposals about how to do that, the principal one being governments or other private parties buying the remaining forests.

Metals and Mining

License-to-operate risks have become increasingly apparent in the mining industry. Barrick Gold was forced to close its Pascua-Lama mine project in 2014 following a US $8 billion investment, US $6 billion of which had to be written down. The closure reflected Barrick's inability to convince local and national regulators that it had an adequate water pollution plan regarding groundwater pollution—but it also seems plausible that Barrick essentially forfeited its license-to-operate in the region through a series of misjudgments. Elsewhere, Barrick admitted in September 2015 that the amount of arsenic spilled in an Argentine river was considerably higher than initially stated. We note in passing that Barrick is now the object of an investor class action in the United States over misrepresentation of developments at Pascua-Lama. Furthermore, Barrick is hardly the only mining company to experience such problems. Newmont Mining's Conga project (partially funded by the International Finance Corporation) was indefinitely halted in 2014 because of community protests, and its reopening remains uncertain. Freeport-McMoRan's Grasberg Mine project in Indonesia has suffered repeated setbacks. More recently, Rio Tinto's knowing destruction of an Aboriginal gravesite has generated some genuine license-to-operate risks for the company in Australia, leading the company's CEO to resign.[118] And at the time of writing, a court in Australia struck down the development of one of the world's largest coal mines, partly as a result of potential climate impacts.[119] We expect such litigation trends to continue. We also expect the real costs of mining in general to increase, affecting margins, as price pressures on products will continue to increase on the regulatory front.

We note that the steel industry, like other process heating–dependent industries, is currently pursuing a range of decarbonization methods. Steel is integral not only to current infrastructure profiles, but also to expected adaptation initiatives going forward. Reducing its carbon impact in the manufacturing process, which is considerable, is an active target among steelmakers and public policy makers. There are actually a number of potential measures that can be adopted in the manufacturing process, depending on the sort of technology being used to produce the steel in the first place, and depending on a variety of scenarios for steel demand. That there will be demand there is no doubt. As is usually the case in undertaking this analysis, the question for investors and lenders is what will be the cost impacts of decarbonization technologies, how will they be paid for, and will those costs be passed on to customers. At bottom, though, the basic decision for steelmakers will be whether to replace oxygen furnaces with electric arc furnace technologies, or else to continue with existing plant and scale up CCS. Both of these options are expensive, and will likely involve capital market access. Margins will clearly be affected. Whatever technologies are adopted, steel production costs will be increasing;[120] whether (and how) these might be passed on to customers is an open question at present.

Renewables Technologies

By this, we simply mean the potential risks associated with the manufacturing of critical components of solar cells and wind turbine engines, as well as broader applications such as communications equipment. Like many other industries discussed here, the technology sector (broadly defined) requires components that involve some serious water use in the manufacturing process. We believe this is an issue that may well affect the siting of new semiconductor fabrication plants, for example. More to the point, many of the mineral components found in modern technological devices—phones and computers, for example—require significant energy (and water) for production.

Additionally, the process of extracting the required minerals is not necessarily a "green" one. The range of minerals required for clean energy technologies, for example, is significant[121]—comparable, in fact, to the range of minerals found in your phone, as shown in Figure 6.14.

We would not expect the current cost structure of the extraction of these minerals to decline—in fact, the reverse appears more likely to be the case. Additionally, the mining waste issue mentioned elsewhere in this book is likely to be exacerbated by the interesting mix of mining waste from these particular minerals.

In the event of shortages, perhaps from supply chain disruption (as we have seen) there may be short-term pricing impacts. Over the longer term, however, much will depend on the ease or difficulty with which such minerals can be extracted from current locations. In terms of raw material availability, we discuss this issue Chapter 7—specifically in terms of potential depletion concerns. We would note that the manufacturing processes

The rapid deployment of clean energy technologies as part of energy transitions implies a significant increase in demand for minerals

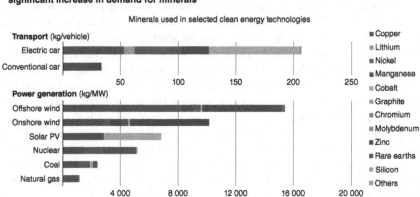

FIGURE 6.14 Metals used in clean energy technologies.
Source: Lawton et al., 2021. /https://www.iea.org/reports/the-role-of-critical-minerals-in-clean-energy-transitions. Last accessed December 12, 2022 /

associated with these products, and technology components in general, are very thirsty processes. Semiconductor fabrication facilities consume lots of water. Complementing this issue, both the disposal of mining wastewater and the disposal of manufacturing waste also raise critical water issues.

A COMMENT ON TIPPING POINTS

Although we mentioned the usefulness of predicting tipping points early on, the lack of discussion of these with reference to physical and adaptation risks should be telling. As the old saying goes, "prediction is very difficult, especially of the future." Ironically, given the sheer breadth of the range of potential climate risks under the mitigation risk rubric, many of these bring with them the fact that potential tipping points may be easier to identify than in other risk domains. This unusual situation derives from the fact that a number of these risks, particularly those on the regulatory and litigation side, are risks ultimately contingent on public policy discussions and implementation. And these will carry a time (and often a scope) horizon. In fact, in many cases—chemical regulation in the European chemical industry, for example—the industry has been involved in the negotiations establishing revisions to existing regulations. This has also been the case in the processes and discussions associated with determining a potential global carbon price—if one is ever achieved, its introduction will be telegraphed well in advance to affected parties.

NOTES

1. There may very well be some on the buy-side, but these are generally not publicly available.
2. See, for example, Donovan, Charles, Milica Fomicov, and Anastasiya Ostrovnaya, *Transition Finance: Managing Funding to Carbon-intensive Firms*. London: CCFI, September 2020.
3. We note that the Energy Transition has received considerable attention over the past few years, which is not surprising given its importance to efforts to reduce GHG growth. However, we believe this should be regarded as just one component of a broader transition of economic activity—any "transition" that does not encompass the broaching of the Boundary conditions that support planetary life, or even a simple metric such as topsoil loss, really shouldn't be called a transition. One of the most complete discussions of these risks, with detailed discussions and suggestions regarding how to assess them, was recently published by Natixis (Merle, Cedric and Orith Azoulay. *Brown Industries: The Transition Tightrope*. Paris: Natixis, 2021). While not intended as a risk taxonomy, the report contains some of the best discussion of transition risks we have come across.
4. Flowers, Simon. *Who Will Fund the Energy Transition?* The Edge, Wood McKenzie, November 27, 2020.
5. Mazengarb, Michael. *Five Years After Carbon Price Repeal, Australia Remains in Policy Abyss*. Renew Economy, July 17, 2019.
6. Khan, Mehreen. How the EU Plans to Reshape Its Economy to Limit Climate Change. *The Financial Times*, July 14, 2021.
7. The specific reasons and mechanisms underlying these potential increases in industry and company costs, especially in resource-dependent industries, are discussed in detail in Chapter 7.
8. IPCC, 2019: Summary for Policymakers. In *Climate Change and Land: An IPCC Special Report on Climate Change, Desertification, Land Degradation, Sustainable Land Management, Food Security, and Greenhouse Gas Fluxes in Terrestrial Ecosystems*. Edited by P. R. Shukla et al. Cambridge and New York: Cambridge University Press, 2019; Fujimori, S. et al. Land-based Climate Change Mitigation Measures Can Affect Agricultural Markets and Food Security. *Nature Food* 3: 110–121, 2022.
9. Mazengarb, Michael. *Five Years After Carbon Price Repeal, Australia Remains in Policy Abyss*. Renew Economy, July 17, 2019.
10. Burke, Josh. *What Is Net Zero?* Grantham Research Institute on Climate Change and the Environment, London School of Economics, April 30, 2019.
11. Murray, James. *Net Zero Faces Fierce Criticism*. GreenBiz, May 10, 2021; Buck, Holly Jean. *Ending Fossil Fuels: Why Net Zero Is Not Enough*. London: Verso Books, 2021.

12. de Pee, Arnout et al. *Decarbonization of Industrial Sectors: The Next Frontier.* McKinsey and Company, July 2018.
13. Carbone, Sante et al. *The Low-carbon Transition, Climate Commitments and Firm Credit Risk.* European Central Bank, Working Paper Series No. 2631, December 2021.
14. Eurostat. Publications Office of the European Union, Luxembourg, 2011.
15. We note that process heating in industry is often agnostic as to the energy source of the required heat. In some cases, this is derived from electricity consumption internally or from elsewhere. In other cases, it derives from on-site power generation, usually directly from fossil fuels, or from steam. See, for example, Bellevrat, Elie and Kira West. *Clean and Efficient Heat for Industry.* International Energy Agency Commentary, January 23, 2018.
16. Which include the consumption of artificial fertilizers, which not only have significant agricultural impacts both positive and negative but also are hugely energy-intensive to manufacture.
17. McKinley, G. A. et al. External Forcing Explains Recent Decadal Variability of the Ocean Carbon Sink. *AGU Advances* 1(2), 2019.
18. Fleming, Sean. *Methane Levels Are Increasing—and Scientists Aren't Sure Why,* World Economic Forum, March 11, 2019; McSweeney, Robert. *Methane Emissions from Fossil Fuels "Severely Underestimated."* Carbon Brief, February 19, 2020.
19. Rockström, J. et al. A Safe Operating Space for Humanity. *Nature* 461: 472–475, 2009.
20. It is important to distinguish between naturally occurring sources of GHGs as opposed to human-made sources. There are four naturally occurring GHGs: water vapor, CO_2, N_2O, and CH_4. Other GHGs are entirely the result of industrial activities, but are less relevant (i.e., less common) than CO_2 or CH_4.
21. Carbon Disclosure Project. *Sector Insights: What Is Driving Climate Change Action in the World's Largest Companies?* Global 500 Climate Change Report 2013, September 2013.
22. Lilliston, Ben. *Latest Agricultural Emissions Data Show Rise of Factory Farms.* Institute for Agriculture and Trade Policy, March 26, 2019.
23. Environmental Protection Agency. *Draft Inventory of US Greenhouse Gas Emissions and Sinks, 1990–2017,* 2019.
24. International Energy Agency. *Methane Emissions from the Energy Sector Are 70% Higher Than Official Figures.* February 23, 2022. See the IES Global Methane Tracker report, 2022.
25. As has recently been pointed out, fracking has been a money-losing activity for most of its lifetime. See Wallace-Wells, David. Hardly Anyone Talks About How Fracking Was an Extraordinary Boondoggle. *The New York Times,* July 27, 2022.
26. Harvey, Fiona. Shipping Fuel Regulation to Cut Sulphur Levels Comes into Force. *The Guardian,* January 1, 2020.
27. Apuzzo, Matt and Sarah Hurtes. Tasked to Fight Climate Change, a Secretive UN Agency Does the Opposite. *The New York Times,* June 3, 2021.

28. Tongia, Rahul. *Net Zero Carbon Pledges Have Good Intentions. But They Are Not Enough.* Brookings, October 25, 2021.
29. Stokes, Leah C. and Matto Mildenberger. The Trouble with Carbon Pricing. *Boston Review*, September 24, 2020.
30. Colmer, Jonathan et al. *Does Pricing Carbon Mitigate Climate Change? Firm-level Evidence from the European Union Emissions Trading Scheme.* CEPR Discussion Paper No. DP16982, January 1, 2022.
31. Cui, Bei et al. *The Real Carbon Price Index,* Monash University, 2021.
32. Ryan, Deb. *Guest Opinion: A Heightened Focus on CO2 Emissions Stokes Interest in the Carbon Markets.* S&P Global Ratings, September 21, 2021.
33. World Bank. *State and Trends of Carbon Pricing 2022.* Washington, DC: World Bank, 2022.
34. Parry, Ian, Simon Black, and James Roaf. *Proposal for an International Carbon Price Floor Among Large Emitters.* International Monetary Fund, June 18, 2021.
35. Hook, Leslie, Max Seddon, and Nastassia Astrasheuskaya. EU Plan for World's First Carbon Border Tax Provokes Trading Partners. *The Financial Times,* July 16, 2021.
36. Morris, Adele. *The Many Benefits of a Carbon Tax.* Brookings, February 26, 2013.
37. Romel, Valentina. IMF urges Europe to Pass on Energy Costs to Consumers. *The Financial Times,* August 3, 2022.
38. Lex. *Carbon Pricing: Twists on the Winding Road to Net Zero. The Financial Times,* December 29, 2021.
39. Parry, Ian. *What Is Carbon Taxation? Carbon Taxes Have a Central Role in Reducing Greenhouse Gases.* International Monetary Fund, June 2019.
40. Liboreiro, Jorge. COP27: *EU left "Disappointed" by Lack of Ambition in Final Deal, Calling It a "Small Step Forward."* Euronews, November 23, 2022.
41. Jan Ahrens, personal communication.
42. Shankelman, Jess. *Bank of England Tells Banks to Brace for Sky-High Carbon Price.* Bloomberg Green, January 14, 2021.
43. Executive Summary: *Energy Efficiency Progress Recovers in 2021 but Needs to Double for Net Zero by 2050.* International Energy Administration, Energy Efficiency 2021.
44. Finkelstein, Jason, David Frankel, and Jesse Noffsinger. Fully Decarbonizing the Power Industry. *McKinsey Quarterly,* 2020; Cleary, Kathryne and Karen Palmer. *Renewables 101: Integrating Renewable Energy Resources into the Grid.* Resources for the Future, April 15, 2020.
45. Moore's Law, named after Gordon Moore who first proposed it in 1965, states that the number of semiconductors on a square inch of an integrated circuit had doubled every year since 1958, and that this would continue for another ten years. Moore later changed this period of doubling to eighteen months rather than one year. In fact, it held up until the 2010s. While solar cells have certainly increased in efficiency over the past two decades, Moore's Law does not appear to apply to this domain.

46. Vaughan, Adam. Most Major Carbon Capture and Storage Projects Haven't Met Targets. *New Scientist*, September 1, 2022; Food and Water Watch. *Capture: Billions of Federal Dollars Poured into Failure*, September 27, 2022; Jacobs, Justin. "Put Up or Shut Up": Can Big Oil Prove the Case for Carbon Capture? *The Financial Times*, October 20, 2022.

47. McKinsey Global Institute. *Resource Revolution: Meeting the World's Energy, Material, Food, and Water Needs*, November 2011; *Resource Revolution: Tracking Global Commodity Markets*, September 2013.

48. Commodity Futures Trading Corporation. *Managing Climate Risk in the US Financial System*, September 9, 2020.

49. Amadeo, Kimberly. *Oil Price Forecast 2020–2050*. The Balance, October, 6, 2020.

50. Raval, Anjli. Oil Companies Face Up to Plunging Asset Values. *The Financial Times*, July 2, 2020.

51. Berwyn, Bob. *Five Years after Paris, Where Are We Now? Facing Urgent Choices*. Climate Home News, December 23, 2020.

52. Wallace-Wells, David. Hardly Anyone Talks About How Fracking Was an Extraordinary Boondoggle. *The New York Times*, July 27, 2022.

53. Charleton, Emma. *Who's Promised Net Zero, and Who's Likely to Get There*. World Economic Forum, December 13, 2019.

54. Harvey, Fiona. Electric Cars Produce Less CO_2 than Petrol Vehicles, Study Confirms. *The Guardian*, March 23, 2020.

55. Henry, Ian. *EVs Are Transforming the Automotive Workforce as Well as the Market*. Automotive Manufacturing Solutions, December 6, 2019.

56. Birkett, Ed and William Nicolle. *Charging Up: Policies to Deliver a Comprehensive Network of Public EV Chargepoints*. Policy Exchange, February 2, 2021.

57. Boucher, Julien and Damien Friot. *Primary Microplastics in the Oceans: A Global Evaluation of Sources*. International Union for Conservation of Nature and Natural Resources, Gland Switzerland, 2017.

58. Ellis-Petersen, Hannah. Treated like Trash: South-East Asia Vows to Return Mountains of Rubbish from West. *The Guardian*, May 28, 2019.

59. Terazono, Emiko. Big Meat: Facing Up to the Demands for Sustainability. *The Financial Times*, January 17, 2021.

60. Piper, Kelsey. *The Rise of Meatless Meat, Explained*. Vox, February 20, 2020.

61. As Michael Mann has noted, this is mostly because of the sizable impact of North American consumption.

62. Sharma, Shefali. *The Meaty Side of Climate Change*. Heinrich Boll Foundation, January 9, 2018.

63. Note that, as is often the case, what appear to be simple issues are actually more complicated. For example, there does not appear to be any solution to topsoil regeneration that does not involve animals.

64. As did comments from Nestle's CEO that some observers interpreted as implying that water should not be considered a human right—what he actually said was arguing water was a human right was an extreme position. The company later clarified this—he does believe it's a human right after all.

65. Deloitte. *Reputation@Risk: 2014 Global Survey on Reputational Risk*, October 20, 2014.

66. Hellerstein, Erica and Ken Fine. *Million Tons of Feces and an Unbearable Stench: Life Near Industrial Pig Farms. The Guardian*, September 20, 2017.

67. Buhr, Bob. *ESG for Credit Investors: Operational, Climate and Natural Capital Risks.* London: Société Générale, 2014.

68. Kaminski, Isabella. Dutch Supreme Court Upholds Landmark Ruling Demanding Climate Action. *The Guardian*, December 20, 2019.

69. Rankin, Jennifer. *Belgium's Climate Failures Violate Human Rights, Court Rules. The Guardian*, June 18, 2021.

70. Gayle, Damien. Court Orders UK Government to Explain How Net Zero Policies Will Reach Targets. *The Guardian*, July 18, 2022.

71. Ekardt, Felix and Katherine Heyl. The German Constitutional Verdict Is a Landmark in Climate Legislation. *Nature Climate Change* 12: 607703, August 2022.

72. Smith, Jamie. Australia Faces Legal Challenge Over Bonds' Climate Risks. *The Financial Times*, July 22, 2020.

73. Schwartz, John. New York Loses Climate Change Fraud Case Against Exxon Mobil. *The New York Times*, December 10, 2019.

74. Reuters. *New York City Sues Exxon, BP, Shell in State Court Over Climate Change*, April 22, 2021.

75. Raymond, Nate. *Exxon Must Face Massachusetts Climate Change Lawsuit, Court Rules.* Reuters, May 24, 2022.

76. Golnaraghi, Maryam et al. *Climate Change Litigation—Insights into the Evolving Global Landscape.* Zurich: The Geneva Association, April 2021; Setzer, Joanna and Catherine Higham, *Global Trends in Climate Change Litigation: 2022 Snapshot.* Grantham Research Institute on Climate Change, London School of Economics, June 2022.

77. Keck, Kristy. *Big Tobacco: A History of Its Decline.* CNN, June 19, 2009.

78. Thomas, Helen. No One Is Ready for the Rising Tide of Climate Litigation. *The Financial Times*, May 26, 2022.

79. World Economic Forum. *Building Resilience in Supply Chains*, January 2013.

80. Berry, Alex. *Taiwan Drought Could Threaten Global Supply of Electronic Chips.* Deutsche Welle, May 27, 2021.

81. Yatsovskaya, Katya, Jagsit Singh Srai, and Mukesh Kuimar. Local Water Stress Impacts on Global Supply Chains: Network Configuration and Natural Capital Perspectives. *Journal of Advances in Management Research*, 13(3), September 2016.

82. Gross, Daniel. *The Ash Economy: How the Volcano Eruption Exposed the Vulnerability of the Global Supply Chain.* Slate, April 23, 2010.

83. Alicke, Knut, Ed Barriball, and Vera Trautwein. *How Covid-19 Is Reshaping Supply Chains.* McKinsey and Company, November 23, 2021.

84. See our discussion of aquifer depletion elsewhere in this volume.

85. US Department of Energy, Energy Information Administration. *World Energy Outlook*, 2014; International Monetary Fund. *Energy Subsidy Reform: Lessons and Implications*, January 2013; OECD. *Inventory of Estimated Budgetary Support and Tax Expenditures for Fossil Fuels 2013*, 2012.

86. US Department of Energy, Energy Information Administration. *World Energy Outlook*, 2014; International Monetary Fund. *Energy Subsidy Reform: Lessons and Implications*, January 2013; OECD. *Inventory of Estimated Budgetary Support and Tax Expenditures for Fossil Fuels 2013*, 2012.

87. Crowley, Kevin. *Biden Tax Plan Targets Fossil Fuel Subsidies Worth $35 Billion*, Bloomberg Green, 7 April 2021.

88. Bove, Tristan. *The Cost of Subsidizing Agriculture*. Earth.org, February 12, 2021.

89. Toledano, Perrine and Clara Roorda. *Leveraging Mining Investments in Water Infrastructure for Broad Economic Development: Models, Opportunities and Challenges*. New York: Columbia Center on Sustainable Investment, March 2014.

90. Talberth, John and Ernest Niemi. *Environmentally Harmful Subsidies in the US. Issue #1: The Federal Logging Program*. Center for Sustainable Economy, May 2019.

91. Chernicoff, David. *US Tax Breaks, State by State: Which US States Are Offering Tax Incentives to Attract Data Center Investment?* DCD, January 6, 2016. Note that this article only concerns tax breaks for data centers. The overall scope of such tax breaks for any sort of plant construction is considerably more generous.

92. Naumann, G. et al. Increased Economic Drought Impacts in Europe with Anthropogenic Warming. *Nature Climate Change* 11: 485–491, 2021.

93. Thiel, Gregory P. and Addison K. Stark. To Decarbonize Industry, We Must Decarbonize Heat. *Joule* 5, 531–550, March 21, 2021.

94. Worrell, Ernst and Gale Boyd. Bottom-up Estimates of Deep Decarbonization of US Manufacturing in 2050. *Journal of Cleaner Production* 330, January 2022.

95. de Pee, Arnout et al. *How Industry Can Move Toward a Low-carbon Future*. McKinsey & Company, 2018.

96. de Pee, Arnout et al. *Decarbonization of Industrial Sectors: The Next Frontier*. McKinsey and Company, July 2018.

97. Global Carbon Capture and Storage Institute. *Carbon Capture and Storage: Global Status Report 2019*. HSBC, January 24, 2020; but see also Horth, Maggie. *Why Carbon Capture Hasn't Saved Us from Climate Change Yet*. FiveThirtyEight, October 30, 2019; Budinis, Sara et al. An Assessment of CCS Costs, Barriers and Potential. *Energy Strategy Reviews* 22: 61–81, 2018.

98. Lynn, Mark. *End of the Line*. New York: Doubleday, 2005.

99. Duke Energy News Center. *Duke Energy Aims to Achieve Net-zero Carbon Emissions by 2050*. September 17, 2019; Dominion Energy. *Carbon Reduction*, 2019 Sustainability Report.

100. Hook, Leslie, Max Seddon, and Nastassia Astrasheuskaya. EU Plan for World's First Carbon Border Tax Provokes Trading Partners. *The Financial Times*, July 16, 2021.

101. Note that these summaries are generally quite short. They also are highly arbitrary. There are extensive discussions of risks potentially affecting these various sectors (and others) in reports from consultancies, NGOs, credit rating agencies and investment banks (some of which are publicly available), and central

banks and financial regulators. Not only are many of them quite good, but they are also freely available online.

102. Schaps, Karolin. *Royal Dutch Shell Pulls Plug on Arctic Exploration.* Reuters, September 28, 2015.
103. Morison, Rachel. *Gas Is the New Coal with Risk of $100 Billion in Stranded Assets.* Bloomberg Green, April 17, 2021.
104. Carbon Tracker. *Taxpayers May Have to Pay £280 Billion in Onshore Plugging Costs for Oil and Gas Wells,* October 1, 2020.
105. TCFD. *Implementing the Recommendations of the Task Force on Climate-related Financial Disclosures,* June 2017.
106. Egis and the UK Met Office. *Climate Change Risks for European Aviation.* EUROCONTROL. 6 September 2021.
107. Wieldon, Esther. *Your Climate Change Goals May Have a Maritime Shipping Problem.* S&P Global, 2021; Stone, Maddie. The Shipping Industry Faces a Climate Crisis Reckoning: Will It Decarbonize? *The Guardian,* November 12, 2021.
108. Zawadzki, Annika et al. *Riding the Rails to Sustainability.* Boston Consulting Group, February 28, 2022.
109. Fletcher, Luke, Kane Marcell, and Tom Crocker. *Driving Disruption.* CDP, January 2018; Hannon, Erik et al. *Mobility's Net-zero Transition: A Look at Opportunities and Risks.* McKinsey & Company, April 25, 2022.
110. Miller, Joe. Electric Car Costs to Remain Higher than Traditional Engines. *The Financial Times,* August 31, 2020.
111. Cogan, Doug and Joe Kruger. *Automaker Roadmap for Climate Scenario Analysis.* CERES, October 2021.
112. Tickner, Joel, Ken Geiser, and Stephanie Baima. Transitioning the Chemical Industry: The Case for Addressing the Climate, Toxics, and Plastics Crises. *Environment: Science and Policy for Sustainable Development* 63(6): 4–15, 2021; Tickner, Joel, Ken Geiser, and Stephanie Baima. Transitioning the Chemical Industry: Elements of a Roadmap Toward Sustainable Chemicals and Materials. *Environment: Science and Policy for Sustainable Development* 64(2): 22–36, 2022; Sharp, Jonathan. *Climate Risks Abound for the US Chemical Industry,* Geopolitical Monitor, April 24, 2022.
113. A depth of 10,975 meters (36,000 feet). See Carrington, Damien. Plastic Pollution Discovered at Deepest Point of Ocean. *The Guardian,* December 20, 2018.
114. Institute for Agriculture and Trade Policy. *New Research Shows 50-year Binge on Chemical Fertilisers Must End to Address the Climate Crisis,* November 1, 2021; Menegat, Stefano, Alicia Ledo, and Reyes Tirado. Greenhouse Gas Emissions from Global Production and Use of Nitrogen Synthetic Fertilisers in Agriculture. *Scientific Reports* 12, 14490, 2022.
115. Wlodarczak, Dominik. *Innovating for a Low Carbon Transition of European Cement.* The Cement Transition Initiative, 2020; Favier, Aurelie et al. *A Sustainable Future for the European Cement and Concrete Industry.* ETH Zurich and École Polytechnique Fédérale de Lausanne, 2018; Fennell, Paul S., Steven J. Davis, and Aseel Mohammed. Decarbonizing Cement Production. *Joule* 5(6): 1305–1311, 2021.

116. Czigler, Thomas et al. *Laying the Foundation for Zero-carbon Cement.* McKinsey & Company, May 2020.
117. Favier, Aurelie et al. *A Sustainable Future for the European Cement and Concrete Industry.* ETH Zurich and École Polytechnique Fédérale de Lausanne, 2018.
118. Newmont Mining's Conga Project Could Be Delayed Another Four Years. *Mining,* October 17, 2020; Burton, Melanie. *Aboriginal Group Says Rio Tinto Ignored Pleas to Save Sacred Cave from Blast.* Reuters, September 25, 2020.
119. Hook, Leslie. Australian Court Blocks Clive Palmer Coal Mine on Climate Grounds. *The Financial Times.* November 25, 2022.
120. Rootzén, J. and F. Johnsson. Paying the Full Price of Steel: Perspectives on the Cost of Reducing Carbon Dioxide Emissions from the Steel Industry. *Energy Policy* 98: 459–469, 2016; Muslemani, Hasan et al. Opportunities and Challenges for Decarbonizing Steel Production by Creating Markets for "Green Steel" Products. *Journal of Cleaner Production* 315, September 15, 2021; Vu, H., F. Cecchin, and N. Iacob. *Climate-neutral Steelmaking in Europe: Decarbonisation Pathways, Investment Needs, Policy Conditions, Recommendations.* European Research Executive Agency, 2022.
121. Lawton, Graham. Net Zero's Dirty Secret. *New Scientist,* November 13, 2021.

CHAPTER 7

Natural Capital Risks

*Man—despite his artistic pretensions, his sophistication, and his
many accomplishments—owes his existence to six inches of topsoil and the fact that it rains.*

—Anonymous

O f all the risk groupings proposed here, our classification of natural capital risks is the most speculative—again, largely because we know of
no previous attempt to codify such risks into an organized taxonomy for
investors.[1] How this category will continue to evolve is an interesting question. We would expect the taxonomy itself to evolve as our understanding
of the breadth and complexity of natural capital risks increases. The major
indicators chosen here—subsidy loss risks, depletion risks, boundary condition risks, and geopolitical event risks—are, in fact, presently being tracked
by a range of organizations, and all are manifesting themselves to varying
degrees. We believe these four general metrics accommodate the wide range
of natural capital issues currently unfolding, many of which (e.g., biodiversity loss and ocean acidification) are receiving increased attention from
public policy makers and investors. However, we would not be surprised to
see this framework evolve as more information on the actual natural capital
risks firms are exposed to receive more attention.

While this issue has not figured prominently in climate or ESG analysis
in the recent past, both Moody's[2] and S&P Global Ratings[3] now incorporate

natural capital considerations in the credit rating process. Moody's basic Environmental Issuer Profile Score now consists of five "exposures":

1. carbon transition,
2. physical climate risks,
3. water management,
4. waste and pollution, and
5. natural capital.

Similarly, some recent publications on assessing natural capital risk have appeared from major investors, for example, particularly from Allianz in 2018 (discussed in more detail later).[4] In addition, there are now numerous publications on these issues from a range of NGOs and consultancies such as PWC and McKinsey. We expect this trend to continue, especially as investors appear interested in stepping up their natural capital investments.

Our organization of the natural capital risks is shown in Figure 7.1. Note that, as with the adaptation and mitigation risks discussed in previous sections, several of these risks derive from multiple sources. Again, as in previous figures, the right-hand column represents a selected indicator of the broader risk—there are others not included in this figure. Boundary condition risks, for example, encompasses nine categories as put forward by the Stockholm Resilience Institute, who first proposed this framework. We will discuss these in more detail later. Note that of the four major risk categories,

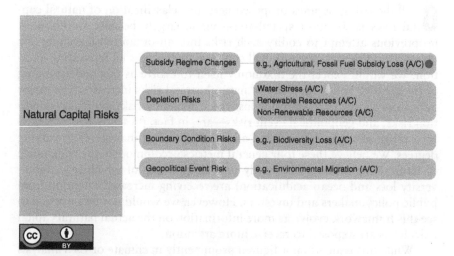

FIGURE 7.1 Proposed natural capital risk taxonomy.
Source: Green Planet Consulting Ltd. *What Is Climate Risk? A Field Guide for Investors, Lenders and Regulators.* London: Centre for Climate Finance and Investment, Imperial College Business School, February 2022.

two are probably more likely to be impactful over the near term (depletion risks and boundary condition risk).

By "natural capital risks" we mean the usual specific risks discussed throughout this book—asset values, profitability, cash flows, or margins stemming from natural events involving outright resource depletion, or the disruption of resources flow. Many of these are potentially being accelerated as a result of global heating impacts. For example, the apparent increase in the number of droughts worldwide is having a short-term impact on some industries (e.g., agriculture in California). But droughts can also have a geopolitical impact, as evidenced by many events in North Africa and the Middle East over the past decade that stem from long-term, drought-driven insufficient domestic agricultural production. Indeed, as we note in this chapter (and throughout this book), water availability is becoming an increasingly important issue for industries such as agriculture and mining.

These types of natural events—droughts, for example—have always occurred, and in the past, they have been treated as idiosyncratic risks since they occurred irregularly and unpredictably. But droughts, like the range of natural disasters that seem to be occurring with increased frequency, remains difficult to accurately forecast in its particulars. Scientists had been warning about drought in the Southwest United States for a number of years, in fact, the actual potential assessments of severity were, and remain, difficult. To take another example, the east coast of North America experiences an annual hurricane season between June and November, but no one can accurately predict the exact number of storms in any particular season, or their potential severity. Many of these risks are becoming more frequent, more numerous, and perhaps more predictable than they used to be.

The concept of natural capital risks is relatively new. Hence, in order to define such risks, we first need to define natural capital. As put forward by the Natural Capital Coalition,[5]

Natural capital is another term for the stock of renewable and non-renewable resources (e.g. plants, animals, air, water, soils, minerals) that combine to yield a flow of benefits to people. All this means is that any part of the natural world that benefits people, or that underpins the provision of benefits to people, is a form of natural capital. Natural capital is a stock, and from it flows ecosystem services or benefits. These services (where service is defined as "a system supplying a public need") can provide economic, social, environmental, cultural, spiritual or eudemonic benefits, and the value of these benefits be understood in qualitative or quantitative (including economic) terms, depending on context. Biodiversity is an essential component of natural capital stocks and an indicator of their condition and resilience. Biodiversity itself provides benefits directly to people.

The critical point for any discussion of natural capital risk is that a variety of forms of natural capital are being depleted. If they are renewable resources (e.g., forests, fisheries, and farmland), then they currently are being depleted more rapidly than they are being replenished—"at an unsustainable rate," as UNEP has noted.[6] If the resources are nonrenewable (e.g., fossil fuels, many minerals and, perhaps, the capacity of the atmosphere and the oceans and atmosphere to absorb CO_2 without untoward effects), then the narrative becomes a bit more straightforward, because at least there is a theoretical end date for consumption of a particular resource. Dependence upon natural capital is a fundamental fact of all economies, and risk assessment relating to natural capital risks is likely to become more important going forward.

In our taxonomy we distinguish, as is customary, between renewable and nonrenewable depletion risks, given that these reflect two different types of resources. We also discuss water risks as being perhaps the most significant depletion risk. Water never truly disappears—it simply changes its state. However, at present, as we indicated in our discussion of hydrological cycle disruption, the trend is for much of the world's water to move from ice to liquid water to water vapor (sometimes skipping the intermediate step), and the speed with which this is occurring appears to be accelerating globally. We discuss this trend in more detail later in this chapter. We also note that efforts over the past two decades to move toward a circular economy[7] relate directly to attempting to reduce natural consumption usage trends, and efforts to reduce their impact.

The four areas of natural capital risk outlined in this chapter are considerably more diffuse than many of the risks discussed in the previous chapters, and their impacts can be considerably broader, both for sovereign nations and on broad industries. As we discuss, however, a number of industries, such as agriculture, chemicals, mining, forestry, and fisheries, are particularly vulnerable to significant changes in natural capital depletion trends. The Natural Capital Finance Alliance (now the Capitals Coalition) has published a guide for financial institutions for developing natural capital assessment procedures.[8]

We note that the natural capital area is receiving a robust increase in attention over the past several years—it is now not uncommon to see regular updates on biodiversity efforts by firms, often in specific reports devoted solely to natural capital issues, or broader frameworks such as sustainability reports, which occasionally deliver less than they promise. More broadly, as a natural follow-on to TCFD, a number of organizations, including investors, have formed the Task Force on Nature-related Financial Disclosures. This group is specifically interested in developing a framework for assessing and implementing nature-based risk disclosure, very much along the lines of those being suggested here, with the intention of providing an initial frame-work in 2023.[9]

RESOURCE DEPLETION

While resource depletion occasionally still carries some neo-Malthusian overtones, particularly those related to agriculture, with the correspond-ing impression that technological progress will continue to render the issue moot, this appears to not be the case. McKinsey,[10] for example, has argued that resource depletion is already occurring, and is likely to accelerate in some categories. As McKinsey pointed out in 2013:

> Progressively cheaper resources underpinned global economic growth during the 20th century. During the 20th century, the price of key resources, as measured by MGI's index, fell by almost half in real terms. This was astounding given that the global population quadrupled in this era and global economic output increased by approximately 20-fold, together resulting in a jump in demand for different resources of between 600 and 2,000 percent. Resource prices declined because of faster technological progress and the discovery of new, low-cost sources of supply. Moreover, in some cases resources were not priced in a way that reflected the full cost of their production (e.g. energy subsidies or unpriced water) and externalities associated with their use (e.g. carbon emissions).
>
> The world could be entering an era of high and volatile resource prices. The past decade alone has reversed a 100-year decline in resource prices as demand for these commodities has surged. . . . With the excep-tion of energy in the 1970s, the volatility of resource prices today is at an all-time high. . . .

And, in fact, such depletion, while only hitting global economic accounts in a very general way, are becoming increasingly visible each year—topsoil loss[11] and aquifer depletion[12] being the two most obvious (and perhaps most worrying) examples.

Note that what is at issue here is not necessarily the imminent deple-tion of most resources to the point of nonavailability. More relevant is the increased difficulty and expense of recovering resources that are more difficult, for whatever reasons (such as physical location, or geopolitical issues), to extract. So, are there resources in actual danger of depletion?

This depends on several factors—not just the natural stock of whatever the resource is, but also whether that resource will be the subject of accelerating demand from emerging middle classes in Asia and Latin America. Nonrenewable resources are finite, clearly. Renewable resources are not, in theory. It should be apparent that in many cases, even if the resource in question is not near depletion levels, it is still likely to cost more to extract or develop than it used to.

In the case of climate risks, the concern here is with the impacts of those physical impacts described earlier on other natural capital trends—particularly the depletion of forests, agricultural land, and other renewable resources, and especially water. Desertification of parts of the world will likely be accelerated even under current trajectories, and more rapidly under more draconian global heating scenarios. In some areas, this already appears to be the case.[13] Again, we are dealing with uncertainties, but highly plausible uncertainties, and the uncertainty relates more to the scope and timing of these events, rather than to whether they will actually occur. But for industries affected—agriculture, mining, forestry in particular, and global trade in general—the impacts here will be tangible.

Depletion Risks—Renewable

There are numerous renewable resources where the consumption of the resource is faster than its replenishment—most of them, in fact. Topsoil loss is perhaps the most prominent example, but other critical resources display similar patterns. Forests continue to be logged faster than they are being replanted, although with significant regional variability[14] (and the replanted forests are never as biodiverse as those they are replacing). Water, as noted, is a renewable resource, but many critical aquifers continue to be depleted at rates faster than replenishment, primarily for increased rates of evaporation, but also the fact that many areas that rely on snowmelt for water availability are finding reduced snowfall levels are becoming a constraint. Water and topsoil represent the two most critical resources being depleted too rapidly.

Moreover, a wide range of biological resources are also being rapidly depleted. Fisheries represents perhaps the best example in terms of a product for human consumption.[15] And while afforestation trends continue to increase, total forest cover, including tropical rainforest, continues to decline on a global basis.[16]

Depletion Risk—Nonrenewable

Resource constraints provide a salutary example of how traditional analysis can lead to some complacency. We know, for example, that extraction of nonrenewable resources has escalated sharply over the past several decades. Many of these resources are those reported on by companies in their CSR or sustainability reports. Moreover, it is likely that commodity prices will continue to trend higher on a long-term basis, in spite of some recent price breakdowns, such as iron ore and oil. The general commodity price increases we have seen since 2000 are unlikely to be broadly reversed over the longer term.[17] Note that what is at issue here is not necessarily the imminent depletion of resources, but rather the costs of their extraction.

Water Risks   Water-related risk is the prime example of depletion risk. Even aside from climate change issues, water is emerging as a major environmental concern of interest to investors and managements. The Water Resources Group of the World Bank has estimated that by 2030, global water demand looks set to exceed current supply by an estimated 40% without substantial efficiency gains.[18] In some parts of the world the lack of water availability is already triggering climate migrations.

Water is a resource facing rising—and often conflicting—demands. There is already intense competition for water resources between agriculture, energy resources, and urban development in some areas (e.g., parts of China).[19] While the water cycle will continue to be a physical process, consumption trends appear to be running well ahead of the cycle's capacity to replenish adequate supplies. All industries use water. But some use water much more intensively than others, and these industries are already, in many cases, engaging with the issues that surround concerns about longer-term availability. The two industries dominating water consumption are agriculture and energy.

Agriculture, of course, necessarily involves water, and the more agriculture there is, the higher the levels of water consumption. However, as noted earlier, there are a number of global regions where water stress is becoming an issue for agriculture—including the Great Plains in the United States, which is the world's largest provider of maize. Increasing water constraints have the potential to provide constraints on agricultural production. There are concerns that this will limit the ability to provide basic subsistence to a global population of 8 billion. Such concerns have been raised before, of course.[20]

The energy industry, from extraction to distribution (utilities), is an intensive water consumer—electric power generation is the single largest industrial use of water because of its dependence on stream-powered turbine engines. Whether this will continue to be the case as more electricity is provided from renewable energy sources (solar and wind, primarily) remains unclear, but actually seems unlikely—water is required for cooling purposes, which is generally not needed in wind or solar electricity generation.[21] However, this still leaves a number of industries that currently are heavy users of water exposed to declining availability concerns.

The metals and mining sector spent nearly US $12 billion on water infrastructure in 2013 alone,[22] and this amount has certainly risen. Mining is indeed a very thirsty industry, as water is used for multiple purposes—process, dust control, and tailings disposal being the most significant. Other very thirsty industries include chemicals, the food and beverage industries (including both direct and indirect use), textiles, cement, steel, automobile manufacturing, and paper. The obvious impacts on firms from this degree of water risk will be on operating margins as the costs of water availability increase, and on cash flows if CAPEX requirements for ensuring availability and disposal increase—which appears likely for certain portions of the mining industry, for example.

However, water depletion concerns are escalating sharply.[23] This trend is even discounting the impact of what appear to be increasingly frequent droughts on a global basis—the current and severe droughts in Brazil, California and the western United States, Australia, Colombia, Pakistan, and China, amidst a host of others. These droughts have their own economic impacts, of course; the World Economic Forum estimates that worldwide drought costs the global economy about US $8–12 billion annually—a figure that is relatively small in terms of the global economy, but one that can reflect significant regional impacts. And this is certainly a figure that will rise as well in coming years.

SUBSIDY REGIME CHANGE RISKS

As discussed previously in this book, subsidies play an important role in the modern economy. This is particularly true for the fossil fuels industry. A recent report from BloombergNEF and Bloomberg Philanthropies highlighted the fact that OECD countries have supplied billions in subsidies to the industry since the Paris Agreement in 2015.[24] As inexplicable as this seems, especially given promises to reduce such subsidies that were made in Paris, this simply represents the political power and the economic importance of the industry.

In developed nations, it is rare to find a construction project that does not involve some sort of government subsidy, for example. Likewise, resource industries often receive generous government subsidies, in part because they typically provide employment opportunities that might otherwise not be available. In fact, firms and entire sectors often receive tax breaks specifically so that they will locate in a particular region and provide such opportunities.[25] These issues are especially important in emerging market nations with a dependence on natural resource development and extraction. For instance, agricultural subsidies are based on multiple rationales—food availability, employment, and the potential for developing agricultural exports. Mining and forestry are two other industries where companies benefit directly from government "incentives" (as subsidies are sometimes referred to).

In this way, changes in national subsidy regimes have the potential to alter the industrial landscape in a number of sectors. In the case of agriculture, it is difficult to quantify direct impacts on various sectors of the global agricultural system. Companies involved in this system range from producers to retailers, with a frequently complex supply chain connecting the two. As a result, changes in subsidy regimes at present appear to be very diffuse. Going forward, there is an increased likelihood of incorporating nature-based factors as part of agricultural reform. In the United Kingdom, for example, there is significant interest in replacing volume-based subsidies with those that encompass increasing environmental protection, with increased subsidies for these measures.[26]

Outright extraction industries may face a more difficult operating environment in the event of significant changes in subsidy regimes. This is particularly true in the case of the mining industry, which often relies on a range of generous subsidies relating to land access and water availability and disposal.[27] For example, the Institute of Energy Economics and Financial Analysis notes that the controversial Adani Carmichael mine project in Australia, which would become the world's largest coal mine if completed, requires considerable Australian government subsidies in order to be profitable.[28]

Likewise, access to public lands is often determined by a range of processes for forestry and paper products. Some firms in these sectors own their own resources but many do not, and thus rely on such access. In addition, as has been noted, agricultural incentives designed to expand agricultural development are having a significant impact on deforestation.[29]

BOUNDARY CONDITION RISKS

In 2009, researchers at the Stockholm Resilience Institute (SRI) proposed that for the past 10,000 years, humanity has been operating under a set of favorable "boundary conditions," which have together acted to provide a supporting "safe space" for the emergence of human civilization. However, they also noted that some of these conditions (or "planetary boundaries") have been breached, and others are nearing a tipping point.

The nine (originally seven) boundary conditions are:

1. climate change;
2. change in biosphere integrity (biodiversity loss and species extinction);
3. stratospheric ozone depletion;

4. ocean acidification;
5. biogeochemical flows (phosphorus and nitrogen cycles);
6. land-system change (e.g., deforestation);
7. freshwater use;
8. atmospheric aerosol loading (microscopic particles in the atmosphere that affect climate and living organisms); and
9. the introduction of novel entities (e.g., organic pollutants, radioactive materials, nanomaterials, and micro-plastics).

The effects of crossing these boundaries remain unclear. Researchers at SRI and the Potsdam Institute for Climate Research have suggested that at least four of the boundaries—climate change, loss of biosphere integrity, land-system change, and altered biogeochemical cycles—have already been crossed, with potentially negative implications,[30] as shown in Figure 7.2. In 2022 the SRI suggested that a fifth condition—freshwater use—has also been breached.

The impacts of these changes are likely to be broad and diffuse, and are already proceeding at differential rates. Much of this book has discussed potential climate change impacts. Often these impacts, especially in terms of biodiversity loss and land-system changes, are more difficult to quantify at anything other than very general macroeconomic levels. Altered biogeochemical cycles, on the other hand, carry direct risks to two large economic sectors: agriculture and chemicals (particularly agricultural chemicals). As SRI has commented:

> The biogeochemical cycles of nitrogen and phosphorus have been radically changed by humans as a result of many industrial and agricultural processes. Nitrogen and phosphorus are both essential elements for plant growth, so fertilizer production and application is the main concern. Human activities now convert more atmospheric nitrogen into reactive forms than all of the Earth's terrestrial processes combined. Much of this new reactive nitrogen is emitted to the atmosphere in various forms rather than taken up by crops. When it is rained out, it pollutes waterways and coastal zones or accumulates in the terrestrial biosphere. Similarly, a relatively small proportion of phosphorus fertilizers applied to food production systems is taken up by plants; much of the phosphorus mobilized by humans also ends up in aquatic systems. These can become oxygen-starved as bacteria consume the blooms of algae that grow in response to the high nutrient supply. A significant fraction of the applied nitrogen and phosphorus makes its way to the sea, and can push marine and aquatic systems across ecological thresholds of their own. One regional-scale example of this effect is the decline in the

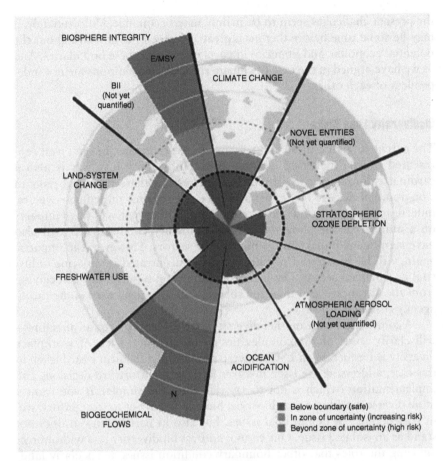

FIGURE 7.2 SRI proposed boundary conditions.
Source: Steffen, W. et al. 2015. Planetary Boundaries: Guiding Human Development on a Changing Planet. *Science* 347(6223), quoted by Stockholm Resilience Institute, 2022. https://www.stockholmresilience.org/research/planetary-boundaries.html

shrimp catch in the Gulf of Mexico's "dead zone" caused by fertilizer transported in rivers from the US Midwest.[31]

There is a pressing need for more research to determine the specific industrial impacts of changes to these boundary conditions. In the case of climate change, the potential risks (as previously discussed) are fairly well identified, if not yet quantified. In the case of the other planetary boundaries, the present challenges seem to be mainly macroeconomic. Unfortunately, it may be some time before there is a greater degree of confidence about the potential economic and financial impacts of crossing these boundaries. And as we have argued in the case of climate risks, these conditions are not independent of each other.

Biodiversity Loss Risks

The extent to which these factors can be intertwined is, in fact, well represented by the increased concern over biodiversity loss.[32] It is also a cardinal example of the difficulties in assessing these potential risks in isolation. Species are being lost at a pace not seen for millennia—we are, indeed, in the midst of a sixth extinction.[33] This event will have impacts on a number of the above-mentioned boundary conditions. It will also have significant impacts on a number of sectors. However, the impacts, again, will be broad and not necessarily concentrated in any one industrial or financial sector. The increasing attention biodiversity is receiving from the corporate and investor spheres has also generated some rating agency comment.[34]

A comparison with another diversity sphere—workplace and directors—will clarify some of the complexities of biodiversity. Lack of workplace diversity is frequently an ESG target, particularly at the firm board level. In this case, addressing the issue involves fairly straightforward decisions and implementation (which is not to say that these are simple). If you want a more diverse workforce, you hire one. Biodiversity is not so straightforward, in part because of definitional issues, but also in part because it does not stand as an isolated issue. One cannot address biodiversity loss without recognizing the roles that other boundary condition issues, particularly land-system change[35] and biogeochemical flows[36] have occupied. As is the case in climate, picking out an issue to be solved in isolation is difficult.[37]

We note that central banks have started to take an interest in biodiversity issues as well. A recent assessment of potential bank review has indicated that biodiversity risks may become a pressing issue sooner than many climate risks, and suggests that central banks adopt a "precautionary" approach to assessing the implications of biodiversity deterioration.[38] This seems like suitable advice for investors and lenders as well.

GEOPOLITICAL EVENT RISKS

This subcategory may not have the breadth of the others in terms of potential credit impacts outside of a few industries. But it does capture a certain aspect of resources—they are unevenly distributed globally, often in what some industries may regard as politically inconvenient countries. There are numerous examples, but two examples will point up the types of risks being addressed here.

First, demand for certain rare earth minerals has been high, because of its importance in the technology industry, particularly among aerospace, handset, and lighting manufacturers. (We should note that these metals actually are not particularly rare—most are about as common as copper.) Most of these are now mainly to be found in China, which accounts for about 80% of global production, and where demand is also highest in the world. This has led to concerns that prices would also remain high, and would continue to spike, as they did in 2011. In fact, this turned out not to be the case— demand fell over the 2010s because of increased efficiencies by manufacturers. As a result, while prices may continue to increase, the sort of price spike that occurred in 2011 does not appear likely to be repeated.[39] Nonetheless, given the already high extraction costs for rare earth metals, these costs are likely to rise as well as extraction issues become more complex. Political considerations such as a further United States/China trade conflict, coupled with increased extraction difficulties, could result in increased constraints on production and availability. These concerns also apply to other mined substances, such as lithium.

Second, phosphate fertilizer is a critical component of modern agriculture, and, indeed, to organic life. Demand trends continue to rise, and there are concerns that supplies from the United States and several other countries may be exhausted by 2040. Moreover, 70% of the required raw material— phosphorus—is found in one country—Morocco—and most other countries with some supply tend to be countries with potentially unstable politics— such as Saudi Arabia, Algeria, Iraq, and Syria.[40]

Neither of these situations represents the kind of raw material stability that buyers would like to see. We have seen numerous instances of supply-chain disruptions in the automobile and technology industries following a warehouse fire, or a tsunami—it can take months, or even years in the case of earthquakes and tsunamis, to recover. The belief that resources under the control of one or two countries should be immune to that sort of disruption should be resisted.

Finally, while not events as such, increased migration as a result of climate-driven natural resource failures is likely to increase in the decades ahead—especially in those situations where water scarcity is a driving force.[41] The substantial migration of people from Syrian and other Middle East countries as a result of drought impacts is likely to be replicated going forward. This type of risk will probably manifest itself most robustly at the level of sovereign government finances, and therefore credit profiles. The potential for these trends to turn into "events" is clear.

IMPLICATIONS FOR SELECT SECTORS

Sectoral Impacts of Biodiversity Loss

Perhaps the most visible sectoral manifestation of this loss will be in the global tourism industry.[42] Tourism is one of the world's largest industries by revenues, and is often reliant on the strength of biodiversity in popular destinations. It likely follows that a meaningful loss of biodiversity in those areas where biodiversity is a tourism generator will be negative for local industries and sovereign governments. More broadly, sovereign governments are likely to bear the impact of this loss if it affects the potential accessibility and availability of natural areas, as many are dependent on tourism revenues for financial stability.

In addition, the global food industry will be under pressure from two sources. First, much biodiversity loss is attributable to agricultural expansion—not only because of large industrial processes (e.g., for products like palm oil), but also because of the fact that much of the world's population continues to rely on local environments for critical resources such as wood for fuel. As industrial farming expands, it is generally at the expense of biodiversity. This can be the case for subsistence farming as well, which often can involve deforestation of large areas to be replaced by farmland.

Second, as biodiversity declines, so does the biological support that agricultural depends on for processes such as pollination; the collapse of the bee population in a number of regions is directly linked to agricultural practices. While honeybee populations appear to be stable in some countries (such as the United States), on a global basis, these populations continue to decline.[43] This development will likely have negative impacts on the levels of pollination that the global food industry requires, especially if agricultural production expands as expected. Other industries likely to be affected include the cosmetics and pharmaceutical industries, due to the loss of a wide range of raw materials, and the automotive sector, over raw material concerns and the sector's impact on biodiversity loss trends.

Recently, there has been significant research on biodiversity economics. In a seminal report, the UK government has published a broad assessment of current biodiversity trends, both in the United Kingdom and globally.[44] We imagine this report will become the template for further investigations in this area. In addition, S&P Global Ratings recently published a whitepaper on natural capital and biodiversity,[45] and we expect more institutional attention on these issues going forward.

In addition to the above, a number of other sectors appear vulnerable to natural capital disruption and a broader range of risks.

The Food Sector

The global food system is the main contributor to current destabilization of global boundary conditions.[46] Hence, it is also the most likely to be disrupted by any further destabilization, or by significant major efforts to reverse current trends. Given the global importance of this system, it is sure to receive increased attention in the future. Current agricultural production systems may be unsustainable, meaning the modern use of fertilizer and agricultural chemicals may be at risk. As Rockström and colleagues[47] point out,

> Building resilient food systems requires a systems-approach integrating carbon, nitrogen, phosphorus, water, soils, biodiversity and biome stability; and taking a truly inter-disciplinary planetary health approach by addressing food cultures, nutritional security and geopolitical stability, as well as the role of governance, trade and equity. In light of the significant lag time to drive global progress on climate mitigation, we cannot afford to have succeeded in tackling climate before moving on to other planetary boundaries. Approaches must be developed and tested at a scale that operationalizes a global commons framework for the stewardship of all food-related planetary boundaries. The social costs of our current global food system are unprecedented in both inter-temporal and inter-regional scales, providing crucial information for effective governance of the commons.

The concerns described above pertain to two sectors in particular, both of which are currently under scrutiny.

The first, the global industrial meat production industry, which occupies vast amounts of land devoted to grazing and the growing of grain feed, has consolidated considerably over the past two decades. As mentioned earlier in this book, consumers have helped drive the development and market acceptance of "meatless meat," which, if it proves durable, should change some of the dynamics of the global meat industry (which has been consolidating aggressively over the past two decades).

The second, palm oil production, involves significant demand from major international food companies and also invariably involves deforestation in developing countries. There have been a number of agreements to phase out palm oil from processed foods over the past decades, but their success has been only partial—forests continue to be replaced by palm oil plantations in southeast Asia.

We note that agriculture in a broader sense is receiving increased attention. This is not simply over concerns that the impacts of agriculture are largely negative from biodiversity concerns. Rather, these appear to be motivated by understanding how nature-based solutions can have a positive impact on newer agricultural practices.[48]

Oil and Gas

As discussed throughout this book, the oil and gas sector is particularly vulnerable to depletion concerns, especially in areas of water scarcity. At present, the sector is benefiting from strong demand in the face of lost Russian supplies in some parts of the world (such as Europe). Drilling in general consumes water, although traditional drilling also generates well-specific water. Fracking, however, is hugely water consumptive, and has already been negatively affected in areas where competition over water resources has increased or where water scarcity limits the potential for fracking.[49] We note that the industry's response has been to expand the range of Exploration and Production (E&P) activities, often into more inhospitable environments (polar regions, for example). Some of this recent interest has been driven by the awkward natural gas availability crisis resulting from the Ukraine invasion. However, this conflict will end at some point, allowing global gas markets some return to normalcy, with less-pressing demand for natural gas products.

Over the longer term, we expect that demand for fossil fuels assets will likely decline, although at what pace remains uncertain. Certainly, the sharp decline in renewables pricing over the past decade will have an increasing impact of electricity generation and distribution. In addition, in the oil and gas drilling sectors, there are two other areas of concern over asset values. The first relates to Liquified Natural Gas (LNG), which has grown rapidly over the past year and shows no signs of slowing while the Ukraine situation is still in effect. The United States has for years been trying to get the EU to accept US-exported LNG, and this looks as if it is currently happening. The long-term success of this approach will depend on how likely it is that "natural gas as a transition fuel" remains a durable public policy strategy.

Second, there are considerable assets tied up in oil and gas pipelines, especially in the United States. To the extent that demand for fossil fuels can be expected to decline, as a result of renewable power sources and the electrification of transport, these assets are likely to come under pressure. While this impact is not imminent, it is certainly feasible.

Metals and Mining

In a 2015 report,[50] CDP identified factors relating to water risks (principally availability) currently being faced by a number of mining companies, based on the surveyed companies' responses. This assessment of water-stress exposure was just the most recent in a series of reports on the mining industry and its potential issues relating to water availability, or to permitting issues relating to water pollution. Using the AQUEDUCT global model mapping tool, CDP determined in 2015 that nearly "50% of facilities for the companies in [the] study are located in areas of medium or higher water stress." Numerous reports in the past five years indicate that this trend continues.[51] This percentage has certainly increased since then. As CDP and Planet Tracker have noted in a recent report, declining water availability in much of the world is itself becoming a significant generator of stranded assets.[52] A number of examples cited in that report are mining companies with significant exposures to water-dependent projects that have gone amiss.

Additionally, mining waste, including wastewater, has been a major contributor to water and land degradation, especially in terms of causing increases in heavy metals in the environment. Although we discussed this earlier as a water-related natural capital depletion risk, it is also a boundary condition risk, particularly in terms of biogeochemical flows and biodiversity integrity.

Electric Utilities

Electric power generation is the single largest industrial usage of water, which explains why most electric power plants are located on or near rivers and coasts—the need to recycle water is integral to electricity generation in classical utility plants. As we discussed elsewhere, an abundance of water, either through sea level rise and/or flooding, can cause considerable problems for utilities. So can the lack of it, as many utilities discovered (again) this year as a result of significantly reduced river volumes—decreased water availability can have negative consequences on the ability of individual plants to maintain operations. Most US utilities, for example, are required by regulators to develop contingency operating plans in the event of water shortages in order to avoid temporary shutdowns, similar to the shutdowns imposed by utilities in the event of wildfires. In the summer of 2022 France, which relies heavily on nuclear power, faced an array of such situations.

It is worth pointing out that the continued shift to renewables entails moving away from large steam-powered utility plants. Accordingly, this vulnerability may decline—although the stranded asset potential may not.

Forestry

Deforestation remains a major issue relating to global heating. It is also a central boundary condition concern, given its potential role in land use changes (as forests continue to be burned for agricultural land in many developing countries) and in biodiversity preservation (as natural forests are natural preserves of biodiversity). We suspect that risks of this type do not arise in established European or North American paper and forest products companies, as these are generally intensely monitored by investors and NGOs, and where there are generally ongoing (and often visible) afforestation efforts. However, such companies in developing countries are less observable, and many are either government owned or government controlled by proxy. In these countries, the risks of deforestation pass up to the sovereign. Countries associated with palm oil production, where native forests are being eliminated at rapid rates, may be particularly vulnerable.

Chemicals

As noted, the agricultural chemical industry is intertwined with the modern food production system. As such, it is vulnerable to significant changes in how that system works. Agricultural runoff is the major contributor to disruption of the biogeochemical flows condition—which, as mentioned, has likely been breached, with significant consequences already observable. Given global population trends, continuing with existing practice is likely to exacerbate these disruptions. It is difficult to envision alternatives to current practice, other than a massive and wholesale shift to organic production (for which sufficient agricultural land currently does not exist). The fact that the agricultural sector has consolidated significantly over the past two decades increases the risk to the sector.

Note also that much of the chemicals industry is based on ethylene, usually derived from ethane or naphtha. As a result, the fracking revolution has allowed the industry to alter its cost structure where ethane is the primary material, to the benefit of the industry and to investors. However, it has been suggested that this entire chain is dependent on inexpensive water availability and disposal in the fracking industry. Removal of support for inexpensive water would have a knock-on impact on much of the US chemical industry, the world's largest.

GLOBAL HEATING IMPACT ON NATURAL RESOURCES

Like adaptation risk, global heating impacts and risks have a longer tail risk than several of the others being discussed. Again, we are dealing with uncertainties, but plausible uncertainties, and the uncertainty relates more to the scope and timing of these events, rather than to whether they will actually occur. For industries affected—agriculture and forestry in particular—the impacts here will be tangible.

At this point, it is difficult to envision that the continued loss of agricultural land will have a direct credit impact on any rated bond issuers *within current ratings horizons*—although an indirect impact on the food business appears plausible. A similar argument can be made about fisheries. In the case of forests, however, there is a more plausible scenario under which paper and forest products companies find a more limited set of opportunities for developing assets, particularly in developing countries. While deforestation remediation and zero-deforestation corporate and national pledges have had some modest success to date,[53] the pace of global deforestation continues, particularly in poorer countries—wood remains the principal fuel for much of the world.[54] However, again it is difficult to envision current trends having a credit impact on these companies over the near to intermediate term. In addition, it seems clear that global consumer demand for products such as palm oil or meat continue to be a significant driver of deforestation in some parts of the world, and these trends show no signs of reversing in the near term.[55]

A broader set of concerns arises regarding a number of emerging market debt issuers, particularly those dependent upon resource development and exports for economic growth. However, we note that a number of agencies and organizations have addressed the issue of the possible impact of climate change on a range of emerging market sovereigns, particularly those with a high dependence on natural resource or agricultural exports, or those with substantial exposure to physical climate risks. These are sectors where the impacts are generally believed to be potentially negative.[56] As we mentioned elsewhere, the focus of this research was on natural catastrophes and the possible mitigating impact of insurance. Rating agencies are mindful of the potential impacts of a range of physical phenomena—changing rainfall patterns, for example—and are beginning to factor these issues into their analysis. We have discussed some of these trends and their potential impacts elsewhere.[57]

NOTES

1. The TNFD framework, currently under development, and in its third iteration, will invariably contain some taxonomic elements but is not intended as a taxonomy *per se*. See Taskforce on Nature-related Financial Disclosures, TNFD Releases Third Iteration of Beta Framework, November 4, 2022.

2. Moody's Investors Service, *General Principles for Assessing Environmental, Social and Governance Risks Methodology*, December 14, 2020; *Sovereigns— Global. Explanatory Comment: New Scores Depict Varied and Largely Credit-negative Impact of ESG Factors*, January 18, 2021.

3. S&P Global Ratings, *General Criteria | Request for Comment: Request for Comment: Environmental, Social, and Governance Principles in Credit Ratings*, May 17, 2021; *Natural Capital and Biodiversity: Reinforcing Nature as an Asset*, April 22, 2021.

4. Bonnet, Chris and Alina Morozova. *Measuring and Managing Environmental Exposure: A Business Sector Analysis of Natural Capital Risk*. Allianz Global Corporate and Specialty, June 2018.

5. Natural Capital Coalition. *Natural Capital Protocol*, 2016.

6. UNEP. International Resource Panel, *Global Resources Outlook 2019*, April 3, 2019.

7. Raworth, Kate. *Doughnut Economics*. London: Random House Business Books, 2017.

8. Natural Capital Finance Alliance (NCFA) and UN Environment World Conservation Monitoring Centre. *Exploring Natural Capital Opportunities, Risks and Exposure: A Practical Guide for Financial Institutions*. Geneva, Oxford and Cambridge: NCFA, 2018.

9. Taskforce on Nature-related Financial Disclosures. *TNFD Releases Third Iteration of Beta Framework*, November 4, 2022.

10. McKinsey Global Institute. *Resource Revolution: Meeting the World's Energy, Material, Food, and Water Needs*, November 2011; *Resource Revolution: Tracking Global Commodity Markets*, September 2013; *Reverse the Curse: Maximizing the Potential of Resource-driven Economies*, December 2013.

11. Arsenault, Chris. Only Sixty Years of Harvests Left if Soil Degradation Continues. *Scientific American*, December 5, 2014; Cosier, Susan. The World Needs Topsoil to Grow 95% of Its Food—But It's Rapidly Disappearing. *The Guardian*, May 30, 2019; Thaler, Evan A. et al. The Extent of Soil Loss Across the US Corn Belt. *Proceedings of The National Academy of Sciences*, April 15, 2021; UN News. FAO *Warns 90 Per Cent of Earth's Topsoil at Risk By 2050*, July 27, 2022.

12. American Geophysical Union. *Groundwater Resources Around the World Could Be Depleted by 2050s*. Phys.Org, December 15, 2016; Mrad, Aassad et al. Peak Grain Forecasts for the US High Plains Amid Withering Waters. *Proceedings of the National Academy of Sciences*, October 5, 2020; Taylor, Richard and Mohammad Shamsudduha. *Groundwater: Depleting Reserves Must Be Protected Around the World*, The Conversation, March 21, 2022.

13. Mirzabaev, Alisher and Jianguo Wu, Desertification. In *Climate Change and Land: An IPCC Special Report on Climate Change, Desertification, Land Degradation, Sustainable Land Management, Food Security, and Greenhouse Gas Fluxes in Terrestrial Ecosystems,* 2019, ch. 3.

14. FAO and UNEP. 2020. *The State of the World's Forests 2020. Forests, Biodiversity and People.* Rome: FAO.

15. Woody, Todd. The Sea Is Running Out of Fish, Despite Nations' Pledge to Stop It. *National Geographic,* October 8, 2019; Carrington, Damian. Fisheries Collapse Confirms Silent Spring Pesticide Prophecy. *The Guardian,* October 31, 2019.

16. FAO and UNEP. *The State of the World's Forests 2020.* Rome: FAO, 2020.

17. McKinsey Quarterly. *Are You Ready for the Resource Revolution?* March 2014; KPMG International. *A New Vision of Value: Connecting Corporate and Societal Value Creation,* September 2014.

18. The 2030 Water Resources Group. *Charting Our Water Future: Economic Frameworks to Inform Decision-making.* The World Bank, 2009.

19. Global Water Partnership. *China's Water Resources Management Challenge: The Three "Red Lines,"* 2015.

20. Note that the conjectures of Thomas Malthus—that population growth would eventually exceed the ability of agriculture to provide sufficient food—are once again becoming a subject of debate. It is generally accepted that technology has enabled humanity to avoid the Malthusian trap to date, and there are expectations that this will continue to be the case. As David Rieff has pointed out, however, Malthus only needs to be right once.

21. Bryan, Alyssa et al. *Managing Water and Climate Risk with Renewable Energy.* McKinsey & Company, October 22, 2021.

22. Gordon, Julie. *Water: Critical Resource and Costly Risk for Miners.* Mineweb, May 30, 2013; International Council on Metals and Mining, and IFC. *Water in the Mining Sector,* 2017.

23. Burks, Beth. *Water Scarcity and Its Credit Implications Across the Value Chain,* S&P Global Ratings, June 16, 2021.

24. Carrington, Damian. *"Reckless": G20 States Subsidised Fossil Fuels by $3tn Since 2015, Says Report.* July 20, 2021.

25. US Cities and States Give Big Tech $9.3bn in Subsidies in Five Years. *The Guardian,* July 2, 2018, *The Realities of Economic Development Subsidies.* The American Prospect, January 1, 2018.

26. Department for Environment, Food, and Rural Affairs. *New Farming Policies and Payments in England,* July 2022. These proposals have generated some degree of controversy, not least over whether they actually will achieve their stated objectives—See UK Parliamentary Accounts Committee, *Defra's Plan for Post-EU Land and Farming Subsidies Based on "Blind Optimism,"* January 2022.

27. *Tax Incentives in Mining: Minimizing Risks to Revenue.* The International Institute for Sustainable Development and the Organisation for Economic Co-operation and Development, 2018.

28. Adani Mine Would Be "Unviable" Without $4.4bn in Subsidies, Report Finds. *The Guardian*, August 29, 2019.

29. *Subsidies to Key Commodities Driving Forest Loss*. Overseas Development Institute, 2015.

30. Steffen, W. et al. 2015. Planetary Boundaries: Guiding Human Development on a Changing Planet. *Science* 347(6223).

31. Rockström, J. et al. Planetary Boundaries: Exploring the Safe Operating Space for Humanity. *Ecology and Society* 14(2): 32, 2009; Rockström, J. et al. A Safe Operating Space for Humanity. *Nature* 461: 472–475, 2009; Steffen, W. et al. Planetary Boundaries: Guiding Human Development on a Changing planet. *Science* 347: 736, 1259855, 2015.

32. Convention on Biological Diversity. *Global Biodiversity Outlook 5*, September 2020.

33. Carrington, Damian. Sixth Mass Extinction of Wildlife Accelerating, Scientists Warn. *The Guardian*, June 1, 2020.

34. Fitch Ratings. *Collaboration and Standardization Key to Halting Biodiversity Loss*, April 28, 2021.

35. Forests are being depleted at a steady but ultimately alarming rate, see Bologna, Mauro and Gerardo Aquino. Deforestation and World Population Sustainability: A Quantitative Analysis. *Scientific Reports* 10, May 2020.

36. Tang, Fiona H.M. et al. Risk of Pesticide Pollution at the Global Scale. *Nature Geoscience* 14: 206–210, 2021; Hough, Rupert Lloyd. A World View of Pesticides. *Nature Geoscience* 14: 183–184, 2021.

37. "When we try to pick out anything by itself, we find it hitched to everything else in the Universe." John Muir. *My First Summer in the Sierra*. New York: Dover Publications, 1911/2004.

38. Kedward, Katie, Josh Ryan-Collins, and Hughes Chenet. Biodiversity Loss and Climate Change Interactions: Financial Stability Implications for Central Banks and Financial Supervisors. *Climate Policy*, August 2, 2022.

39. Majcher, Kristin. What Happened to the Rare-earths Crisis? *MIT Technology Review*, February 25, 2015; Hsu, Jeremy. Don't Panic about Rare Earth Elements. *Scientific American*, May 31, 2019.

40. Carpenter, Damian. Phosphate Fertiliser "Crisis" Threatens World Food Supply. *The Guardian*, 6 September 2019.

41. Beth Burks, *Water Conflicts Are Heightening Geopolitical and Social Tensions Globally*. S&P Global Ratings, July 7, 2020.

42. Convention on Biological Diversity. *Mainstreaming Biodiversity into Tourism Development*, 2018.

43. Zattara, Eduardo E. and Marcelo A. Aizen. Worldwide Occurrence Records Suggest a Global Decline in Bee Species Richness. *One Earth* 4(1): 114–123. For historical context, See Buchmann, Stephen L. and Gary Paul Nabhan, *The Forgotten Pollinators*. Washington, DC: Island Press, 1996.

44. Dasgupta, P. *The Economics of Biodiversity: The Dasgupta Review*, London: HM Treasury, 2021.

45. Bryson, Maurice and Michael Wilkins. *Natural Capital and Biodiversity: Reinforcing Nature as an Asset.* S&P Global Ratings, April 12, 2021.
46. Rockström, J. et al. Planet-proofing the Global Food System. *Natural Food* 1: 3–5, 2020. Retrieved from: https://www.sochob.cl/web1/wp-content/uploads/2020/01/Planet-proofing-the-global-food-system.pdf
47. Rockström, J. et al. Planet-proofing the Global Food System. *Natural Food* 1: 3–5, 2020. Retrieved from: https://www.sochob.cl/web1/wp-content/uploads/2020/01/Planet-proofing-the-global-food-system.pdf
48. Holtedahl, Pernille, Alexandre Köberle, and Michael Wilkins. *Future of Food Part 3—Can Markets Save Nature? Investing in Nature to Tackle Biodiversity Loss and Enhance Food Security.* Centre for Climate Finance and Investment, Imperial College Business School, October 2020.
49. Kondash, Andrew J., Nancy E. Lauer, and Avner Vengosh. The Intensification of the Water Footprint of Hydraulic Fracturing. *Science Advances* 4, August 15, 2018
50. CDP, *Making the Grade: Are Some Miners Chasing Fool's Gold?* November 2015.
51. Deloitte. *Tracking the Trends 2018: The Top 10 Issues Shaping Mining in the Year Ahead,* 2018.
52. CDP. *High and Dry: How Water Issues Are Stranding Assets.* Planet Tracker and CDP, May 2022.
53. Delgado, C., M. Wolosin, and Purvis, N. Restoring and Protecting Agricultural and Forest Landscapes and Increasing Agricultural Productivity. Working paper for: *Seizing the Global Opportunity: Partnerships for Better Growth and a Better Climate.* London and Washington, DC: New Climate Economy, 2015.
54. Bailis, R. et al. The Carbon Footprint of Traditional Woodfuels. *Nature Climate Change* 5: 266–272, 2015.
55. Biggest Food Brands "Failing to Banish Palm Oil Deforestation." *The Guardian,* January 17, 2020.
56. Mrsnik, Marko. The Heat Is On: Climate Change and Sovereign Ratings. In *Climate Risk: Rising Tides Raise the Stakes,* Standard & Poor's Rating Services, December 2015; Moody's Investors Service, *Understanding the Impact of Natural Disasters: Exposure to Direct Damages Across Countries,* 28 November 2016; Moody's Investors Service. *How Moody's Assesses the Physical Effects of Climate Change on Sovereign Issuers,* November 7, 2016; S&P Global Ratings, *Sovereign Postcard: ESG and Sovereign Ratings,* 7.
57. Buhr, Bob and Ulrich Volz. *Climate Change and the Cost of Capital in Developing Nations: Assessing the Impact of Climate Risks on Sovereign Borrowing Costs.* London: Centre for Climate Finance and Investment and SOAS University, 2018.

CHAPTER 8

Concluding Observations

In this book, we have introduced a climate risk taxonomy designed to assess the risks to firms posed by the physical and transition impacts associated with climate change. Many of the specific categories chosen mirror those found in any compendium of climate risks, although not all of these are organized along the same lines. Others had to be imputed based on traditional risks employed by financial analysts. In general, however, there is increasing recognition that the basket of potential risk covered by the rubric "climate risks" is moving from a group of idiosyncratic risks to more secular risks that will be more difficult for investors and lenders to diversify away from.

There is a general recognition of the utility of, and the differences between, physical risks, transition/adaptation risks, and transition/mitigation risks, and it is difficult to find discussions of financial impacts of global heating that do not employ these categories. The category of natural capital risks, on the other hand, represents a novel taxonomy and for that reason is more speculative than other potential risk categories proposed here. Nonetheless, as we have suggested, the motivation for such a risk category is well documented at this point, as are some of the potential difficulties.[1]

Climate risks actually constitute a broad set of risks of various types. As we have seen, one approach to the issue of risk assessment is to granulate these risks in a taxonomy so that relations between risks can be assessed in a more straightforward manner. Yet, few of these risks exist in isolation. The potential for feedback loops here is high and, in many cases, is not well understood. This issue does not pertain only to physical feedback; as companies in several sectors are well aware, the feedback loops between litigation and reputational risks can be rapid and unforgiving—all the more reason to have as complete a picture of risk exposure as possible.

As investors and lenders have discovered over the past decade, and as we noted in our Introduction (Chapter 1), the assessment of climate risks is as much an art as a science at present. In part, this ambiguity reflects horizon issues. Assessing risks that may not manifest themselves for several decades is indeed a highly speculative process. But at this point, the emergence of most of these risks (at least the physical ones) is essentially a certainty. We know that something is highly likely to occur, even if we are not yet certain about the timing or the scope. Hence, it is vital that we do not underestimate (or even worse, ignore) these risks simply because we lack the appropriate framework for assessing them.

The taxonomy presented here is designed to provide investors and lenders with a toolkit for potential risk identification and assessment. We recognize that it does have some differences from the Basel framework employed by lenders, but these do not present themselves as being insurmountable. The key issue is to identify where financial risks will be coming from. It may be that another tool for this work will come along but at present, this appears to be the only risk-based toolkit that considers both physical and transition risks at the firm level.

Over the past decade, the perception of potential climate risks among the financial community has changed, moving from idiosyncratic risks to systemic risks. Potential climate risks are no longer regarded as extraneous. Rather, they are becoming central as risk categories. In fact, broader environmental, social, and governance (ESG) concerns are becoming more central to the investment and finance industry.[2] Green taxonomies, while necessary, are not in themselves sufficient. More systematic risk taxonomies are equally critical to achieving a successful energy and broader economic transition. Therefore, as the scale of potential risks becomes clearer, we expect that taxonomies like this one will be more widely adopted as part of the process of integrating potential climate risks into general risk analysis.

NOTES

1. Fiedler, T. et al. Business Risk and the Emergence of Climate Analytics. *Nature Climate Change* 11: 87–94, 6, 2021.
2. Mutua, David Caleb. *Goldman Says ESG Finance to Become "Core Part" of Strategy*. Bloomberg Green, February 12, 2021.

Selected Bibliography

Bank of England. *A Framework for Assessing Financial Impacts of Physical Climate Change: A Practitioner's Aide for the General Insurance Sector*, May 17, 2019.

Bonneuil, Christophe and Jean-Baptiste Fressoz. *The Shock of the Anthropocene.* London: Verso Books, 2017.

Brown, Lester R. *The Great Transition: Shifting from Fossil Fuels to Solar and Wind Energy.* New York: W.W. Norton, 2015.

Buck, Holly Jean. *After Geoengineering: Climate Tragedy, Repair and Restoration.* London: Verso Books, 2019.

Buck, Holly Jean. *Ending Fossil Fuels: Why Net Zero Is Not Enough.* London: Verso Books, 2021.

Buhr, B. *ESG for Credit Investors: Operational, Climate and Natural Capital Risks,* London: Société Générale, 2014.

Cambridge Institute for Sustainability Leadership. *ClimateWise Physical Risk Framework: Understanding the Impacts of Climate Change on Real Estate Lending and Investment Portfolios,* February 2019.

Cambridge Institute for Sustainability Leadership. *ClimateWise Transition Risk Framework: Managing the Impacts of the Low Carbon Transition on Infrastructure Investments,* February 2019.

Climate Bonds Initiative. *Climate Bond Taxonomy.* London: CBI, January 2020.

Cocker, Mark. *Our Place: Can We Save Britain's Wildlife Before It Is Too Late?* London: Jonathan Cape, 2018.

Dallas, George and Mike Lubrano. *Governance, Stewardship and Sustainability* (2nd edition). London: Routledge, 2022.

Daly, Herman E. and John B. Cobb, Jr. *For the Common Good.* Boston: Beacon Press, 1989.

Daly, Herman E. and Kenneth N. Townsend. *Valuing the Earth: Economy, Ecology, Ethics.* Cambridge, MA: MIT Press, 1993.

Danen, Marcel, UBS, PRI, and MASCI. *Sustainable Investing Handbook.* 2019.

Dasgupta, P. *The Economics of Biodiversity: The Dasgupta Review.* London: HM Treasury, 2021.

Dodds, Klaus. *Ice: Nature and Culture.* London: Reaktion Books, 2018.

European Central Bank. *Climate Change and Financial Stability.* Financial Stability Review, May 2019.

EU Technical Expert Group on Sustainable Finance. *Taxonomy: Final Report of the Technical Expert Group on Sustainable Finance,* March 2020.

EU Technical Expert Group on Sustainable Finance. *Financing a Sustainable European Economy Taxonomy Report: Technical Annex,* March 2020.

Flannery, Tim. *Here on Earth*. London: Allen Lane, 2010.

Flyn, Cal. *Islands of Abandonment: Life in the Post-human Landscape*. London: William Collins, 2021.

Funk, McKenzie. *Windfall: The Booming Business of Global Warming*. New York: Penguin, 2014.

Ghosh, Amitav. *The Great Derangement: Climate Change and the Unthinkable*. London: University of Chicago Press, 2016.

Ghosh, Amitav. *The Nutmeg's Curse: Parables for a Planet in Crisis*. London: John Murray, 2021.

Gies, Erica. *Water Always Wins: Thriving in an Age of Drought and Deluge*. Chicago: University of Chicago Press, 2022.

Glantz, Michael H. *Currents of Change: El Nino's Impact on Climate and Society*. Cambridge: Cambridge University Press, 1996.

Goodell, Jeff. *Goodbye, Miami. Rolling Stone*, June 20, 2013.

Helm, Dieter. *Natural Capital: Valuing the Planet*. London: Yale University Press, 2015.

Helm, Dieter. *Green and Prosperous Land: A Blueprint for Rescuing the British Countryside*. London: William Collins, 2019.

Helm, Dieter. *Net Zero: How to Stop Causing Climate Change*. London: William Collins, 2020.

Intergovernmental Panel on Climate Change. *Fifth Assessment Report: Climate Change 2014: Impacts, Adaptation and Vulnerability*, 2014; *Global Warming of 1.5°C, Summary for Policymakers*, 2018.

Intergovernmental Panel on Climate Change. Summary for Policymakers. In *IPCC Special Report on the Ocean and Cryosphere in a Changing Climate*, 2019.

Intergovernmental Panel on Climate Change. *The Concept of Risk in the IPCC Sixth Assessment Report: A Summary of Cross-working Group Discussions*. Guidance for IPCC authors, September 2020.

Intergovernmental Panel on Climate Change. *Climate Change 2022: Mitigation of Climate Change, Working Group III: Contribution to the Sixth Assessment Report of the Intergovernmental Panel on Climate Change*. Summary for Policymakers, 2022.

Jensen, Derrick and George Draffan. *Strangely Like War: The Global Assault on Forests*. White River Junction: Chelsea Green, 2000.

Juniper, Tony. *What Nature Does for Britain*. London: Profile Books, 2015.

Kolbert, Elizabeth. The Siege of Miami. *The New Yorker*, December 21, 2015.

Kolbert, Elizabeth. *Under a White Sky*. London: The Bodley Head, 2021.

Krosinsky, Cary and Sophie Purdom. *Sustainable Investing: Revolutions in Theory and Practice*. London: Routledge, 2017.

Leggett, Jeremy. *The Carbon War: Dispatches from the End of the Oil Century*. London: Allen Lane, 1999.

Lewis, Simon L. and Mark A. Maslin, *The Human Planet: How We Created the Anthropocene*. London: Pelican, 2018.

Lustgarten, Abraham. How Climate Migration Will Reshape America. *The New York Times Magazine*, September 2020

Lynas, Mark. *Six Degrees: Our Future on a Hotter Planet.* New York: Harper, 2008.

Lynas, Mark. *Our Final Warning: Six Degrees of Climate Emergency.* New York: Fourth Estate, 2020.

Lynn, Mark. *End of the Line.* New York: Doubleday, 2005.

Lynn, Mark. *Cornered: The New Monopoly Capitalism and the Economics of Destruction.* New York: Wiley, 2010.

Malm, Andreas. *Fossil Capital.* London: Verso Books, 2016.

Malm, Andreas. *How to Blow Up a Pipeline.* London: Verso Books, 2020.

Mann, Michael. *The New Climate War: The Fight to Take Back Our Planet.* London: Scribe, 2021.

McGuire, Bill. *Hothouse Earth: An Inhabitant's Guide.* London: Icon Books, 2022.

McKibben, Bill. *The End of Nature.* New York: Viking Press, 1990.

McKibben, Bill. *The Global Warming Reader.* New York: Penguin, 2012.

McKinsey Global Institute. *Resource Revolution: Meeting the World's Energy, Material, Food, and Water Needs,* November 2011.

McKinsey Global Institute. *Resource Revolution: Tracking Global Commodity Markets,* September 2013.

McKinsey Global Institute. *Reverse the Curse: Maximizing the Potential of Resource-driven Economies,* December 2013.

McKinsey Global Institute. *Climate Risk and Response,* January 2020.

McKinsey Global Institute. *Will Infrastructure Bend or Break Under Climate Stress?* June 2020b.

Mitchell, Alana. *Dancing at the Dead Sea.* London: Transworld Publishers, 2005.

Natural Capital Coalition. *Natural Capital Protocol,* 2016.

Neher, Agnes L. *ESG Risks and Responsible Investment in Financial Markets.* Marburg: Metropolis Books, 2015.

OECD. *Developing Sustainable Finance Definitions and Taxonomies: A Guide for Policymakers,* Geneva: October 2020.

Patel, Raj. *Stuffed and Starved.* London: Portobello Books, 2007.

Porritt, Jonathan. *Hope in Hell: A Decade to Confront the Climate Emergency.* London: Simon & Schuster, 2020.

Quarmby, Lynn. *Watermelon Snow: Science, Art, and a Lone Polar Bear.* Montreal: McGill-Queen's University Press, 2020.

Rawlence, Ben. *The Treeline: The Last Forest and the Future of Life on Earth.* London: Jonathan Cape, 2022.

Raworth, Kate. *Doughnut Economics.* London: Random House Business Books, 2017.

Rich, Nathaniel. *Losing Earth: The Decade We Could Have Stopped Climate Change.* New York: Picador, 2019.

Rich, Nathaniel. *Second Nature: Scenes from a World Remade.* New York: Farrar, Strauss and Giroux, 2021.

Rush, Elizabeth. *Rising: Dispatches from the New American Shore.* New York: Milkweed Editions, 2018.

Sagoff, Mark. *The Economy of the Earth.* Cambridge: Cambridge University Press, 1984.

Schwartz, Judith D. *Cows Save the Planet*. White River Junction, VT: Chelsea Green, 2013.

Schwartz, Judith D. *Water in Plain Sight*. White River Junction, VT: Chelsea Green, 2017.

Schwartz, Judith D. *The Reindeer Chronicles*. White River Junction, VT: Chelsea Green, 2020.

Simard, Suzanne. *Finding the Mother Tree*. London: Allen Lane, 2021.

Stern, Nicholas. *The Economics of Climate Change: The Stern Review*. Cambridge: Cambridge University Press, 2007.

TCFD. *Final Report: Recommendations of the Task Force on Climate-related Financial Disclosures*, December 2016.

TCFD. *Task Force on Climate-related Financial Disclosures Status Report*, October 2021.

Turner, Adair. *Just Capital: The Liberal Economy*. London: Macmillan, 2001.

Van Dieren, Wouter. *Taking Nature into Account: A Report to the Club of Rome*. New York: Springer-Verlag, 1995.

Vince, Gaia. *Adventures in the Anthropocene*. London: Vintage, 2014.

Vince, Gaia. *Nomad Century*. London: Penguin Books, 2022.

Wadham, Jemma. *Ice Rivers*. London: Allen Lane, 2021.

Wallace-Wells, David. *The Uninhabitable Earth: A Story of Our Future*. London: Allen Lane, 2019.

World Commission on Environment and Development. *Our Common Future*. New York: Oxford University Press, 1987.

World Resources Institute and UNEP Finance Initiative. *Carbon Asset Risk: Discussion Framework*, 2020.

Worldwatch Institute. *State of the World*. Washington, DC: Worldwatch Institute and Island Press, 1984–present.

Worldwatch Institute. *Vital Signs*. Washington, DC: Worldwatch Institute and Island Press, 1994–present.

Worster, Donald. *Nature's Economy: A History of Ecological Ideas*. Cambridge: Cambridge University Press, 1977.

Worster, Donald. *The Wealth of Nature: Environmental History and the Ecological Imagination*. New York: Oxford University Press, 1993.

Organizational Information

(Another highly arbitrary list)

Bank of England (BoE) https://www.bankofengland.co.uk

Cambridge Institute for Sustainability Leadership (CISL) https://www.cisl.cam.ac.uk

Capitals Coalition (formerly Natural Capital Coalition) https://capitalscoalition.org

Carbon Disclosure Standards Board https://www.cdsb.net (Now part of International Sustainability Standards Board [ISSB], but research still available here.)

CDP (formerly the Carbon Disclosure Project) https://www.cdp.net/en

Centre for Climate Finance and Investment (CCFI) https://www.imperial.ac.uk/business-school/faculty-research/research-centres/centre-climate-finance-investment/

CERES https://www.ceres.org/homepage

Client Earth https://www.clientearth.org

Climate Bonds Initiative (CBI) https://www.climatebonds.net

Climate Central https://www.climatecentral.org

Climate Policy Initiative https://www.climatepolicyinitiative.org

Convention on Biological Diversity https://www.cbd.int

Council on Economic Policies https://www.cepweb.org

Ecologic Institute https://www.ecologic.eu

The Ellen Macarthur Foundation https://ellenmacarthurfoundation.org

EU Technical Expert Group on Sustainable Finance (TEG) https://finance.ec.europa.eu/publications/technical-expert-group-sustainable-finance-teg_en

European Banking Authority (EBA) https://www.eba.europa.eu

European Central Bank (ECB) https://www.ecb.europa.eu/home/html/index.en.html

Food and Agricultural Organization of the United Nations (FAO) https://www.fao.org/home/en

Global Carbon Capture and Storage Institute https://www.globalccsinstitute.com

Global Center on Adaptation https://gca.org

Global Water Policy Project https://www.globalwaterpolicy.org

Grantham Institute—Climate Change and the Environment, Imperial College https://www.imperial.ac.uk/grantham/

Grantham Research Institute on Climate Change and the Environment, London School of Economics https://www.lse.ac.uk/granthaminstitute/

Institute for Agricultural and Trade Policy (IATP) https://www.iatp.org

Integrated Drought Management Programme https://www.drought-management.info

Intergovernmental Panel on Climate Change (IPCC) https://www.ipcc.ch

International Accounting Standards Board (IASB) https://www.ifrs.org/groups/international-accounting-standards-board/

International Energy Agency (IEA) https://www.iea.org

International Institute for Sustainable Development (IISD) https://www.iisd.org

International Maritime Organization (IMO) https://www.imo.org

International Monetary Foundation (IMF) https://www.imf.org/en/Home

International Sustainability Standards Board (ISSB) https://www.ifrs.org/groups/international-sustainability-standards-board/

International Union for the Conservation of Nature (IUCN) https://www.iucn.org

NACE (Nomenclature of Economic Activities) https://ec.europa.eu/eurostat/statistics-explained/index.php?title=Glossary:Statistical_classification_of_economic_activities_in_the_European_Community_(NACE)

NAISC https://www.naics.com/search/

National Academy of Sciences (NAS) https://www.nasonline.org

Natural Capital Finance Alliance https://naturalcapital.finance

Network for Greening the Financial System (NGFS) https://www.ngfs.net/en

New Climate Economy https://newclimateeconomy.net

Organization for Economic Co-operation and Development (OECD) https://www.oecd.org

Pacific Institute https://pacinst.org

Planet Tracker https://planet-tracker.org

Potsdam Institute for Climate Impact Research (PIK) https://www.pik-potsdam.de/en/home

Principles of Responsible Investment (PRI) https://www.unpri.org

Resources for the Future (RFF) https://www.rff.org

RMI (formerly Rocky Mountain Institute) https://rmi.org

Stockholm International Water Institute (SIWI) https://siwi.org

Stockholm Resilience Institute (SRI) https://www.stockholmresilience.org

Sustainable Accounting Standards Board (SASB) https://www.sasb.org

Task Force on Climate-related Financial Disclosures (TCFD) https://www.fsb-tcfd.org

Task Force on Nature-related Financial Disclosures (TNFD) https://tnfd.global

UK Department for Environment, Farming and Rural Affairs (DEFRA) https://www.gov.uk/government/organisations/department-for-environment-food-rural-affairs

Union of Concerned Scientists https://www.ucsusa.org

United Nations Environmental Program Finance Initiative (UNEPFI) https://www.unepfi.org

United Nations Environment World Conservation Monitoring Centre https://www.unep-wcmc.org/en

United Nations Framework Convention on Climate Change (UNFCCC) https://unfccc.int

US Commodity Futures Trading Corporation (CFTC) https://www.cftc.gov

US Department of Energy, Energy Information Administration https://www.eia.gov

US Environmental Protection Administration (EPA) https://www.epa.gov

US Federal Reserve https://www.federalreserve.gov

US Global Change Research Program https://www.globalchange.gov

US National Oceanic and Atmospheric Administration (NOAA) https://www.noaa.gov

US Securities and Exchange Commission (SEC) https://www.sec.gov

Verisk Maplecroft https://www.maplecroft.com

The World Bank https://www.worldbank.org/en/home

World Commission on Environment and Development (WCED) https://sustainabledevelopment.un.org/milestones/wced

World Economic Forum (WEF) https://www.weforum.org

World Meteorological Organization (WMO) https://public.wmo.int/en

World Resources Institute (WRI) https://www.wri.org

Acknowledgments

This book had an earlier incarnation as a series of ESG-related reports from Société Générale. I am grateful to Tim Barker, Simon Surtees, and Guy Stear for their support and encouragement. More recently the subject was expanded into a report from the Centre for Climate Finance and Investment at Imperial College Business School, released in February 2022: *What Is Climate Risk? A Field Guide for Investors, Lenders and Regulators.* If nothing else, we have shortened the title a bit. I am indebted to a number of people for guidance on various portions of this book, particularly Caroline Harrison at Climate Bonds; Anastasiya Ostrovnaya, Pernille Holtedahl, and Stella Whitaker at CCFI; Jan Ahrens of Sparkchange; and Lenora Suki. Rahul Ghosh provided valued assistance and insight. Earlier versions were ably reviewed by Christoph Klein, Carmen Nuzzo, Prashant Vaze, and Mike Wilkins, all of whom provided insightful comments. Any mistakes are not theirs, of course, although they probably should have caught them. Colleagues at CCFI have been very supportive, particularly the Centre's former Director, Charles Donovan; Raul Rosales, whose idea this was in the first place; Mili Fomocov; and Anastasiya Ostrovnaya (again), for whom a simple acknowledgment is insufficient. Thankfully, Eva Klein and Dalia Daou were there to make sure the report got done. Caty Phares made the earlier version readable, and Cato van Schalkwyk provided some excellent graphics. And thanks to Jenni, of course. I am grateful to all.

Some of this work has been funded by the International Network for Sustainable Financial Policy Insights, Research, and Exchange (INSPIRE). INSPIRE is a global research stakeholder of the Network for Greening the Financial System (NGFS). It is philanthropically funded through the ClimateWorks Foundation and co-hosted by ClimateWorks and the Grantham Research Institute on Climate Change and the Environment at the London School of Economics.

About the Author

Bob Buhr is an Honorary Research Fellow at the Centre for Climate Finance and Investment (CCFI), Imperial College Business School. Bob retired in 2017 from a 30-year career as a corporate bond analyst, and now focuses on areas of interest to investors, particularly climate risks and adaptation strategies. He has published numerous ESG and climate-related reports and, since joining CCFI, has published on climate vulnerable countries and sovereign risks, and firm-based risks relating to climate risk impacts. Bob received a BA from Ithaca College, and a PhD from Brown University. He lives in London.

Index